Keyboarding and Word Processing

Microsoft® Word 2002

SUSIE H. VANHUSS, PH.D.
University of South Carolina

CONNIE M. FORDE, PH.D.
Mississippi State University

DONNA L. WOO
Cypress College, California

SOUTH-WESTERN
™
THOMSON LEARNING

Australia · Canada · Mexico · Singapore · Spain · United Kingdom · United States

College Keyboarding and Word Processing, Microsoft Word® 2002, Lessons 1-60
by Susan H. VanHuss, Connie M. Forde, Donna Woo

Team Leader:
Karen Schmohe

Consulting Editor:
Diane Durkee

Cover Design:
Paul Neff Design

Project Manager:
Jane Phelan

Production Manager:
Tricia Boies

Cover Image:
©Getty Images/Joseph Drivas

Editor:
Martha Conway

Manufacturing Coordinator:
Charlene Taylor

Internal Design:
Grannan Graphic Design Ltd.

Channel Manager:
Chris McNamee

Design Project Manager:
Stacy Jenkins Shirley

Compositor:
D&G Limited, LLC

Marketing Coordinator:
Lori Pegg

Rights and Permissions Manager:
Linda Ellis

Printer:
Quebecor World, Dubuque

For more information, contact
South-Western
5101 Madison Road
Cincinnati, OH 45227-1490
Or you can visit our internet site at www.swep.com.

For permission to use material from this text or product, contact us by
Phone: 1-800-730-2214
Fax: 1-800-730-2215
www.thomsonrights.com

SOUTH-WESTERN™
THOMSON LEARNING

FAMILY OF PRODUCTS

Texts

Keyboarding Course (Lessons 1-25) – Lessons cover alphabetic, numeric, and symbol keys, and skillbuilding. Combined with *Keyboarding Pro* software, you have a system that guarantees a strong keyboarding foundation.

Keyboarding and Word Processing (Lessons 1-60) – Develop marketable skills with this all-in-one keyboarding, formatting, and word processing text. Formats include business letters, standard memos, reports, tables, and newsletters with graphics. Microsoft Certified: Core Level.

Advanced Word Processing (Lessons 61-120) – Advances students to the expert level of word processing as they master document design. Microsoft Certified: Expert Level.

Keyboarding and Word Processing, Complete Course, (Lessons 1-120) – Students progress from that of a beginner to an expert user without having to change texts. Microsoft Certified: Core and Expert Levels.

Integrated Applications – Combines instruction on all Microsoft Office XP tools. Microsoft Certified: Core Level.

Microsoft Word Applications – Project-based instruction that reinforces word processing, document design, Internet research, and communication skills. Reviews both Core and Expert level skills.

Instructor's Manual/Key – Available for both Lessons 1-60 and 61-120. Traditional printed format.

Technology Solutions

Keyboarding Pro, Ver. 3 – Covers alphabetic, numeric, keypad, and skillbuilding instruction. Excellent instruction for learning and reviewing keyboarding. Student version available.

CheckPro 2002 – Assessment software that provides immediate feedback on keyboarding and proofreading skills. Checks drills, timings, selected documents, and production assessments for speed and accuracy. Student version available.

WebTutor for College Keyboarding 15E – Online supplement that includes multimedia activities, Web links, presentations, quizzes, flashcards, enrichment materials, model documents, and more for each text. Available for WebCT or Blackboard.

MicroPace Pro – Timed writing, paced skill development, drills, and error diagnostics software. Correlates with *College Keyboarding, 15E*. Student version available.

KeyChamp – Unique program that develops speed by analyzing a student's two-stroke key combinations and providing drills that build speed on slow key combinations.

Instructor CD – Solutions, data files, teaching tips, and objective and performance assessments, Keyboarding Pro User's Manual, and more—all in an easy-to-use format.

www.collegekeyboarding.com

PREFACE

COLLEGE KEYBOARDING, KEYBOARDING AND WORD PROCESSING, MICROSOFT® WORD 2002 is a learning package designed to prepare you for the career of your choice. This ultra-successful learning package combines *Windows 2000*, state-of-the-art operating system; *Microsoft Word 2002*, leading word processing software; ***KEYBOARDING PRO***, a very effective all-in-one keyboarding instruction program; and well-written learning materials presented in an easy-to-learn format. This winning combination ensures that you will have marketable skills regardless of the career you choose.

Career Skills

Pick your career—manager, engineer, scientist, physician, attorney, administrative employee, educator, sales executive, accountant, computer specialist, factory worker, or any one of a host of other choices. The critical skills for success are the ability to access and manage knowledge and to communicate effectively. Knowledge management and communication tools include keyboarding, word processing, Internet usage, and the other software applications in the *Microsoft Office XP* suite. *College Keyboarding* will enable you to master these knowledge management and communication skills required in virtually every profession.

Keyboarding Skill

Keyboarding is the foundation skill required for effective computer usage. As with the development of any high-level skill, you must consistently use proper techniques and meaningful practice to develop the skill. *Keyboarding Pro* will teach you the alphabetic, numeric, and symbol keys, and the keypad. And your practice won't be dull! When you are ready, you can access Skill Builder to boost your speed and accuracy. Challenging games, along with progress graphs, color photos, sound effects, and a full-featured word processor, will keep you motivated. *CheckPro 2002* will check your speed and accuracy on all of your *Word* documents beginning with Lesson 29.

Word Processing

The features of word processing are taught in a systematic, easy to-learn manner. The approach used in *College Keyboarding, Microsoft® Word 2002* ensures that all of the skills required for Core certification are taught by the end of Lesson 60, and the skills required for Expert certification are taught in Lessons 61-120. Whether you choose to pursue certification or not, you will have mastered the skills required to use *Microsoft Word 2002* effectively.

Document Design

Effective document design enhances both the readability and the image of documents—which are critical components of effective communication. You will learn to prepare and produce documents efficiently using the standard formats required for most professions.

Learning New Software

Much of what you learn today will be outdated in a few years. In addition to learning the features of the most state-of-the-art software available today, you will learn how to use new software that will be developed after you complete your education. Understanding word processing concepts and the key words necessary to access information makes it easy for you to use online help effectively. Learning how to use new software ensures that your skills will never be outdated!

TABLE OF CONTENTS

Make a Lasting Impression
with Key Features from College Keyboarding 15E

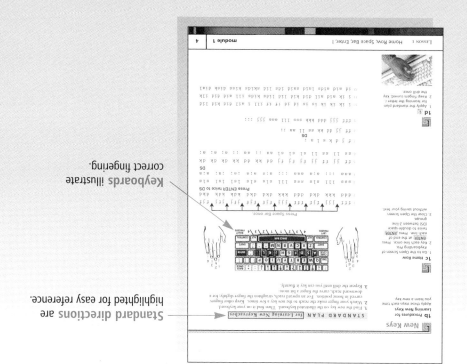

Keyboards illustrate correct fingering.

Standard directions are highlighted for easy reference.

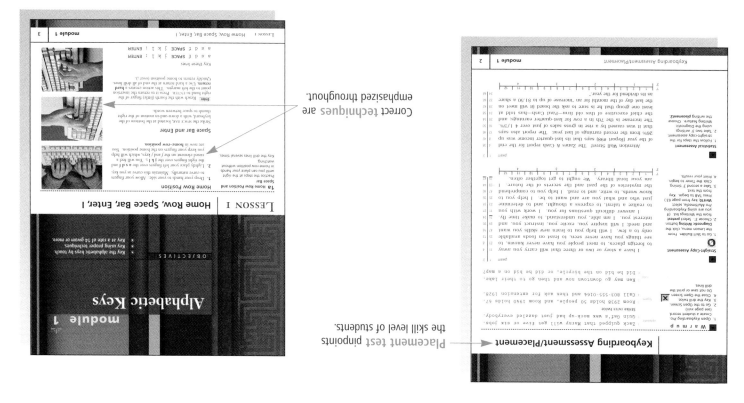

Correct techniques are emphasized throughout.

Placement test pinpoints the skill level of students.

A **diagnostic report** of errors on timed writings is available.

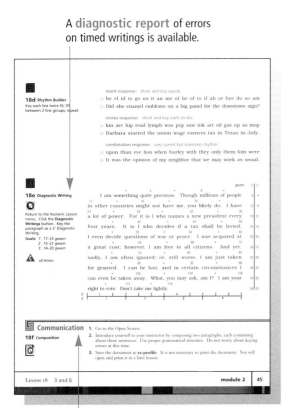

Communication activities are completed in the word processor within *Keyboarding Pro*.

Labels focus learning.

Help keywords teach how to learn new functions.

Drills immediately reinforce new functions.

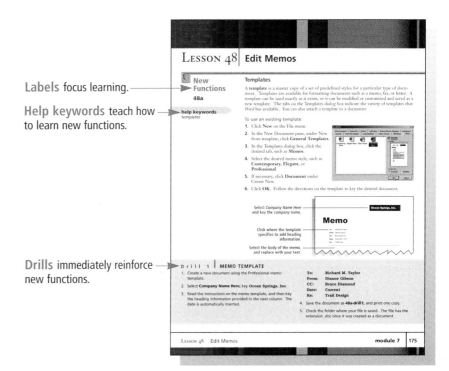

New formats are explained and illustrated with model documents.

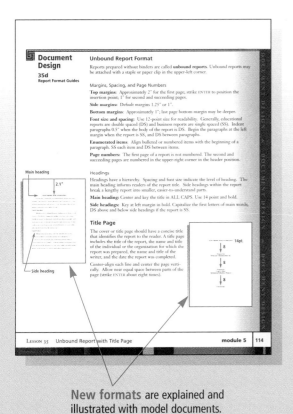

Applications reinforce new learning.

Icon identifies use of data file.

Discover extends the depth of word processing coverage.

Directions and copy to be keyed are easy to read.

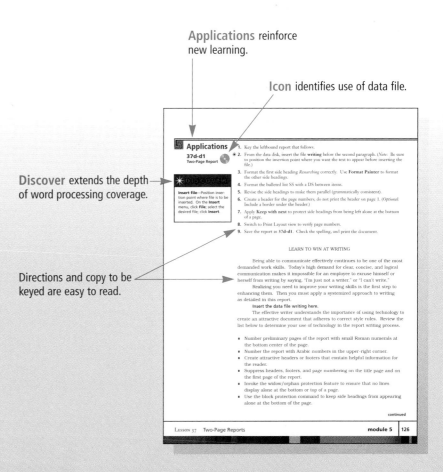

APPROVED COURSEWARE

What Does This Logo Mean?

It means this courseware has been approved by the Microsoft®, Office User Specialist Program to be among the finest available for learning *Microsoft Word 2002*. It also means that upon completion of this courseware, you may be prepared to become a Microsoft Office User Specialist.

What is a Microsoft Office User Specialist?

A Microsoft Office User Specialist is an individual who has certified his or her skills in one or more of the Microsoft Office desktop applications of Microsoft Word, Microsoft Excel, Microsoft PowerPoint®, Microsoft Outlook®, or Microsoft Access, or in Microsoft Project. The Microsoft Office User Specialist Program typically offers certification exams at the "Core" and "Expert" skill levels.* The Microsoft Office User Specialist Program is the only Microsoft approved program in the world for certifying proficiency in Microsoft Office desktop applications and Microsoft Project. This certification can be a valuable asset in any job search or career advancement.

More Information:

To learn more about becoming a Microsoft Office User Specialist, visit www.mous.net

To purchase a Microsoft Office User Specialist certification exam, visit www.DesktopIQ.com

To learn about other Microsoft Office User Specialist approved courseware from South-Western, Thomson Learning, visit www.swep.com/careered/index.html.

---

* The availability of Microsoft Office User Specialist certification exams varies by application, application version, and language. Visit www.mous.net for exam availability.

Microsoft, the Microsoft Office User Specialist Logo, PowerPoint and Outlook are either registered trademarks or trademarks of Microsoft Corporation in the United States and/or other countries.

KNOW YOUR COMPUTER

The numbered parts are found on most computers. The location of some parts will vary.

1. **CPU (Central Processing Unit)**: Internal operating unit or "brain" of computer.

2. **Disk drive**: Reads data from and writes data to a disk.

3. **Monitor**: Displays text and graphics on a screen.

4. **Mouse**: Used to input commands.

5. **Keyboard**: An arrangement of letter, figure, symbol, control, function, and editing keys and a numeric keypad.

Keyboard Arrangement

1. **Alphanumeric keys**: Letters, numbers, and symbols.

2. **Numeric keypad**: Keys at the right side of the keyboard used to enter numeric copy and perform calculations.

3. **Function (F) keys**: Used to execute commands, sometimes with other keys. Commands vary with software.

4. **Arrow keys**: Move insertion point up, down, left, or right.

5. **ESC (Escape)**: Closes a software menu or dialog box.

6. **TAB**: Moves the insertion point to a preset position.

7. **CAPS LOCK**: Used to make all capital letters.

8. **SHIFT**: Makes capital letters and symbols shown at tops of number keys.

9. **CTRL (Control)**: With other key(s), executes commands. Commands may vary with software.

10. **ALT (Alternate)**: With other key(s), executes commands. Commands may vary with software.

11. **Space Bar**: Inserts a space in text.

12. **ENTER (RETURN)**: Moves insertion point to margin and down to next line. Also used to execute commands.

13. **DELETE**: Removes text to the right of insertion point.

14. **NUM LOCK**: Activates/deactivates numeric keypad.

15. **INSERT**: Activates insert or typeover.

16. **BACKSPACE**: Deletes text to the left of insertion point.

WELCOME TO WINDOWS®

Microsoft® Windows® is an **operating system,** a program that manages all other software applications on your computer and its peripherals such as the mouse and printer. Software applications that run under *Windows* have many common features. Depending on the version of your operating system, some features may look, work, or be named slightly differently on your computer.

The Desktop

When your computer is turned on and ready to use, it will display a **desktop,** the main working area. The illustration shows a *Windows® 2000* desktop. Your desktop will have many of the same features. Depending on what programs are on your computer and how the desktop has been arranged, it may look different.

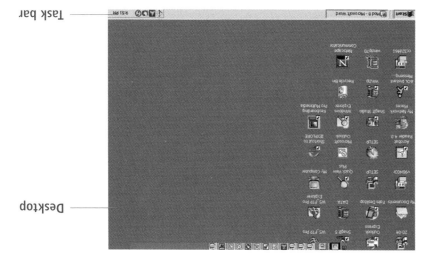

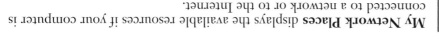

Task bar

Desktop

The desktop displays icons and a taskbar. **Icons** provide an easy way to access programs and documents that you use frequently. *Note* three icons in particular:

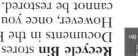

My Computer displays the disk drives, CD-ROM drives, and printers that are attached to your computer.

My Network Places displays the available resources if your computer is connected to a network or to the Internet.

Recycle Bin stores files and folders that have been deleted from the hard drive. Documents in the Recycle Bin may be restored and returned to their folders. However, once you empty the Recycle Bin, the documents are deleted and cannot be restored.

The bar at the bottom of the desktop is the taskbar. The **taskbar** displays the Start button on the left, a button for each program or document that is open, and the system clock on the right (your taskbar may have additional icons). The taskbar enables you to open programs and navigate on your computer.

The Start Button

 The **Start button** opens the Start menu, which lists a variety of items from which to choose such as programs and documents.

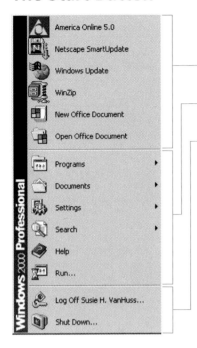

The Start menu is divided into three sections.

The *top* section contains applications or shortcuts you may have added to your computer such as an antivirus program.

The *center* section contains a list of options such as Programs, Documents, Search, and Help.

The *lower* section contains basic commands such as Log On/Off and Shut Down.

To open an item listed on the Start menu, point to the item and click the left mouse button. A right arrow beside a menu item indicates that a cascading or submenu with more options is available for that item. (*Note:* If an icon is displayed on the desktop, you can double-click the icon to open the program, document, or folder that it represents.)

The Mouse

 *Windows* requires the use of a mouse or other pointing device such as a touch pad built into your keyboard. A mouse has two buttons. The left button is used to select text or commands, to open files or menus, or to drag objects. The right button is used to display shortcut menus.

To move the pointer, you must move the mouse. If you have a touch pad on your keyboard, move the pointer by moving your finger on the touch pad. The mouse or touch pad is used to perform four basic actions:

Point: Move the mouse so that the pointer touches something displayed onscreen.

Click: Point to an item, quickly press the mouse button once, and release it.

Double-click: Point to an item; quickly press the mouse button twice, and release it.

Drag: Point to an item, then hold down the mouse button while you move the mouse to reposition the item.

The mouse pointer changes in appearance depending on its location on the desktop and the task being performed.

| The *vertical blinking bar* indicates the current position of the cursor.

I The *I-beam* indicates the location of the mouse pointer. To reposition the cursor at this point, you must click the mouse button.

The *arrow* indicates that you can select items. It displays when the mouse is located outside the text area. You can point to a toolbar icon to display the function of that icon.

The *hourglass* indicates that *Windows* is processing a command.

A *double-headed arrow* appears when the pointer is at the border of a window; it is used to change the size.

Windows Features

Windows displays folders, applications, and individual documents in windows. A **window** is a work area on the desktop that can be resized or moved. To resize a window, point to the border. When the pointer changes to a double-headed arrow, drag the window to the desired size. To move a window, point to the title bar, drag it to the new position, and release the mouse button.

Menu bar ——
Toolbar ——
Desktop ——
Drives ——

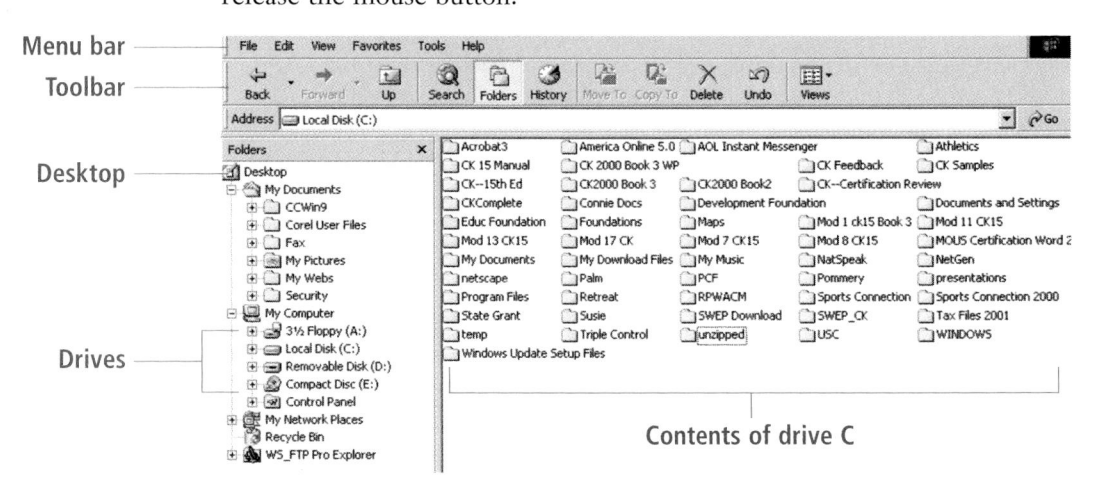

Contents of drive C

The basic features of all windows are the same. Each window contains the following:

Title bar: Displays the name of the application that is currently open and the path (folder name). The Title bar also includes several buttons at the right.

Minimize button: Reduces the window to a button on the taskbar. To restore the window, click the button on the taskbar.

Maximize button: Enlarges a window to full-screen size.

Restore button: When you maximize a window, the Maximize button is replaced with a Restore button that, when clicked, returns the window to its original size.

Close button: Closes the application.

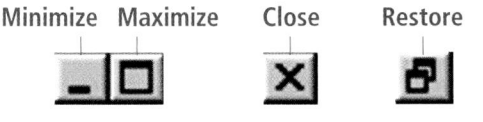

Minimize Maximize   Close   Restore

Menu bar: Displays commands available in the software.

Toolbars: Display icons that offer a convenient way to access frequently used commands. Applications programs often have different toolbars for different tasks.

Scroll bars: Enable you to see material that does not fit on one screen. You can click the arrows on the scroll bars or drag the scroll box to move through a document.

Help

Help is available for *Windows*. Help is also available with each software application that you use. Generally you will use the Help feature provided with the application. To access *Windows* Help, click the Start button, and then click Help. A list of topics will be displayed. From the list, choose the appropriate one by highlighting the topic and clicking on it.

You can also click **Index** to display a list of specific items in alphabetical order. As you key the characters of the topic in the entry box, the program automatically moves to items beginning with the keyed letters. When the correct topic is displayed, highlight it and choose display. If you prefer, you can scroll through the list of topics until you find what you are looking for.

To search for a topic, key the topic in the Search box and press ENTER to see a display of Help pages that contain the topic. Select the topic and click **Display** to present the information.

Shut Down

Before you exit *Windows*, be sure that all programs have been closed. To exit *Windows*, click the **Start** button, and then click **Shut Down** to display the Shut Down dialog box. Check to be sure Shut down is displayed, and then click **OK**. If Shut down is not displayed, click the down arrow at the right, then select **Shut down**. Never just turn your computer off. Windows may notify you when the computer can be turned off, or it may automatically shut down once you click OK. This will vary depending upon how your computer was set up.

FILE MANAGEMENT

As with paper files, it is important to establish a logical and easy-to-use computer file management system to organize your files efficiently so that you can find them quickly and easily. You can manage files from the desktop or from My Computer or Windows Explorer.

Understand the File System

Computer files are stored on **disks** specified by their location. The desktop of the computer in the example below has a hard disk drive (C), a floppy disk drive (A), a removable drive (D), and a CD-ROM drive (E). Drives are illustrated and named.

Drives on the computer

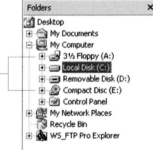

View Contents of a Drive

To view the contents of a drive:

- Click the **My Computer** icon on the desktop.

- When the drives display in the first column, double-click the drive you want to see. Note in the Address box below that Drive A is displayed. The folders contained in Drive A are displayed in the right half of the screen.

Drive indicator

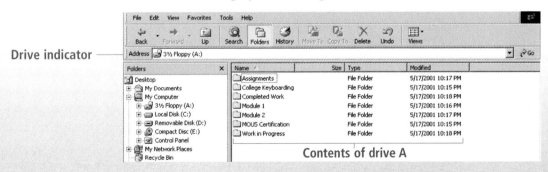

Contents of drive A

Working with Folders and Files

Folders are extremely important in managing files. You will want to create folders to organize and store related files or other folders. You can do so using My Computer on the desktop or Windows Explorer.

View Contents of a Folder

Folders are listed in alphabetic order. (In the illustration, Assignments is listed first.) To see the contents of a folder, double-click the folder. Folders may contain files, other programs, and folders. (*Note:* You can also use Windows Explorer to view a hierarchal list of files on your computer by clicking Start, pointing to Programs, pointing to Accessories, and clicking Windows Explorer.)

View Data and Arrange Files

Files and folders within My Computer can be viewed in different ways: as Large Icons, Small Icons, List, or Details. In the illustration above, items are shown in List view.

To change the view, click **View** on the menu; then choose a view. You may want to experiment with each of the views to decide which one you prefer.

Folders are usually listed in alphabetical order. You can also arrange them in descending order by date, size, or type of file. To rearrange the order of files or folders, select **Details** from the View menu, and then click on one of headings displayed above the files or folders such as size, date, or type.

Create Folder

To create a folder, click **My Computer;** then double-click the drive or folder that will contain the new folder. (Drive A has been selected in the example.) In the window that opens, from the menu bar, click **File,** point to **New,** and click **Folder.** Select and replace **New Folder** with the folder name you want.

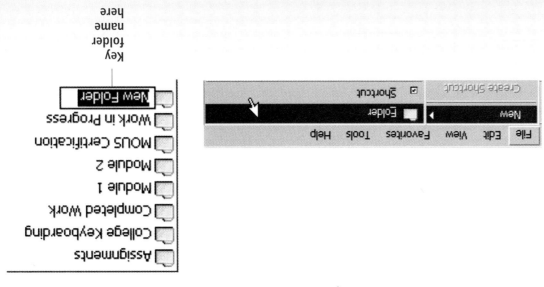

Key folder name here

Name Files and Folders

Good file organization begins with giving your folders and files names that are logical and easy to understand. In the example, the user created a folder on Drive A for Completed Work and a second folder for Work in Progress. Another option is to create a folder called College Keyboarding and then within this folder, create a folder for Module 3, in which you save files for all documents created in Module 3 (Lessons 26-28). You would save the files by the exercise name such as **26b-d1** or **26b-d2** (See the documents on page 79). You would create a second folder for Module 4, etc. A system like this makes finding files simple.

Rename Files and Folders

Occasionally, you may want to rename a file or folder. To do so, right-click the file or folder, choose **Rename**, key the new name, and press ENTER. You can also rename files using the Windows Explorer menu.

Move and Copy Files and Folders

To move files or folders, double-click My Computer on the desktop. Double-click the drive that contains the file or folder you want to move, and then locate the item. Be sure the place you want to move the file or folder to is visible. Press and hold down the left mouse button and drag the pointer to the new location.

To copy a file or folder, press and hold down CTRL while you drag.

Note: If you drag a file or folder to a location on the same disk, it will be moved. If you drag an item to a different disk, it will be copied. To move the item, press and hold down SHIFT while dragging.

When you are moving or copying items, selecting (clicking) several items at once can save time. To select consecutive items, click the fist item, hold down SHIFT, and click the last item. To select items in different places, hold down CRTL while you click each item.

Delete Files and Folders

You can select and delete several files and folders at once, just as you can select several items to move or copy. If you delete a folder, you automatically delete any files and folders inside it.

To delete a file or folder and send it to the Recycle Bin, right-click on the file or folder, and choose **Delete**. Answer **Yes** to the question about sending the item to the Recycle Bin. (*Note:* You can also delete files and folders using Windows Explorer.)

Restore Deleted Files and Folders

When you delete a file or folder, the item goes to the Recycle Bin. If you have not emptied the Recycle Bin, you can restore files and folders stored there.

- Minimize the working window, and then double-click the Recycle Bin on the desktop to open the Recycle Bin window.
- Select the file you want to restore, right-click to display the shortcut menu, and choose **Restore**. You can also choose **Restore** from the File menu.

Close the Recycle Bin window. Click the folder where the file was originally located, and it should now be restored.

Welcome to Keyboarding Pro

Keyboarding Pro combines the latest technology with South-Western's superior method for teaching keyboarding. The Alphabetic and Numeric and Skill modules of *Keyboarding Pro* or *Keyboarding Pro Multimedia,* correspond to Lessons 1–25 in *College Keyboarding.* Use Skill Builder to boost your speed and accuracy after you learn the alphabetic keys. Use the Numeric Keypad to learn the keypad by touch.

Getting Started

1. Click the **Start** button and then select **Programs.** Select the South-Western Keyboarding program group and click **Keyboarding Pro.** If you chose to add an icon to your desktop during the install, you may also double-click on the icon to start the program.

2. Click anywhere on the splash screen to remove it and bring up the Log In dialog box.

The first time you use *Keyboarding Pro,* you must enter your user information and indicate where you will store your data. This process creates a student record. You will create a student record **only once** so that the results of all lessons are stored in one file.

1. From the Log In dialog box, click **New User.**

2. Enter your name (first name then last name), your Class ID, and a password. Write down the password and store it in a safe place. You will need to use this password each time you enter the program.

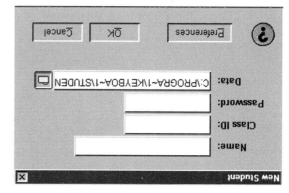

3. Specify the data location. The default storage path is **c:\Program Files\Keyboarding Pro Multimedia\ Students.** If you will be storing on Drive A or if you have a student subdirectory on the network, set the path accordingly. Click the **Folder** icon to change the page to Drive A or browse to locate your network folder.

4. If desired, click the **Preferences** button and update the information. Click **OK** to complete the registration.

Each time you enter *Keyboarding Pro* after the first time, the Log In dialog box displays. Click your name and enter your password. If you do not see your name, click **Locate** to locate the drive where your student record is located (Drive A or your folder on the network.)

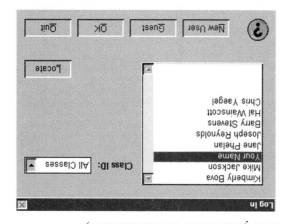

Main Menu

The Main menu displays after you have logged in. Note these special features. Other features will be explained as you move through the program.

Open Screen is a word processor with a timer. You can practice your keyboarding or take a timed writing.

Animations demonstrate proper posture and hand positions. Review techniques frequently.

Quick Review includes numerous keyboarding drills for improving techniques and keyboarding skill.

Diagnostic Writings are timed writings (1', 3', or 5') with extensive error analysis. They are accessed from the Lesson menus of Numeric and Skill and Skill Builder. Writings are keyed from the textbook.

WELCOME TO CHECKPRO 2002

CheckPro 2002 verifies the accuracy of the keystrokes in drills, timed writings, and selected documents that you key beginning in Module 4. The drill practice and timed writings features are built right into the *CheckPro 2002* program. For the document exercises, *CheckPro 2002* works in conjunction with *Microsoft Word 2002*. You will key documents using *Word* and then *CheckPro2002* error-checks your work.

Getting Started with *CheckPro 2002*

To launch the program, click the **Start** button and then select **Programs**. Select the South-Western Keyboarding program group and click **CheckPro 2002**. Once the splash screen is removed, the Student Registration dialog box appears.

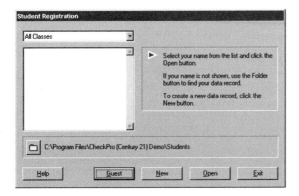

When you first use the *CheckPro 2002* software, you must enter your user information and indicate where you will store your data. This process creates a student record. You will create a student record only once.

1. From the Student Registration dialog box, click **New**. This launches the New Student dialog box.

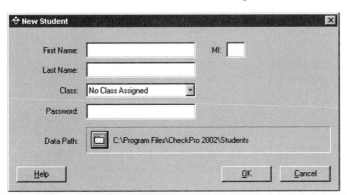

2. Enter your name and password and select your class if it is available on the drop-down list.

3. Specify the data location. The default storage path is **c:\Program Files\CheckPro 2002\Students**. If you will be storing on Drive A or if you have a student subdirectory on the network, set the path accordingly.

Each time you enter *CheckPro 2002* after the first time, the Student Registration dialog box displays. Click your name and enter your password. If you do not see your name, click the folder icon and browse either Drive A or the folder on the network where your data is being saved to locate your data record.

Main Screen

After you start the program and log in, the program displays the *CheckPro 2002* main screen. The main screen is the central navigation point for the entire program. From here you can select a lesson, e-mail a data file, or access the supplemental timings/documents. Supplemental timings refer to timed writings that are not located in a numbered lesson (for example, Skill Builders 2, 3, etc.). Supplemental documents include documents that cannot be accessed from numbered lessons (CheckPoints, projects, tests, and documents created by your instructor) .

Choose a lesson by keying the lesson number or clicking on the arrows to the right of the Go To field. Then click on the **Go To** button or strike ENTER. You are now at a lesson screen.

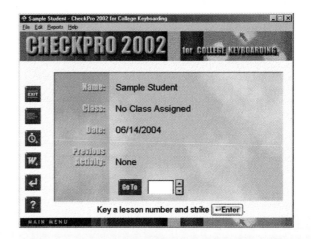

Lesson Screen

The lesson screen contains more activity options. Each activity corresponds directly with the activities for that lesson in your textbook. Click on the button next to an activity title to complete that activity. Drills and timed writings will be completed within the *CheckPro 2002* software. *CheckPro 2002* will launch *Word 2002* for you to complete documents or production tests.

Drill Practice: For a drill practice activity, key each drill line as it appears on the screen. You can choose to repeat the activity when you finish the drill practice. A check mark appears next to the menu option on the lesson screen when you complete it.

Timed Writings: Click a **Timed Writing** button to take a timed writing. Then select the timing length and source. Key the timed writing from your textbook. The program shows the gwam, error rate, and actual errors when you finish the writing. You can print the timed writing report or save it to disk.

Documents and Production Tests: Select a document or assessment activity and choose **Begin new document.** You'll get a dialog box with important information, and then your word processor will be launched. *CheckPro 2002* creates a document for you with the correct filename. The *CheckPro* toolbar will appear on top of the *Word 2002* document window. When you are finished proofreading the document, do not save the file. Instead, click on the check mark on the *CheckPro* toolbar. *CheckPro 2002* will then save your document and open a checked version of it back in *CheckPro 2002* for you to review your errors. To finish an exercise or revise a checked document, select the activity and choose

Open existing document.

Check document.

Save without checking.

Reports

There are a number of reports available in *CheckPro 2002*. Click on the **Reports** menu to see the selection. The Lesson Report provides a snapshot of your results for a specific lesson. Click on the **Activity Checklist** to see an overview of which activities have been completed. This report indicates the date each activity was completed, but provides no further information. Choose the **Reports** menu, **Summary Report** to view Drill, Timed Writing, Document, and Production Test summaries. All of the information for creating these reports is saved in your record file.

Sending Files to Your Instructor

If you are using *CheckPro 2002* in a distance learning environment, you may need to send your record file and work to your instructor electronically. *CheckPro 2002* includes a feature that lets you send these files as an attachment to an e-mail. However, this feature works with MAPI-compliant e-mail programs only. So you may need to manually launch your e-mail program and attach the files yourself.

If you accepted the default data location when you registered as a new student, your data files and your record file should be in the folder c:\Program Files\CheckPro 2002\Students\ **Your Name**. Your record file is entitled **your name.ckc**. You will go to the Students folder and attach your .ckc file in an e-mail to your instructor. Your instructor may want you to attach actual documents in addition to your record file. If so, you would attach the appropriate .ctw files for timed writings and .doc files to attach the documents you keyed.

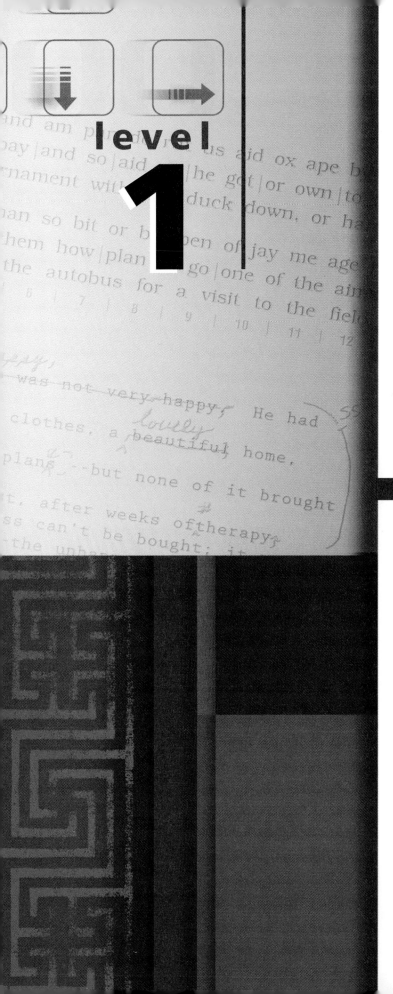

level 1

Developing Keyboarding Skill

KEYBOARDING

To key the alphabetic and number keys by touch with good technique.

To key approximately 25 *wam* with good accuracy.

COMMUNICATION SKILLS

To apply proofreaders' marks and revise text.

To create simple documents in a basic word processor.

Document 9

Table with Hyperlinks

Key the table at the right in landscape format so that all entries appear on a single line.

Include the title and subtitle in the first row of merged cells.

Center the column headings and add 10% shading. Change the line spacing of rows 2–8 to 1.5. Save the table as **mod9-d9**.

WEB SITE INFORMATION Nelson, Canada		
Subject	**Name of Site**	**Web Site Address**
Nelson and surrounding areas	Nelson Area Communities Connect	http://www.kics.bc.ca
Schools	School District 81 Fort Nelson	http://www.schdist81.bc.ca
City of Nelson	City of Nelson	http://www.city.nelson.bc.ca
Library	Nelson Municipal Library	http://www.kics.bc.ca/~library
Newspaper	Nelson Daily News	http://www.sterlingnews.com/Nelson/home.html
Sports	Nelson Mid-summer Curling Bonspiel	http://www.midsummerbonspiel.nelson.bc.ca

Document 10

Announcement

Key the following information as a 2-column announcement with balanced columns and a line between them. Use *WordArt* for the title and add an appropriate graphic to the second paragraph.

Add the following hyperlink to Nelson and Area Communities Connect: http://www.kics.bc.ca.

Save it as **mod9-d10**.

Consider Relocating to Nelson

As you are all aware, the Board of Directors voted to move the corporate headquarters of Selkirk Communications from Portland, Oregon, to Nelson, British Columbia.

Nelson is surrounded by the Selkirk Mountains and sits on the shores of Kootenay Lake. Its heritage, charm, and stunning scenery create the quintessential small-town setting. The city, with a population of 9,500, has a unique mix of urban sophistication and rural ambience.

We would like you to consider relocating with us to Nelson. To help acquaint you with the area, please take the time to view Nelson and Area Communities Connect. Additional information on Nelson can be found in the Web sites posted on our intranet.

Keyboarding Assessment/Placement

Warmup

1. Open *Keyboarding Pro*. Create a student record. (see page xviii)
2. Go to the Open Screen.
3. Key the drill twice.
4. Close the Open Screen . Do not save or print the drill lines.

alphabetic
1 Zack quipped that Marny will get five or six jobs.
2 Quin Gaf's wax mock-up had just dazzled everybody.

Strike ENTER twice

figures
3 Room 2938 holds 50 people, and Room 1940 holds 67.
4 Call 803-555-0164 and then ask for extension 1928.

easy
5 Ken may go downtown now and then go to their lake.
6 Did he bid on the bicycle, or did he bid on a map?

gwam   1' 3'

Straight-Copy Assessment

1. Go to Skill Builder. From the Lesson menu, click the **Diagnostic Writing** button.
2. Choose 3'. Select **pretest** from the Writings list. (If you are using *Keyboarding Pro Multimedia*, select **Writ10**; key from page 63.) Press TAB to begin. Key from the text.
3. Take a second 3' timing. Click the Timer to begin.
4. Print your results.

| | I have a story or two or three that will carry you away | 11 | 4 |

     I have a story or two or three that will carry you away   11   4
to foreign places, to meet people you have never known, to   23   8
see things you have never seen, to feast on foods available   35 12
only to a few. I will help you to learn new skills you want 47 16
and need; I will inspire you, excite you, instruct you, and   59 20
interest you. I am able, you understand, to make time fly.   71 24

     I answer difficult questions for you. I work with you   11 27
to realize a talent, to express a thought, and to determine   23 31
just who and what you are and want to be. I help you to   35 35
know words, to write, and to read. I help you to comprehend 47 40
the mysteries of the past and the secrets of the future. I   59 44
am your local library. We ought to get together often.   70 47

| 1' | 1 | 2 | 3 | 4 | 5 | 6 | 7 | 8 | 9 | 10 | 11 | 12 |
| 3' | | 1 | | | 2 | | | 3 | | | 4 | |

gwam   1' 3'

Statistical Assessment

1. Follow the steps for the straight-copy assessment.
2. Take two 3' writings using the Diagnostic Writing feature. Choose the writing **placement2**.

     Attention Wall Street! The Zanes & Cash report for the end   4 38
of the year (Report #98) says that its last-quarter income was up   8 42
26% from the record earnings of last year. The report also says 12 46
that it was caused by a rise in gross sales of just over 4 1/3%.   16 50
The increase is the 7th in a row for last-quarter earnings; and   20 54
the chief executive of this old firm—Paul Cash—has told at   24 58
least one group that he is sure to ask the board (it will meet on 28 62
the last day of the month) for an "increase of up to $1.50 a share 32 66
as its dividend for the year."   34 68

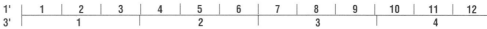

| 1' | 1 | 2 | 3 | 4 | 5 | 6 | 7 | 8 | 9 | 10 | 11 | 12 |
| 3' | | 1 | | | 2 | | | 3 | | | 4 | |

Document 7
Multi-page Report with Table

Open **steeringcommittee** from the data files. Add the text at the right to the end of the document.

Use full alignment for this report, and watch closely for any errors that may not be marked. Check for words that need to be changed to Canadian spelling.

Create a header to number the pages at the top right.

Add a comment to Patzy Frazier's telephone number to check the phone number.

Prepare a title page. The report was prepared for **Nelson Chamber of Commerce by Richard R. Holmes, President**. Date the report March 15.

Delete the comment.

Save the report as **mod9-d7**, and save the title page as **mod9-d7a**.

Recommended facilitators include: *teamleaders and* (set this up as a table) *the following*

Team	Team Leaders	Facilitators
Education	Dale Coppage, Nelson BC	Ellen Obert, Spokane WA
Youth Services	Lawrence Riveria, Portland, OR	Jack Jones, Vancouver BC
Recreation	Bradley Greger, Nelson BC	Carolos Pena, Calgary AB
Economic Development	Jon Guyton, Nelson BC	Harvey Lewis
Crime	Monica Brigham, Toronto ON	Shawn McNullan, NC

DS After the first breakout sessions, participants will join for lunch in the H. L. Calvert Union Building. The Steering Committee recommends that Mayor Alton johnson address the topic of meeting educational challenges of the next century. A repeat of the morning breakout sessions will begin at 1:30 *a.m.* This repeat will allow participants to contirube to another topic. In the closing session breakout facilitators will present the goals and plans to the audience. *During*

Sponsors

The Steerting Committee has discussed the sponsorship of a goals conference with a number of partners in the Nelson area. The following organizations have agreed to serve as sponsors: Nelson Economic Development Foundation, Bank of Canada, Northeast Bottling Company, ~~and~~ Bank of Nelson, and Farthington's Clothiers.

Summary

The Steering Committee strongly recommends this goals conference. The committee will be avilable at the Camber of commerce meeting to answer any questions.

Document 8
Agenda

Format the agenda as a table with no lines. Adjust the rows to leave extra space between each time slot. Save it as **mod9-d8**.

Goals Conference Agenda *all caps*

9:30 a.m. - 9:45 a.m.	Welcome
9:45 a.m. - 10:15 a.m.	Opening Remarks
	Overview of Community Quality Initiative
	Purpose of Goals Conference
	Process
	Introduction of Community Leaders and Chamber Officers
10:15 a.m. - 10:35 a.m.	Refreshment Break
10:35 a.m. - 12 noon	Breakout Sessions
12 noon - 1:00 p.m.	Lunch
	Speaker on Educational Challenges of the 21st Century
1:00 p.m. - 2:30 p.m.	~~Goals Setting Workshops~~ Breakout Sessions
2:30 p.m. - 2:45 p.m.	Refreshment Break
2:45 p.m. - 4:00 p.m.	Presentation of Goals

get these from the report.

module 1

Alphabetic Keys

OBJECTIVES

✳ Key the alphabetic keys by touch.
✳ Key using proper techniques.
✳ Key at a rate of 14 *gwam* or more.

LESSON 1 | Home Row, Space Bar, Enter, I

1a Home Row Position and Space Bar

Practice the steps at the right until you can place your hands in home-row position without watching.

Key the drill lines several times.

Home Row Position

1. Drop your hands to your side. Allow your fingers to curve naturally. Maintain this curve as you key.

2. Lightly place your left fingers over the **a s d f** and the right fingers over the **j k l ;**. You will feel a raised element on the *f* and *j* keys, which will help you keep your fingers on the home position. You are now in **home–row position**.

Space Bar and Enter

Strike the SPACE BAR, located at the bottom of the keyboard, with a down-and-in motion of the right thumb to space between words.

Enter   Reach with the fourth (little) finger of the right hand to ENTER. Press it to return the insertion point to the left margin. This action creates a **hard return**. Use a hard return at the end of all drill lines. Quickly return to home position (over ;).

Key these lines

a s d f **SPACE** j k l ; **ENTER**
a s d f **SPACE** j k l ; **ENTER**

Document 4
Memo

Prepare this memo using the Elegant memo template. Use Find and Replace to find and replace any words that should be changed to Canadian spellings.

Save the memo as **mod9-d4**.

TO: Marilyn Smith, Public Relations Media Assistant | **FROM:** Anthony Baker, Public Relations Coordinator | **DATE:** Current | **SUBJECT:** Electronic Presentation

Richard Holmes has been invited to introduce our company at the March 15 meeting of the Nelson Chamber of Commerce. Please prepare a 20-minute electronic presentation for this meeting by extracting the key points from Richard's speech, which is attached.

As you prepare the presentation, remember these key points:

- Write phrases, not sentences, so that listeners focus on the key points.
- Use parallel structure and limit wraparound lines of text.
- Create *builds* to keep the audience alert.
- Add transitions between slides (suggest fade in and out).
- Add graphics and humor—we want them to remember us.

Please have the presentation ready for Richard to review by February 24. After he has made his revisions and the presentation is final, print the presentation as a handout. | xx | Attachment

Document 5
Table

Format this list of purchases as a table. Center the column headings and the data in Column 1.

Calculate the total price for each item; then calculate the final total in cell D7. Save the table as **mod9-d5**.

Quantity	Description	Unit Price	Total Price
2	Posture back task chair	265.00	
2	Under-desk keyboard manager	54.00	
1	10 pack Zip 100 disks	99.95	
1	Carton laser paper (5,000 sheets, 20 lb.)	47.50	
2	Laser address labels, #5168	24.95	
	Total		

Document 6
Letter

Prepare this letter to order supplies. Copy the table you created in Document 5 into the letter. Use the current date and add an appropriate salutation. Key the company name in the closing in all caps.

Insert another row in the table just before the Total with this information: **2 external Zip drives at $89.99 each.** Recalculate the total.

Save the letter as **mod9-d6**.

West Coast Office Supplies
3245 Granville Street
Vancouver BC V6B 5G8

Please ship the following items, which are listed in your current office supplies catalogue.

Insert the table here (Document 5)

Please bill this to our account number 4056278. This order is urgent; therefore, ship it overnight by Loomis.

Yours truly

Selkirk Communications

Allan Burgess, Purchasing Agent

New Keys

1b Procedures for Learning New Keys

Apply these steps each time you learn a new key.

STANDARD PLAN | for Learning New Keyreaches

1. Find the new key on the illustrated keyboard. Then find it on your keyboard.
2. Watch your finger make the reach to the new key a few times. Keep other fingers curved in home position. For an upward reach, straighten the finger slightly; for a downward reach, curve the finger a bit more.
3. Repeat the drill until you can key it fluently.

1c Home Row

1. Go to the Open Screen of *Keyboarding Pro*.
2. Key each line once. Press ENTER at the end of each line. Press ENTER twice to double-space (DS) between 2-line groups.
3. Close the Open Screen without saving your text.

Press Space Bar once.

```
1 fff   jjj   fjf   fff   jjj   fjf   fjf   jfj   jfj   fjf
2 ddd   kkk   dkd   ddd   kkk   dkd   dkd   kdk   kdk   dkd
```
Press ENTER twice to DS
```
3 sss   lll   sls   sss   lll   sls   sls   lsl   lsl   sls
4 aaa   ;;;   a;a   aaa   ;;;   a;s   a;a   ;a;   ;a;   a;a
```
DS
```
5 ff jj ff jj fj fj fj dd kk dd kk dk dk dk
6 ss ll ss ll sl sl sl aa ;; aa ;; a; a; a;
```
```
7 f j d k s l a ;
```
DS
```
8 ff jj dd kk ss ll aa ;;
```
```
9 fff jjj ddd kkk sss lll aaa jjj ;;;
```

1d i

1. Apply the standard plan for learning the letter *i*.
2. Keep fingers curved; key the drill once.

```
10 i ik ik ik is is id id if if ill i ail did kid lid
11 i ik aid ail did kid lid lids kids ill aid did ilk
12 id aid aids laid said ids lid skids kiss disk dial
```

Document 2
Memo with Table

Prepare this memo to the staff. Use the Elegant memo template.

List the words in the table in alphabetical order. Use 10% blue shading in the first row.

Save the memo as **mod9-d2**.

TO: All Staff, Spokane Branch
FROM: Marilyn Josephson, Office Manager
SUBJECT: American vs. Canadian Spelling
DATE: Current

All correspondence addressed to our Canadian office should now include Canadian spelling. Some of the differences are shown in the following table. We will need to get a list of other words that differ as well.

U.S. Spelling	Canadian Spelling
counseling	counselling
honor	honour
endeavor	endeavour
defense	defence
center	centre
check (meaning money)	cheque
color	colour
marvelous	marvellous
labor	labour
theater	theatre

Document 3
Letter

Key the company name a DS below the complimentary closing in all caps (use Change Case to make the autotext all caps). Press ENTER four times and key the writer's name.

Use Find and Replace to find and replace any words that should be changed to Canadian spellings.

Save the letter as **mod9-d3**.

Current date | Chamber of Commerce | 225 Hall Street | Nelson BC V1L 5X4 | CANADA | Ladies and Gentlemen

Selkirk Communications will be relocating its headquarters from Spokane, Washington, to downtown Nelson on April 1. We are an international communications company offering the following services:

1. Written and oral communications refresher workshops
2. Customized training onsite or in our training center
3. Mail-order newsletters
4. Computer training on popular business software
5. Individualized or group training sessions

I would like to attend the Nelson Chamber of Commerce meeting in March to share some of the exciting ways we can help Chamber members meet their training needs. Is there time available for us on your March agenda? Please contact Anthony Baker, public relations coordinator, at our Nelson office at (604) 555-0193.

Selkirk Communications will be holding an open house during the month of April, and we will be inviting you and the Nelson community to attend. We look forward to becoming actively involved with the business community of Nelson.

Yours truly | SELKIRK COMMUNICATIONS | Richard R. Holmes, President

1e Lesson 1 from Software

1. Read the information at the right. Then do Lesson 1 from *Keyboarding Pro*.

1. Select a lesson from Alphabetic by clicking the lesson number. (Figure 1-1)
2. The first activity is displayed automatically. In Figure 1-2, *Learn Home Row* is in yellow because this activity is active. Follow the directions on screen. Key from the screen.

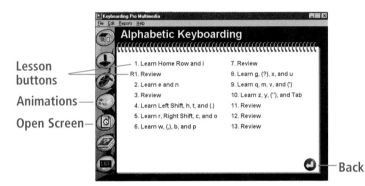

Figure 1-1 Alphabetic Keyboarding Lesson Menu

Figure 1-2 Alphabetic Keyboarding (Lesson 1: Learn Home Row and i)

3. Key the Textbook Keying activity from your textbook (lines 13–18 below). Press ESC to continue.
4. Figure 1-3 shows the Lesson Report. A check mark opposite an exercise indicates that the exercise has been completed.
5. At the bottom, click the **Print** button to print your Lesson Report. Click the **Graph** button to view the Performance Graph.
6. Click the **Back** button twice to return to the Main menu. Then click the **Exit** button to quit the program. Remove your storage disk if necessary. Clean up the work area.

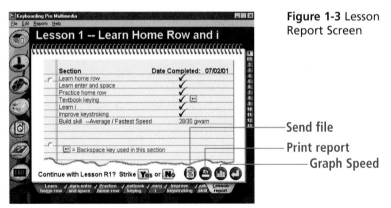

Figure 1-3 Lesson Report Screen

Textbook Keying

2. Key the lines at the right in Textbook Keying. Key each line once. Strike ENTER at the end of each line.
3. When you complete the lesson, print your Lesson Report (step 5 above) and exit the software.

```
13  a  a;  al  ak  aj  s  s;  sl  sk  sj  d  d;  dl  dk  dj
14  j  ja  js  jd  jf  k  ka  ks  kd  kf  l  la  ls  ld  lf
15  a;  sl  a;sl  dkfj  a;sl  dkfj  a;sldkfj  asdf  jk
16  a;  sl  a;sl  dk  fj  dkfj  a;sl  dkfj  fkds;a;  fj
17  f  ff  j  jj  d  dd  k  kk  s  ss  l  ll  a  aa  ;  ;;  fj
18  afj;  a  s  d  f  j  k  l  ;  asdf  jkl;  fdsa  jkl;
```

Selkirk Communications

Selkirk Communications is a training company that is relocating its office from Spokane, Washington, to Nelson, Canada. As an administrative assistant, you will prepare a number of documents using many of the formatting and word processing skills you have learned throughout Lessons 26 to 60. Selkirk Communications uses the block letter format and unbound report style. Before you begin, add Selkirk Communications as autotext so that you do not have to key it repeatedly.

Document 1

Invitation

Format this document attractively. Use a 20-point font for the main heading and add a special text effect. Use a different font for the callouts (Place, Time, etc.), and 14-point font for the text.

Use a fancy bullet for the bulleted list. Position the document attractively on the page. Save it as **mod9-d1**.

OPEN HOUSE

Place: Selkirk Communications
1003 Baker Street
Nelson BC VIL 5N7

Time: 1:00-4:00 p.m.

Date: Saturday and Sunday, April 27 and 28

Selkirk Communications is excited to open its tenth international communications office in downtown Nelson. Please plan to attend our open house.

Come in and meet our friendly staff and learn how we can help meet your training needs. Selkirk Communications specializes in:

- Instructor-led training in our classroom or your facility
- Newsletters designed to meet your needs
- Authorized training center for Microsoft Office
- Oral and written communication refresher courses

LESSON 1R | Review

✳ Warmup

1Ra Review home row

1. Open *Keyboarding Pro* software.
2. Click the ↓ next to *Class ID* and select your section. Click your name.
3. Key your password and click **OK**.
4. Go to *Lesson R1*.

Key each exercise as directed. Repeat if desired.

Fingers curved and upright

```
1  f j fjf jj fj fj jf dd kk dd kk dk dk dk
2  s ; s;s ;; s; s; s; aa ;; aa ;; a; a; a;

3  fj dk sl a; fjdksla; jfkdls;a ;a ;s kd j
4  f j fjf d k dkd s l sls a ; fj dk sl a;a

5  a; al ak aj s s; sl sk sj d d; dl dk djd
6  ja js jd jf k ka ks kd kf l la ls ld lfl

7  f fa fad s sa sad f fa fall fall l la lad s sa sad
8  a as ask a ad add j ja jak f fa fall; ask; add jak
```

▤ Skillbuilding

1Rb Keyboard Review

Key each line once; repeat as time permits.

```
9   ik ki ki ik is if id il ij ia ij ik is if ji id ia
10  is il ill sill dill fill sid lid ail lid slid jail

11  if is il kid kids ill kid if kids; if a kid is ill
12  is id if ai aid jaks lid sid sis did ail; if lids;

13  a lass; ask dad; lads ask dad; a fall; fall salads
14  as a fad; ask a lad; a lass; all add; a kid; skids

15  as asks did disk ail fail sail ails jail sill silk
16  ask dad; dads said; is disk; kiss a lad; salad lid

17  aid a lad; if a kid is; a salad lid; kiss sad dads
18  as ad all ask jak lad fad kids ill kill fall disks
```

MODULE 8 Checkpoint

Objective Assessment   Answer the questions below to see if you have mastered the content of this module.

1. A dynamic, graphic form of print that provides for adding color and shading and that is ideal for formatting banner headings in newsletters is created using the _____ feature.

2. A chart that is used effectively to show percentages of a whole is a(n) _____.

3. Text columns that flow down one column to the top of the next column are known as _____ columns.

4. To change the format of a document and have a different format on the same page, insert a(n) _____ section break.

5. Section breaks are shown as a dotted line with the type of break indicated in _____ view.

6. An informal message that is sent by one computer user to another computer user is referred to as _____.

7. To insert shapes such as an octagon or triangle, click _____ on the Drawing toolbar.

8. To view your Web page in Word as it would appear in your Web browser, click _____ from the View menu.

9. You can recognize hyperlinked text because it is usually _____.

10. The _____ feature is used to show differences between two documents.

Performance Assessment

Document 1
Newsletter

1. Open **Safety Net** from the data files.
2. Change the side margins for the entire document to .75".
3. Use WordArt for the banner.
4. Format the document in two equal-sized columns.
5. Create a Line chart to replace the Workplace Accidents Table. Change the line color to red.
6. Use a 1.5-point line across the column to separate components of the newsletter except when it would be positioned at the top of a column.
7. Insert a picture of a handheld cell phone positioned at the left side of the column after the cell phone is mentioned in the text.
8. Insert a picture of an individual at a computer workstation after the ergonomics seminar has been introduced.
9. Adjust the newsletter so that it will fit on one page with balanced columns.
10. Print and save the document as **checkpoint 8d-1**.

Document 2
Web Page with Hyerlinks

1. Open **checkpoint 8d-1**.
2. Select the line chart; create a hyperlink to the Excel data file **accidents.xls**.
3. Create a link to the e-mail address for Warren Derrick (wderrick@asc.org).
4. Save as a Web page. Save the file as **checkpoint 8d-2**.

LESSON 2 | E and N

Warmup

2a

1. Open *Keyboarding Pro*.
2. Locate your student record.
3. Select Lesson 2.

```
1 ff  dd  ss  aa  ff  dd  ss  aa  jj  kk  ll  ;;  fj  dk  sl  a;  a;
2 fj  dk  sl  a;  fjdksla;  a;sldkfj  fj  dk  sl  a;  fjdksla;
3 aa  ss  dd  ff  jj  kk  ll  ;;  aa  ss  dd  ff  jj  kk  ll  ;;  a;
4 if  a;  as  is;  kids  did;  ask  a  sad  lad;  if  a  lass  is
```

New Keys

2b E and N

Key each line once; DS between groups.

e Reach *up* with *left second* finger.

n Reach down with right first finger.

```
   e
 5 e  ed  ed  led  led  lea  lea  ale  ale  elf  elf  eke  eke  ed
 6 e  el  el  eel  els  elk  elk  lea  leak  ale  kale  led  jell
 7 e  ale  kale  lea  leak  fee  feel  lea  lead  elf  self  eke

   n
 8 n  nj  nj  an  an  and  and  fan  fan  and  kin  din  fin  land
 9 n  an  fan  in  fin  and  land  sand  din  fans  sank  an  sin
10 n  in  ink  sink  inn  kin  skin  an  and  land  in  din  dink

   all reaches learned
11 den  end  fen  ken  dean  dens  ales  fend  fens  keen  knee
12 if  in  need;  feel  ill;  as  an  end;  a  lad  and  a  lass;
13 and  sand;  a  keen  idea;  as  a  sail  sank;  is  in  jail;
14 an  idea;  an  end;  a  lake;  a  nail;  a  jade;  a  dean  is
```

2c Textbook Keying

Key each line once; DS between groups. Repeat.

```
15 if  a  lad;
16 is  a  sad  fall

17 if  a  lass  did  ask
18 ask  a  lass;  ask  a  lad

19 a;sldkfj  a;sldkfj  a;sldkfj
20 a;  sl  dk  fj  fj  dk  sl  a;  a;sldkfj

21 i  ik  ik  if  if  is  is  kid  skid  did  lid  aid  laid  said
22 ik  kid  ail  die  fie  did  lie  ill  ilk  silk  skill  skid
```

Reach with little finger; tap Enter key quickly; return finger to home key.

60c-d2
Web Page with Hyperlink

1. Open **rules** from the data files.
2. Select **Ryan O'Bryant**. Create a link to his e-mail address (jobryant@say.org).
3. Select the word *here* in the last paragraph, and create a hyperlink to http://www.eteamz.com/basketball/instruction/tips/.
4. Change the background; you will be posting this document to your Web page.
5. Save this *Word* document as a Web page. Name the file **60c-d2**.
6. View the document in your Web browser.

60c-d3
E-mail with Attachment

1. Key each enumerated item that follows, correcting the redundancies as you key. (*Hint:* A redundancy is a phrase that repeats an idea in an accompanying word, e.g., *true facts* or *full and complete.*) Save the document as **60c-d3revised**.
2. Compare the data file **60c-d3original** with your file. Merge to a new document and save it as **60c-d3**.
3. Key an e-mail message to your instructor stating that **60c-d3** is attached. Key **Redundancy Drill** as the subject line. Attach the file to your e-mail message.

1. The witness was instructed to tell the honest truth.
2. Attendance is a necessary requirement for a keyboarding course.
3. The two twins were greeted by their brother and sister.
4. Past history should assist us in blocking an appropriate number of rooms for each night of the convention.
5. Please refer back to page 25 for exact wording of the research questions.
6. Would you like my personal opinion?
7. Children left unattended are in serious danger.
8. Let me know whether or not you will attend the meeting at 2 p.m. in the afternoon.
9. Each and every contestant will receive a prize for being on the show.
10. Waiting for my plane to leave, I watched the sun set in the west.

2d Open Screen

The **Open Screen** is a word processor. Exercises to be keyed in the Open Screen are identified with an Open Screen icon. For these exercises, follow the instructions in the textbook and key from your textbook. Keep your eyes on the textbook copy as you key— not on your fingers or the screen.

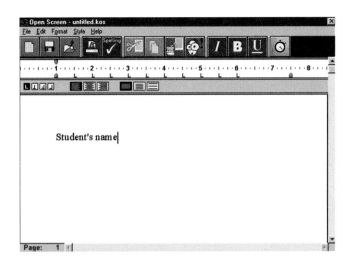

1. Click the **Open Screen** button at the left edge of the Main Menu of *Keyboarding Pro*.
2. Key your name and strike ENTER twice.
3. Follow the directions in the textbook for the drill.
4. Print what you key in the Open Screen.
5. Click the **Close** button in the upper-right corner to exit the Open Screen.

Skillbuilding

2e Reinforcement

1. In the Open Screen, key each line twice. DS between groups of two lines.
2. Print but do not save the exercise.
3. Close the Open Screen and you will return to Lesson 2 in the software.

> **TECHNIQUE TIP**
>
> Keep your eyes on the textbook copy.

i

23 ik ik ik if is il ik id is if kid did lid aid ails
24 did lid aid; add a line; aid kids; ill kids; id is

n

25 nj nj nj an an and and end den ken in ink sin skin
26 jn din sand land nail sank and dank skin sans sink

e

27 el els elf elk lea lead fee feel sea seal ell jell
28 el eke ale jak lake elf els jaks kale eke els lake

all reaches

29 dine in an inn; fake jade; lend fans; as sand sank
30 in nine inns; if an end; need an idea; seek a fee;

2f End the lesson

1. Print the Lesson Report.
2. Exit the software; remove the storage disk if appropriate.

60c-d1
Newsletter

1. Key a newsletter using the information that follows.
2. Set page margins for a 1" top margin and .5" side and bottom margins.
3. Use a banner heading with the design in column 1, row 3 of the WordArt Gallery, and change the color to dark red. Extend the heading from margin to margin.
4. Use 11-point Times New Roman for body text and Heading 1 for all headings.
5. Format the document using two equal columns with .5" spacing between columns.
6. Key the text and balance columns.
7. Copy the radial diagram from **Portfolio Structure** in the data files and paste it at the bottom of the newsletter at the approximate horizontal center.
8. If necessary, adjust the newsletter so that it fits on one page.
9. Save the newsletter as **60c-d1**, and print a copy.

Central Foundation Update
Central University Foundation committees met this past week, and this newsletter is designed to update all Board Members of the actions taken by one of the Investment Committee. At its last meeting, the Foundation Board charged the Investment Committee to work with its consultants to diversify the Foundation's investment portfolio and present the proposed portfolio structure to the full Board for its approval at its next meeting.

Asset Allocation
The Investment Committee agreed on an aggressive asset allocation of 75% equity and 25% fixed income securities. The Foundation endows its assets in perpetuity and spends only 5% of the income earned on these assets each year. Therefore, the extremely long time horizon of the investment portfolio justifies the aggressive investment in equities.

Asset Classes
The Committee considered eight classes of assets: large cap core, large cap value, large cap growth, small cap value, small cap growth, international equities, fixed income, and alternative assets. The Committee included all classes of assets except alternative investments in its recommendation. Alternative investments are so named because these assets have not traditionally been included in the portfolios of foundations. Alternative investments include assets such as hedge funds, venture capital funds, real estate funds, and direct investment in startup ventures. The Committee recommends that investments in alternative investments be deferred for at least a year.

Asset Weightings
Obviously, some of the equity classes deserve higher weightings than other classes. Small cap stocks and international stocks play a less predominate role in traditional foundation portfolios than large cap stocks. The portfolio structure diagram shown below contains the Investment Committee's recommendations for weighting the various asset classes.

LESSON 3 | Review

Warmup

3a

Key each line at a steady pace; strike and release each key quickly. Key each line again at a faster pace.

home 1 ad ads lad fad dad as ask fa la lass jak jaks alas

   n 2 an fan and land fan flan sans sand sank flank dank

   i 3 is id ill dill if aid ail fail did kid ski lid ilk

 all 4 ade alas nine else fife ken; jell ink jak inns if;

Skillbuilding

3b Rhythm Builder

Key each line twice.

Lines 5–8: Think and key words. Make the space part of the word.

Lines 9–12: Think and key phrases. Do not key the vertical rules separating the phrases.

easy words

 5 if is as an ad el and did die eel fin fan elf lens

 6 as ask and id kid and ade aid eel feel ilk skis an

 7 ail fail aid did ken ale led an flan inn inns alas

 8 eel eke nee kneel did kids kale sees lake elf fled

easy phrases

 9 el el|id id|is is|eke eke|lee lee|ale ale|jill jill

10 is if|is a|is a|a disk|a disk|did ski|did ski|is a

11 sell a|sell a|sell a sled|fall fad|fall fad|did die

12 sees a lake|sees a lake|as a deal|sell a sled|all a

3c Technique Practice

Key each 2-line group twice; SS.

> **TECHNIQUE TIP**
>
> Reach with the little finger; tap Enter key quickly; return finger to home key.

home row: fingers curved and upright

13 jak lad as lass dad sad lads fad fall la ask ad as

14 asks add jaks dads a lass ads flak adds sad as lad

upward reaches: straighten fingers slightly; return quickly to home position

15 fed die led ail kea lei did ale fife silk leak lie

16 sea lid deal sine desk lie ale like life idea jail

double letters: don't hurry when stroking double letters

17 fee jell less add inn seek fall alee lass keel all

18 dill dell see fell eel less all add kiss seen sell

LESSON 60 | Assessment

Skillbuilding

60a
Warmup
Key each line twice SS; DS between 2-line groups.

alphabetic	1	Jayne Cox puzzled over workbooks that were required for geometry.
figures	2	Edit pages 308 and 415 in Book A; pages 17, 29, and 60 in Book B.
one hand	3	Plum trees on a hilly acre, in my opinion, create no vast estate.
easy	4	If they sign an entitlement, the town land is to go to the girls.

| 1 | 2 | 3 | 4 | 5 | 6 | 7 | 8 | 9 | 10 | 11 | 12 | 13 |

gwam 3' | 5'

60b
Timed Writings
Take one 3' and one 5' writing at your control level.

A all letters

What is a college education worth today? If you asked that 4 | 2
question to a random sample of people, you would get a wide range of 9 | 5
responses. Many would respond that you cannot quantify the worth of 13 | 8
a bachelor's degree. They quickly stress that many factors other 18 | 11
than wages enhance the quality of life. They tend to focus on the 22 | 13
benefits of sciences and liberal arts and the appreciation they 26 | 16
develop for things that they would never have been exposed to if 31 | 18
they had not attended college. 33 | 20

Data show, though, that you can place a value on a college 37 | 22
education—at least in respect to wages earned. Less than twenty 41 | 25
years ago, a high school graduate earned only about fifty percent 45 | 27
of what a college graduate earned. Today, that number is quite 50 | 30
different. The gap between the wages of a college graduate and 54 | 32
the wages of a high school graduate has more than doubled in the 58 | 35
last twenty years. 59 | 36

The key factor in economic success is education. The new 63 | 38
jobs that pay high wages require more skills and a college degree. 68 | 41
Fortunately, many high school students do recognize the value of 72 | 43
getting a degree. Far more high school graduates are going to 76 | 46
college than ever before. They know that the best jobs are jobs 81 | 48
for knowledge workers and those jobs require a high level of skill. 85 | 51

| 3' | 1 | 2 | 3 | 4 |
| 5' | 1 | 2 | 3 |

Assessment

60c
Timed production: 25'

Continue

Check

With CheckPro 2002:   When you complete a document, proofread it, check the spelling, and preview for placement. When you are completely satisfied with the document, click the **Continue** button to move to the next document. You will not be able to return and edit a document once you continue to the next document. Click the **Check** button when you are ready to error-check the test. Review and/or print the document analysis results.

Without CheckPro 2002: On the signal to begin, key the documents in sequence. When time has been called, proofread all documents again; identify errors, and determine *g-pwam*.

$$g\text{-}pwam = \frac{\text{total words keyed}}{25}$$

3d Keyboard Mastery

Key each line once;
repeat drill.

LEFT FINGERS   4 \ 3 \ 2 \ 1 \ 1 \ 2 \ 3 \ 4   RIGHT FINGERS

TECHNIQUE TIP

Strike keys quickly.
Strike the Space Bar with
down-and-in motion.
Strike Enter with
a quick flick of the little
finger.

reach review

19 ea sea lea seas deal leaf leak lead leas fleas keas

20 as ask lass ease as asks ask ask sass as alas seas

21 sa sad sane sake sail sale sans safe sad said sand

22 le sled lead flee fled ale flea lei dale kale leaf

23 jn jn nj nj in fan fin an; din ink sin and inn an;

24 de den end fen an an and and ken knee nee dean dee

phrases (think and key phrases)

25 and and land land el el elf elf self self ail nail

26 as as ask ask ad ad lad lad id id lid lid kid kids

27 if if|is is|jak jak|all all|did did|nan nan|elf elf

28 as a lad| ask dad| fed a jak| as all ask| sales fad

29 sell a lead|seal a deal|feel a leaf|if a jade sale

30 is a|is as if|a disk|aid all kids|did ski|is a silk

3e Reinforcement

1. In the Open Screen, key
   your name. Insert a hard
   return.
2. Key each line once. DS
   between groups of two
   lines.
3. Print the exercise.
4. Click the **X** box in the
   upper-right corner to close
   the Open Screen.
5. Print your Lesson Report
   and Exit.

d/e

31 den end fen ken dean dens ales fend fens keen knee

32 a deed; a desk; a jade; an eel; a jade eel; a dean

n/a

33 an an in in and and en end end sane sane sand sand

34 a land; a dean; a fan; a fin; a sane end; end land

nj

35 el eel eld elf sell self el dell fell elk els jell

36 in fin inn inks dine sink fine fins kind line lain

all reaches

37 an and fan dean elan flan land lane lean sand sane

38 sell a lead; sell a jade; seal a deal; feel a leaf

Applications

59c-d1
Compare and
Merge

1. Open **grammar practice** from the data files. Save as **59c-d1 revised**.

2. Edit each sentence selecting the proper words from the choices shown in parentheses. Resave.

3. Compare the data file **59c-d1 original** with your file. Merge to a new document and save it as **59c-d1**.

 59c-d2
Compare and
Merge

Ms. Ginger Spivey
Jefferson Realty
12 West Street
Murrieta, CA 92562-2934

1. Key the letter below as a block letter with mixed punctuation. Use the current date. See the Rolodex card at the left for the letter address.

2. Correct the errors in punctuation, capitalization, subject-verb agreement, and word choice. Proofread carefully to ensure an error-free document. Save as **59c-d3 revised**.

3. Compare the data file **59c-d3 original** with your file. Merge to a new document and save it as **59c-d3**.

4. Insert the following comment at the end of the first bulleted list:

   I recommend 850 MHz processor, 512 MB SDRAM, 20 GB hard drive, and 24X variable CD-ROM. Cost is $2,500.

5. Select the total in the last paragraph. Insert the following comment:

   You will need to recalculate this amount if you go with my recommendation.

6. Edit the first comment as follows: **20X variable CD-ROM and cost of $2,450**. Delete the second comment. Resave and print.

   Dear Ms. Spivey

   Recently you asked me to compare several computers and printers and to recommend equipment that Jefferson realty should purchase. These recommendations follow.

   • I recommend the Amina Optima notebook by Finn at $2,199. You agents can use the Amina Optima in the office as well as on the road. This computer has a 366 MHz processor, a 15" XGA active matrix display, 64MB SDRAM, a 6.4GB hard drive, and a 20X variable CD-ROM/floppy drive. The Amina optima comes with the latest version of the Capstone Office Suite.

   • I recommend Ventura's AZ Printer/Copier/Scanner at $499. This multifunctional unit will save you the expense of a separate copier and scanner. The AZ includes integrated desktop software for organizing scanned documents and OCR software for text editing.

   Both pieces of equipment has been rated by Savvy Consumer as being reliable low-maintenance and best buys. You would need 8 notebooks ($17,592). With the printer, this purchase would fall comfortably within your $20,000 budget. If you have any questions or need further assistance please do not hesitate to call me.

   Sincerely | Your Name | Consultant

LESSON 4 | Left Shift, H, T, Period

 Warmup

4a
Key each line twice SS.
Keep eyes on copy.

home row 1 al as ads lad dad fad jak fall lass asks fads all;

e/i/n 2 ed ik jn in knee end nine line sine lien dies leis

all reaches 3 see a ski; add ink; fed a jak; is an inn; as a lad

easy 4 an dial id is an la lake did el ale fake is land a

 **New Keys**

4b Left **Shift** and **h**
Key each line once.

Follow the "Standard procedures for learning new keyreaches" on p. 4 for all remaining reaches.

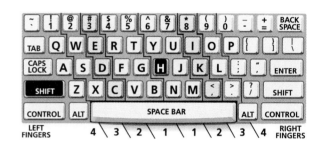

left shift Reach *down* with *left fourth* (little) finger; shift, strike, release.

h Reach to *left* with *right first* finger.

left shift

5 J Ja Ja Jan Jan Jane Jana Ken Kass Lee Len Nan Ned

6 and Ken and Lena and Jake and Lida and Nan and Ida

7 Inn is; Jill Ina is; Nels is; Jen is; Ken Lin is a

h

8 h hj hj he he she she hen aha ash had has hid shed

9 h hj ha hie his half hand hike dash head sash shad

10 aha hi hash heal hill hind lash hash hake dish ash

all reaches learned

11 Nels Kane and Jake Jenn; she asked Hi and Ina Linn

12 Lend Lana and Jed a dish; I fed Lane and Jess Kane

13 I see Jake Kish and Lash Hess; Isla and Helen hike

4c New Key Mastery
Key the drill once; DS and repeat. Strive for good control.

14 he she held a lead; she sells jade; she has a sale

15 Ha Ja Ka La Ha Hal Ja Jake Ka Kahn La Ladd Ha Hall

16 Hal leads; Jeff led all fall; Hal has a safe lead

17 Hal Hall heads all sales; Jake Hess asks less fee;

Comments

help keywords

Insert a comment

Modify a comment

Delete a comment

Members of writing teams also benefit from the Comment feature as it allows each author to add notes to selected text. They may also insert responses to the various comments. A comment is keyed in a comment balloon. If comments are not visible on the screen, click **View**, **Markup** to view the comments.

To insert a comment in a document:

1. Select the text or item you want to comment on or click at the end of the text.
2. Click **Insert**, **Comment**. A comment balloon displays.
3. Type the comment in the comment balloon. To edit a comment, click inside the comment balloon. Make the desired changes.

All defenses must be player-to-player, but double-teaming is allowed within the three-point line. Within the lane, all defenders can go after the ball. Players may switch after picks or help if a defender loses his

> **Comment:** Which term do you recommend—the traditional team man-to-man or player-to-player?

To delete a comment:

1. Display the Reviewing toolbar if not displayed (View, Toolbars, Reviewing).
2. Click the **Reject Change/Delete Comment** button on the Reviewing Toolbar. To delete all comments, click the down arrow and choose **Delete All Comments in Document**.

MOUS TIPS

Right-click comment and click Delete Comment.

Click Insert Comment on Reviewing Toolbar to insert a comment.

Reviewing
Final Showing Markup ▾ Show ▾

To respond to a comment, click in the comment; then click **Insert**, **Comment**. A new comment balloon displays below the original comment. Key the response in the new comment balloon.

Drill 2 | **INSERT COMMENT**

1. Open **rules** from the data files. Save as **59b-drill2**.
2. Find and select the term *player-to-player*. Key the following comment in the comment balloon.

Which term do you recommend—the traditional man-to-man or player-to-player?

3. Resave and print. Do not close this file.

Drill 3 | **EDIT COMMENT**

1. Edit the comment in 59b-drill2 as follows:

Which term do you recommend—the traditional man-to-man or player-to-player? *(Insert the words* ***in the handout to players and parents*** *after the word recommend.)*

2. Save as **59b-drill3** and print. Do not close this file.

Drill 4 | **RESPOND TO COMMENT**

1. Insert the following response to the comment in 59b-drill3:

I prefer man-to-man because that's the term the referees and other coaches will use in the game.

2. Save as **59b-drill4**. Do not close this file.

Drill 5 | **DELETE COMMENTS**

1. You agree with the change suggested in the response created in 59b-drill4. Edit as indicated.

2. Delete both comments. Save as **59b-drill5**.

4d t and . (period)

Key each line once.

t Reach *up* with *left first* finger.

. (period) Reach *down* with *right third* finger.

Period: Space once after a period that follows an initial or an abbreviation. To increase readability, space twice after a period that ends a sentence.

t

18 t tf tf aft aft left fit fat fete tiff tie the tin
19 tf at at aft lit hit tide tilt tint sits skit this
20 hat kit let lit ate sit flat tilt thin tale tan at

. (period)

21 .1 .1 1.1 fl. fl. L. L. Neal and J. N. List hiked.
22 Hand J. H. Kass a fan. Jess did. I need an idea.
23 Jane said she has a tan dish; Jae and Lee need it.

all reaches learned

24 I did tell J. K. that Lt. Li had left. He is ill.
25 tie tan kit sit fit hit hat; the jet left at nine.
26 I see Lila and Ilene at tea. Jan Kane ate at ten.

Skillbuilding

4e Reinforcement

Lines 27–34: Key each line twice in the Open Screen. Try to increase your speed the second time.

Lines 35–38: Key the lines once; repeat.

End the lesson

Print the lines keyed in the Open Screen and print your Lesson Report. Exit the software.

reach review
27 tf .1 hj ft ki de jh tf ik ed hj de ft ki 1. tf ik
28 elf eel left is sis fit till dens ink has delt ink

h/e
29 he he heed heed she she shelf shelf shed shed she
30 he has; he had; he led; he sleds; she fell; he is

i/t
31 it is if id did lit tide tide tile tile list list
32 it is; he hit it; he is ill; she is still; she is

shift
33 Hal and Nel; Jade dishes; Kale has half; Jed hides
34 Hi Ken; Helen and Jen hike; Jan has a jade; Ken is

35 Nan had a sale.
36 He did see Hal.
enter
37 Lee has a desk.
38 Ina hid a dish.

TECHNIQUE TIP

Strike Enter without pausing or looking up from the copy.

LESSON 59 | Workgroup Collaboration

Skillbuilding

59a
Warmup

Key each line twice SS;
DS between 2-line
groups.

alphabet 1 Loquacioius, breezy Hank forgot to jump over the waxed hall floor.

figures 2 Invoices 675 and 348, dated June 29 and August 10, were not paid.

one hand 3 Polk traded Case #789—24 sets of rare carved beads—as rare art.

easy 4 They may dismantle the eight authentic antique autos in the town.

| 1 | 2 | 3 | 4 | 5 | 6 | 7 | 8 | 9 | 10 | 11 | 12 | 13 |

New Functions

59b

help keywords
*Compare and merge
documents*

Compare and Merge

Members of writing teams benefit from the **Compare and Merge** feature as it tracks the differences between two documents. The edited document is compared to the original document. *Word* displays the differences in the two documents in color.

To compare and merge documents:

1. Open the edited copy of the document.

2. From the **Tools** menu, click **Compare and Merge Documents**.

3. Select the original document from the files.

4. Click the down arrow next to the Merge button; select one of these three choices:

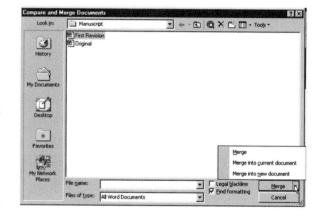

a. **Merge**—to display differences in the orginal document.

b. **Merge into current document**—to display differences in edited document.

c. **Merge into new document**—to display differences in a new document.

D r i l l 1 | **COMPARE AND MERGE**

1. Key the following paragraph exactly as shown. Save it as **59b-drill1 original**.

To avoid copyright infringement, the Internet user must be knowledgeable of copyright laws. 2 important laws include The Copyright Law of 1967, and the Digital Millennium Copyright Act, which was enacted in 1998 to update the copyright law.

2. Edit the paragraph keyed in Step 1 making the changes indicated as follows. Save it as **59b-drill1 revised**.

To avoid copyright infringement, the internet user must be knowledgeable of copyright laws. ② *sp*
important laws include The Copyright Law of 1967 and the Digital Millennium Copyright Act which was enacted in 1998 to update the copyright law s *for the digital age.*

3. Compare the two files prepared in Steps 1 and 2. Merge to a new document and save it as **59b-drill1**.

LESSON 5 | R, Right Shift, C, O

Warmup

5a
Key each line twice.

home keys 1 a; ad add al all lad fad jak ask lass fall jak lad

t/h/i/n 2 the hit tin nit then this kith dint tine hint thin

left shift/. 3 I need ink. Li has an idea. Hit it. I see Kate.

all reaches 4 Jeff ate at ten; he left a salad dish in the sink.

New Keys

5b r and Right Shift
Key each line once.

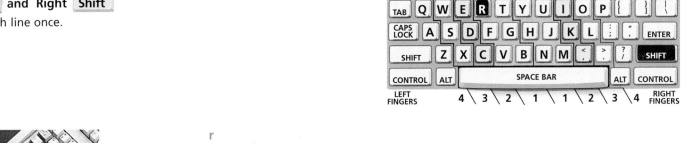

r Reach *up* with *left first* finger.

right shift Reach *down* with *right fourth* finger; shift, strike, release.

r

5 r rf rf riff riff fir fir rid ire jar air sir lair

6 rf rid ark ran rat are hare art rant tire dirt jar

7 rare dirk ajar lark rain kirk share hart rail tart

right shift

8 D D Dan Dan Dale Ti Sal Ted Ann Ed Alf Ada Sid Fan

9 and Sid and Dina and Allen and Eli and Dean and Ed

10 Ed Dana; Dee Falk; Tina Finn; Sal Alan; Anna Deeds

all reaches learned

11 Jane and Ann hiked in the sand; Asa set the tents.

12 a rake; a jar; a tree; a red fire; a fare; a rain;

13 Fred Derr and Rai Tira dined at the Tree Art Fair.

5c New Key Mastery
Key each line twice. DS between groups.

14 ir ir ire fir first air fair fire tire rid sir

15 fir jar tar fir flit rill till list stir dirt fire

16 Feral is ill. Dan reads. Dee and Ed Finn see Dere.

17 All is still as Sarah and I fish here in the rain.

18 I still see a red ash tree that fell in the field.

19 Lana said she did sail her skiff in the dark lake.

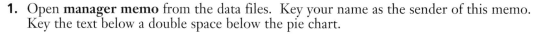

Applications

58c-d1

Create Hyperlinks and a Web Page

1. Open **manager memo** from the data files. Key your name as the sender of this memo. Key the text below a double space below the pie chart.

   The recommendation for providing the Listening Skills Training Program has been accepted by our management team and will be implemented April 1, 200-. In preparation for this training, you are to review resources on the topics listed below. Just click on each topic to hyperlink to valuable resources that have already been identified. After you have viewed these links, please identify additional resources and e-mail them to my assistant, Janice Berryhill, prior to next week's meeting.

   International Listening Association

   The Power of Listening

   Improving Your Listening Skills

2. Create the following hyperlinks:
   a. Select **Janice Berryhill**. Create a link to your instructor's e-mail address.
   b. Select **International Listening Association**. Create a link to www.listen.org.
   c. Select **The Power of Listening**. Create a link to www.smartbiz.com/sbs/arts/bly55.htm.
   d. Select **Improving Your Listening Skills**. Create a link to www.smartbiz.com/sbs/arts/wwt3.htm.

3. Save this *Word* document as a Web page to the folder named Web Page created in Drill 1. Name the file **58c-d1,** and view the document in your Web browser.

58c-d2
Link to E-mail Address and Save as Web Page

1. Open **timings** from the data files.
✳ 2. Create a link to the e-mail address for *Mitchell T. Kiesecker* (mtkiesecker@mtu.edu).
3. Save this *Word* table as a Web page to the folder named *Web Page* created in Drill 1. Name the file **58c-d2**.
4. View the document in your Web browser.

DISCOVER

To link to an e-mail address: under Link to, click **E-mail address** and key the e-mail address in E-mail Address Entry box.

58c-d3
Format Background and Save as Web Page

1. Open **52c-d1**.
2. Change the background of this report. Choose **Background** from the Format menu. Choose one of the colors shown, click **More Colors** to design a custom color, or click **Fill Effects** to choose from a gradient, textured, patterned, or picture background. Experiment with a professional background for this report.
3. Increase the length of the horizontal line at the bottom of the document by dragging the right handle.

 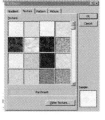

help keywords
Change a background

4. Save this *Word* document as a Web page to the Web Page folder. Name the file **58c-d3**.
5. View the document in your Web browser.

5d c and o
Key each line once.

c Reach *down* with *left second* finger.

o Reach *up* with right *third* finger.

c

20 c c cd cd cad cad can can tic ice sac cake cat sic
21 clad chic cite cheek clef sick lick kick dice rice
22 call acid hack jack lack lick cask crack clan cane

o

23 o ol ol old old of off odd ode or ore oar soar one
24 ol sol sold told dole do doe lo doll sol solo odor
25 onto door toil lotto soak fort hods foal roan load

all reaches learned

26 Carlo Rand can call Rocco; Cole can call Doc Cost.
27 Trina can ask Dina if Nick Corl has left; Joe did.
28 Case sent Carole a nice skirt; it fits Lorna Rich.

Skillbuilding

5e Keyboard Reinforcement
Key each line once SS; key at a steady pace. Repeat, striving for control.

TECHNIQUE TIP

Reach up without moving hands away from your body. Use quick keystrokes.

o/r

29 or or for for nor nor ore ore oar oar roe roe sore
30 a rose|her or|he or|he rode|or for|a door|her doll

i/t

31 is is tis tis it it fit fit tie tie this this lits
32 it is|it is|it is this|it is this|it sits|tie fits

e/n

33 en en end end ne ne need need ken ken kneel kneels
34 lend the|lend the|at the end|at the end|need their

c/o

35 ch ch check check ck ck hack lack jack co co cones
36 the cot|the cot|a dock|a dock|a jack|a jack|a cone

all reaches

37 Jack and Rona did frost nine of the cakes at last.
38 Jo can ice her drink if Tess can find her a flask.
39 Ask Jean to call Fisk at noon; he needs her notes.

1. Create a folder named *Web Page*. You will save the *Word* document used in this drill in this folder.

2. Open **orgchart** from the data files.

3. Save this *Word* document as a Web page to the *Web Page* folder created in step 1. Name the file **58b-drill1**.

4. View the document in your browser.

(*Note:* The file **58b-drill1** and a folder **58b-drill1_files** are created when you save a document as a Web page.)

Hyperlinks

Hyperlinks enable an online reader to move quickly from place to place in the same document or to another file such as a spreadsheet or Web page. Hyperlinked text is usually displayed in a different color than the body text of the document. Images such as clip art, charts, and other graphics may contain hyperlinks. In this lesson you will learn to create a hyperlink to an existing file or Web page.

To create a hyperlink to an existing file or Web page:

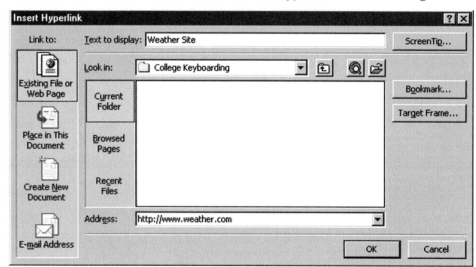

1. Select the text or object to be displayed as a hyperlink.

2. Click the **Insert Hyperlink** button.

3. Click **Existing File or Web Page**.

4. Select the filename or Web page by using either of the following methods:

   a. Key the filename or Web address in the Address entry box.

   b. Select a file from displayed list. Click the category tabs (**Current Folder, Browsed Pages**, and **Recent Files**) to display various files.

5. Click **OK**.

To go to the hyperlinked location:

1. Point to the hyperlinked text or object.

2. Press the CTRL key and click on the hyperlinked text or object. (*Note:* When the *Word* document is saved as a Web page, just click on the hyperlinked text or object.)

1. Open **hyperlink** from the data files.

2. Create hyperlinks as described in the document linking text and graphics to other documents and Web pages.

3. Save the document as **58b-drill2**.

LESSON 6 | W, Comma, B, P

W a r m u p

6a

Key each line twice; avoid pauses.

home row 1 ask a lad; a fall fad; had a salad; ask a sad jak;

o/t 2 to do it; to toil; as a tot; do a lot; he told her

c/r 3 cots are; has rocks; roll cot; is rich; has an arc

all reaches 4 Holt can see Dane at ten; Jill sees Frank at nine.

New Keys

6b w and , (comma)

Key each line once.

> **Comma:** Space once after a comma.

w Reach *up* with *left third* finger.

w

5 w ws ws was was wan wit low win jaw wilt wink wolf

6 sw sw ws ow ow now now row row own own wow wow owe

7 to sew; to own; was rich; was in; is how; will now

, (comma)

8 k, k, k, irk, ilk, ask, oak, ark, lark, jak, rock,

9 skis, a dock, a fork, a lock, a fee, a tie, a fan,

10 Jo, Ed, Ted, and Dan saw Nan in a car lift; a kit

, (comma) Reach *down* with *right second* finger.

all reaches learned

11 Win, Lew, Drew, and Walt will walk to West Willow.

12 Ask Ho, Al, and Jared to read the code; it is new.

13 The window, we think, was closed; we felt no wind.

6c New Key Mastery

Key each line twice; DS between groups.

14 walk wide sown wild town went jowl wait white down

15 a dock, a kit, a wick, a lock, a row, a cow, a fee

16 Joe lost to Ron; Fiji lost to Cara; Don lost to Al

17 Kane will win; Nan will win; Rio will win; Di wins

18 Walter is in Reno; Tia is in Tahoe; then to Hawaii

Skillbuilding

58a
Warmup
Key each line twice SS;
DS between 2-line
groups.

alphabetic 1 Jimmy Favorita realized that we must quit playing by six o'clock.

figure 2 Joell, in her 2001 truck, put 19 boxes in an annex at 3460 Marks.

double letter 3 Merriann was puzzled by a letter that followed a free book offer.

easy 4 Ana's sorority works with vigor for the goals of the civic corps.

| 1 | 2 | 3 | 4 | 5 | 6 | 7 | 8 | 9 | 10 | 11 | 12 | 13 |

New Functions

58b

help keywords
*Create a Web page from
an existing* Microsoft
Word *document*

About ways to view a
Word *document*

*Preview a document as
a Web page*

Save a Word Document as a Web Page

To distribute a *Word* document on the World Wide Web, you must first convert the document to HTML format by saving it as a Web page document. *Word* automatically creates the HTML codes for the desired format. To view the new Web document as it will appear online, choose Web Layout View. After correcting any formatting problems, you may then preview the new Web document in your default Web browser.

To save a *Word* document as a Web page:

1. On the File menu, click **Save as Web Page.**

2. Select the drive and folder where you wish to save the file. (*Hint:* Save Web files in a folder created for that purpose. Storing these files in one location simplifies your work when you are ready to post the files to the Web.)

3. In the File name box, key the filename or accept the name provided. *Word* automatically adds the file extension .htm at the end of the document.

4. Click **Save**. (Click **Continue** if *Word* warns that the document has formatting not supported by the Web browser.)

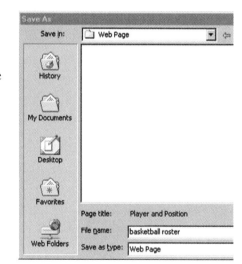

To view a document in Web Layout view:

1. On the View menu, click **Web Layout**. (*Shortcut:* Click the **Web Layout View** button on the status bar.)

2. Make any necessary formatting revisions (e.g., reposition graphics).

To preview the file in your browser:

On the File menu, click **Web Page Preview**. The file opens in your default Web browser. If the browser is not open, *Word* automatically opens it.

(*Note:* Web documents do not always display the same in all browsers. Using *Internet Explorer*, a *Microsoft*-compatible browser, will reduce these formatting differences.)

6d b and p
Key each line once.

b Reach *down* with *left first* finger.

p Reach *up* with *right fourth* (little) finger.

b

18 bf bf bf biff fib fib bib bib boa boa fib fibs rob
19 bf bf bf ban ban bon bon bow bow be be rib rib sob
20 a dob, a cob, a crib, a lab, a slab, a bid, a bath

p

21 p; p; pa pa; pal pal pan pan pad par pen pep paper
22 pa pa; lap lap; nap nap; hep ape spa asp leap clap
23 a park, a pan, a pal, a pad, apt to pop, a pair of

all reaches learned

24 Barb and Bob wrapped a pepper in paper and ribbon.
25 Rip, Joann, and Dick were all closer to the flash.
26 Bo will be pleased to see Japan; he works in Oslo.

Skillbuilding

6e Keyboard Reinforcement
Key each line once; key at a steady pace.

reach review
27 ki kid did aid lie hj has has had sw saw wits will
28 de dell led sled jn an en end ant hand k, end, kin

s/w
29 ws ws lows now we shown win cow wow wire jowl when
30 Wes saw an owl in the willow tree in the old lane.

b/p
31 bf bf fib rob bid ;p p; pal pen pot nap hop cap bp
32 Rob has both pans in a bin at the back of the pen.

6f Speed Builder
1. Follow the standard Open Screen directions on page 8.
2. Key each line twice. Work for fluency.

all reaches
33 Dick owns a dock at this lake; he paid Ken for it.
34 Jane also kept a pair of owls, a hen, and a snake.

35 Blair soaks a bit of the corn, as he did in Japan.
36 I blend the cocoa in the bowl when I work for Leo.

37 to do|can do|to bow|ask her|to nap|to work|is born
38 for this|if she|is now|did all|to see|or not|or if

57d-d2
E-mail Message with Copy Notation

1. Key the following e-mail message to your instructor.
2. Copy the message to one student in your class.
3. Key **Assignment 2 from Your Name** as the subject line.
4. Send the message.

List five things to consider when composing e-mail.

1. Do not use bold or italic or vary fonts.

2. Do not use uppercase for emphasis.

3. Use emoticons or e-mail abbreviations with caution (e.g., :) for smile or BTW for by the way).

4. Write clear, concise messages that are free of spelling and grammatical errors.

5. Do not send an e-mail message in haste or anger. Think about the message carefully before clicking the Send button.

57d-d3
E-mail Message with Attachment

1. Key the following e-mail to your instructor, and send one copy to one student in your class.
2. Key **Chapter Activity Report** as the subject line.
3. Attach the data file **activity**.

I have completed the Chapter Activity Report required for this year's competitive events. The file Activity.doc is attached to this e-mail for your review. Please add the names of the members initiated at the February meeting and review the listing of awards received by our members. Revise the file as needed.

After you have edited the report, please print a laser copy and give to Shandra Pfitzer for inclusion in the national project notebook. I would also appreciate your e-mailing me the revised file for the historian records.

Remember, the reports must be postmarked by March 1. Thanks for your excellent work on this important part of the national competition.

57d-d4
Compose E-mail

1. Compose an e-mail message to three students in your class that states you are attaching new guidelines for a voice mail greeting. Be sure to order names alphabetically.
2. Key **Guidelines for Voice Mail Greeting** as the subject line.
3. Attach the data file **greeting**.
4. Send the message.

LESSON 7 | Review

Warmup

7a

Key each line twice; begin new lines promptly.

all	1 We often can take the older jet to Paris and back.
home	2 a; sl dk fj a;sl dkfj ad as all ask fads adds asks
1st row	3 Ann Bascan and Cabal Naban nabbed a cab in Canada.
3d row	4 Rip went to a water show with either Pippa or Pia.

Skillbuilding

7b Reach Mastery
Key each line once; repeat.

```
 5 ws ws was was wan wan wit wit pew paw nap pop bawl
 6 bf bf fb fb fob fob rib rib be be job job bat back
 7 p; p; asp asp pan pan ap ap ca cap pa nap pop prow

 8 Barb and Bret took an old black robe and the boot.
 9 Walt saw a wisp of white water renew ripe peppers.
10 Pat picked a black pepper for the picnic at Parks.
```

7c Rhythm Builder
Key each line once.

words	11 a an pan so sot la lap ah own do doe el elf to tot
phrases	12 if it|to do|it is|do so|for the|he works|if he bid
sentences	13 Jess ate all of the peas in the salad in the bowl.

words	14 bow bowl pin pint for fork forks hen hens jak jaks
phrases	15 is for|did it|is the|we did a|and so|to see|or not
sentences	16 I hid the ace in a jar as a joke; I do not see it.

TECHNIQUE TIP

words: key as a single unit rather than letter by letter;

phrases: say and key fluently;

sentences: work for fluency.

words	17 chap chaps flak flake flakes prow prowl work works
phrases	18 as for the|as for the|and to the|to see it|and did
sentences	19 As far as I know, he did not read all of the book.

These addresses will receive a copy of the message.

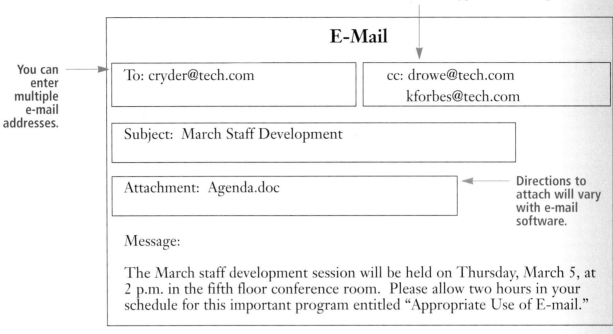

E-Mail

You can enter multiple e-mail addresses.

To: cryder@tech.com

cc: drowe@tech.com
kforbes@tech.com

Subject: March Staff Development

Attachment: Agenda.doc

Directions to attach will vary with e-mail software.

Message:

The March staff development session will be held on Thursday, March 5, at 2 p.m. in the fifth floor conference room. Please allow two hours in your schedule for this important program entitled "Appropriate Use of E-mail."

Applications

Follow these directions for completing all documents in Lesson 57:

Without Internet access: Complete all documents as memos.

With an e-mail address: Complete the documents in your software and send them.

With Internet access but no e-mail address: Your instructor will assist you in setting up a free e-mail account and address.

57d-d1
E-mail Message

1. Key the following e-mail message to your instructor.
2. Key **Assignment 1 from Your Name** as the subject line.
3. Send the message.

List five things to consider when choosing an appropriate e-mail password.

1. Do not choose a password that is named after a family member or a pet.
2. Do not use birth dates as a password.
3. Choose a combination of letters and numbers; preferably, use uppercase and lowercase letters, e.g., TLQ6tEpR.
4. Do not share your password with anyone.
5. Do not write your password on a piece of paper and leave it by your computer or in your desk drawer.

7d Technique Practice

Key each set of lines once SS; DS between 3-line groups.

▼ Space once after a period following an abbreviation.

20 ad la as in if it lo no of oh he or so ok pi be we

21 an ace ads ale aha a fit oil a jak nor a bit a pew

22 ice ades born is fake to jail than it and the cows

spacing/shifting   ▼   ▼

23 Ask Jed.   Dr. Han left at ten; Dr. Crowe, at nine.

24 I asked Jin if she had ice in a bowl; it can help.

25 Freda, not Jack, went to Spain.   Joan likes Spain.

7e Timed Writings in the Open Screen

STANDARD PLAN | **for using the Open Screen Timer** |

You can check your speed in the Open Screen using the Timer.

1. In the Open Screen, click the **Timer** button on the toolbar.
   In the Timer dialog box, check **Count-Down Timer** and time; click **OK**.
2. The Timer begins once you start to key and stops automatically. Do not strike ENTER at the end of a line. Wordwrap will cause the text to flow to the next line automatically.
3. To save the timing, click the **File** menu and **Save as**. Use your initals (xx), the exercise number, and number of the timing as the filename. Example: **xx-7f-t1** (your initials, exercise 7f, timing1).
4. Click the **Timer** button again to start a new timing.
5. Each new timing must be saved with its own name.

7f Speed Check

1. Take two 1' writings on the paragraph in the Open Screen.
2. Follow the directions in 7e. Do not strike ENTER at the ends of the lines.

Goal: 12 *wam*.

```
              •            4          •            8          •
It is hard to fake a confident spirit.  We will do
         12          •           16           •
better work if we approach and finish a job and
20         •           24          •           28          •
know that we will do the best work we can and then
              32
not fret.
|  1  |  2  |  3  |  4  |  5  |  6  |  7  |  8  |  9  |  10  |
```

7g Guided Writing

1. Key each line once for fluency.
2. Set the Timer in the Open Screen for 30". Take two 30" writings on each line. Do not save the timings.

Goal: to reach the end of the line before time is up.

gwam

26 Dan took her to the show.   12

27 Jan lent the bowl to the pros.   14

28 Hold the wrists low for this drill.   16

29 Jessie fit the black panel to the shelf.   18

30 Jake held a bit of cocoa and an apricot for Diane. 20

31 Dick and I fish for cod on the docks at Fish Lake. 20

32 Kent still held the dish and the cork in his hand. 20

| 1 | 2 | 3 | 4 | 5 | 6 | 7 | 8 | 9 | 10 |

LESSON 57 | Electronic Mail

Skillbuilding

57a
Warmup
Key each line twice SS;
DS between 2-line
groups.

adjacent
reaches

1 art try pew sort tree position copy opera maker waste three draft
2 sat coil riot were renew forth trade power grope owner score weed

one hand

3 ad null bar poll car upon deed jump ever look feed hill noon moon
4 get hilly are employ save phony taste union versa yummy wedge fad

balanced
hand

5 aid go bid dish elan glen fury idle half jamb lend make name slam
6 oak pay hen quay rush such urus vial works yamen amble blame pale

| 1 | 2 | 3 | 4 | 5 | 6 | 7 | 8 | 9 | 10 | 11 | 12 | 13 |

57b
Timed Writings
1. Key three 1'
   writings.
2. Key two 2' writings.
   Try to maintain your
   best 1' rate.

 all letters

gwam | 1' | 2'

	1'	2'
Good plans typically are required to execute most tasks	11	6 50
successfully. If a task is worth doing, it is worth investing	24	12 56
the time that is necessary to plan it effectively. Many people	37	18 62
are anxious to get started on a task and just begin before they	49	25 69
have thought about the best way to organize it. In the long run,	63	31 75
they frequently end up wasting time that could be spent more	75	37 81
profitably on important projects that they might prefer to tackle.	88	44 88

1' | 1 | 2 | 3 | 4 | 5 | 6 | 7 | 8 | 9 | 10 | 11 | 12 | 13 |
2' | 1 | 2 | 3 | 4 | 5 | 6 |

Document Design

57c

Electronic Mail

Electronic mail (or **e-mail**) is an informal message that is sent by one computer user to another computer user. To be able to send or receive e-mail, you must have an e-mail address, an e-mail program, and access to the Internet.

Heading: Accurately key the e-mail address of the receiver and supply a specific subject line. The date and your e-mail address will display automatically.

Attachments: Documents can be sent electronically by attaching the document file to the recipient's e-mail message. The attached file can then be opened and edited by the recipient.

Body: SS the body of an e-mail; DS between paragraphs. Do not indent the paragraphs.

Formatting: Do not add bold or italic or vary the fonts. Do not use uppercase letters for emphasis. Use emoticons or e-mail abbreviations with caution (e.g., :- for wink or BTW for by the way).

LESSON 8 | G, Question Mark, X, U

✳ W a r m u p

8a
Key each line twice. Keep eyes on copy.

all 1 Dick will see Job at nine if Rach sees Pat at one.

w/b 2 As the wind blew, Bob Webber saw the window break.

p/, 3 Pat, Pippa, or Cap has prepared the proper papers.

all 4 Bo, Jose, and Will fed Lin; Jack had not paid her.

⌐ New Keys

8b g and ?
Key each line once; repeat.

Question mark: The question mark is usually followed by two spaces.

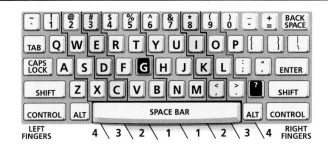

g Reach to *right* with *left first* finger.

? Left SHIFT; reach *down* with *right fourth* finger.

g

5 g g gf gaff gag grog fog frog drag cog dig fig gig

6 gf go gall flag gels slag gala gale glad glee gals

7 golf flog gorge glen high logs gore ogle page grow

?

8 ? ?; ?; ? ? Who? When? Where? Who is? Who was?

9 Who is here? Was it he? Was it she? Did she go?

10 Did Geena? Did he? What is that? Was Jose here?

all reaches learned

11 Has Ginger lost her job? Was her April bill here?

12 Phil did not want the boats to get here this soon.

13 Loris Shin has been ill; Frank, a doctor, saw her.

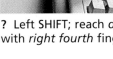

8c New Key Review
Key each line once; DS between groups.

reach review

14 ws ws hj hj tf tf ol ol rf rf ed ed cd cd bf bf p;

15 wed bid has old hold rid heed heed car bed pot pot

g

16 gf gf gin gin rig ring go gone no nog sign got dog

17 to go|to go|go on|go in|go in|to go in|in the sign

▌TECHNIQUE TIP
Concentrate on correct reaches.

?

18 ?; ?;? who? when? where? how? what? who? It is I?

19 Is she? Is he? Did I lose Jo? Is Gal all right?

a series of nine modules ranging from two to four hours long to provide maximum schedule flexibility. The three core modules are required for all employees. At least three modules must be selected from the six modules that are designated as electives. Descriptive information and schedules are available from the Training Department and will be posted on the Crown Lake Online Bulletin Board.

Students Function as Professional Consultants

In late spring, President John Marcus notified us that a team of international MBA students from the Business School at State University would be working with us to develop an export strategy for Crown Lake and asked us to cooperate fully with the team. Most of us felt that we were being asked to take on a project that was essentially a "public service" contribution to the University. Were we ever wrong!!! It only took us one day to realize that these five graduate students were truly professionals in every respect and that they were going to function as a highly effective, results-oriented professional consulting team. A faculty member advised the team, and they had access to a wide range of expertise at the University. This past week the team presented the final results of their field-consulting project to the division management team. The bottom line is that we now have an export strategy for three of our product lines and a viable implementation plan to begin exporting to Canada and Mexico

early next year. The team also performed extensive country analyses of 12 European and South American countries and laid the groundwork for future expansion to those markets. Partnering with the University was truly a win-win situation!

—Roberta C. West
Vice President of Marketing

✉ **Mail from Employees**

—Student's name
Production Associate

8d x and u
Key each line once; repeat.

x Reach *down* with *left third* finger.

u Reach *up* with right first finger.

x

20 x x xs xs ox ox lox sox fox box ex hex lax hex fax

21 sx six sax sox ax fix cox wax hex box pox sex text

22 flax next flex axel pixel exit oxen taxi axis next

u

23 u uj uj jug jut just dust dud due sue use due duel

24 uj us cud but bun out sun nut gun hut hue put fuel

25 dual laud dusk suds fuss full tuna tutus duds full

all reaches learned

26 Paige Power liked the book; Josh can read it next.

27 Next we picked a bag for Jan; then she, Jan, left.

28 Is her June account due? Has Lou ruined her unit?

Skillbuilding

8e Reinforcement
Key each line once; DS between groups. Repeat. Print.

29 nut cue hut sun rug us six cut dug axe rag fox run

30 out of the sun|cut the action|a fox den|fun at six

31 That car is not junk; it can run in the next race.

32 etc. tax nick cure lack flex walls uncle clad hurt

33 lack the cash|not just luck|next in line|just once

34 June Dunn can send that next tax case to Rex Knox.

8f Speed Check
1. Key the paragraph. Press ENTER once to begin the second paragraph.
2. Take two 1' writings. Save the timings as **xx8e-t1** and **xx8e-t2**, with *xx* being your initials.

Goal: 14 *wam*.

```
          •        4        •        8        •
How a finished job will look often depends on how
        12        •        16        •        20
we feel about our work as we do it.  Attitude has
          •        24        •        28        •
a definite effect on the end result of work we do.
```
Press ENTER once
```
          •        4        •        8        •
When we are eager to begin a job, we relax and do
        12        •        16        •        20
better work than if we start the job with an idea
          •        24        •        28        •
that there is just nothing we can do to escape it.
```

Crown Lake News and Views

Current date

Newsletter Staff

Eric Burge
    Editor

Nancy Suggs
Christopher Hess
Anne Reynolds
    Associate Editors

Wayne Martin
    Editorial Assistant

The *Crown Lake News and Views* is a weekly newsletter compiled by the staff of the Human Resources Department, and it is sent to all employees. Employees are invited to share ideas with others by writing a letter to the editor to be included in the Mail from Employees column.

New Development Project

Crown Lake won the bid to develop and construct the new multimillion-dollar Business Center adjacent to Metro Airport. Connie McClure, one of the three senior project managers, has been named as the Business Center project manager. The project is expected to take more than two years to complete. Approximately fifty new permanent employees will be hired to work on this project. All jobs will be posted within the next two weeks. The recruiting referral program is in effect for all jobs. You can earn a $100 bonus for each individual you recommend who is hired and remains with Crown Lake for at least six months. You may pick up your recruiting referral forms in the Personnel Office.

Blood Drive Reminder

The Crown Lake quarterly blood drive is set for Friday, April 4, in the Wellness Center. The Community Blood Bank needs all types of blood to replace the supplies sent to the islands during the recent disaster caused by Hurricane Lana. Employees in all divisions are being asked to participate this quarter because of the current supply crisis. All three donation sites will be used. Several volunteers will be needed to staff the two additional sites. The

regular division rotation will resume next quarter.

Lee Daye Honored

The Community Foundation honored Lee Daye of the Marketing

Department with the Eagle Award for outstanding service this year. The Eagle Award is presented each year to three citizens who have made a significant impact on the lives of others. The Community Foundation recognized Lee for his work with underprivileged children, the Community Relations Task Force, the Abolish Domestic Violence Center, and the Community Transitional Housing Project. Congratulations, Lee, you made a difference in the lives of many citizens in our community. Your award was richly deserved.

New Training Program

The pilot test of the new Team Effectiveness training program was completed last month, and the results were excellent. Thanks to all of you who participated in the development and testing of the program. Your input is vital to the program's success. The program is designed as

LESSON 9 | Q, M, V, Apostrophe

✳ W a r m u p

9a
Key each line twice.

all letters 1 Lex gripes about cold weather; Fred is not joking.

space bar 2 Is it Di, Jo, or Al? Ask Lt. Coe, Bill; he knows.

easy 3 I did rush a bushel of cut corn to the sick ducks.

easy 4 He is to go to the Tudor Isle of England on a bus.

New Keys

9b q and m
Key each line once; repeat.

q Reach *up* with *left fourth* finger.

m Reach *down* with *right first* finger.

q

5 q qa qa quad quad quaff quant queen quo quit quick

6 qa qu qa quo quit quod quid quip quads quote quiet

7 quite quilts quart quill quakes quail quack quaint

m

8 m mj mj jam man malt mar max maw me mew men hem me

9 m mj ma am make male mane melt meat mist amen lame

10 malt meld hemp mimic tomb foam rams mama mire mind

all reaches learned

11 Quin had some quiet qualms about taming a macaque.

12 Jake Coxe had questions about a new floor program.

13 Max was quick to join the big reception for Lidia.

9c New Key Review
Key each line once for control.
DS and repeat the drill.

m/x 14 me men ma am jam am lax, mix jam; the hem, six men

15 Emma Max expressed an aim to make a mammoth model.

q/u 16 qa qu aqua aqua quit quit quip quite pro quo squad

17 Did Quin make a quick request to take the Qu exam?

g/n 18 fg gn gun gun dig dig nag snag snag sign grab grab

19 Georgia hung a sign in front of the union for Gib.

Drill 2 | CONTINUOUS SECTIONS

1. Using document **56d-drill1**, change the Next Page section break to a Continuous section break.

2. Drag the pie chart to the approximate center of the page if it is not centered.

3. Save the document as **56d-drill2**, and print a copy.

Applications

56e-d1
Two-page Newsletter with Unequal Columns

To add an AutoText entry, choose **Tools** menu and **AutoCorrect Options**. On the **AutoText** tab, enter the text in the AutoText entry box.

1. Frequently used text can be added as an AutoText entry so that you don't have to key the entire text each time it occurs. Before keying the newsletter, add **Crown Lake** as an AutoText entry. Then key the newsletter on the next two pages as straight text (no columns). When Word suggests the complete Crown Lake entry, press ENTER to accept it.

2. Set left and right margins of .75".

3. Use WordArt for the banner heading, and adjust the size so the banner spans all columns. Leave two or three blank lines; then insert a continuous break.

4. Use 14-point Times New Roman for headings within the document and 12-point Times New Roman for body text.

5. Format the document after the banner as a three-column document with lines between the columns. Use the following settings:
First Column: 1.5"
Space between all columns: .025"
Second and third columns: 2.5"

6. Use the first column for editorial information as shown; then insert a column break.

7. Insert an Eagle from clip art similar to what is shown. Center it in the column after the Eagle Award is mentioned.

8. When text wraps to the second page, insert a column break in the first column to shift the text to the second column so that you will reserve the first narrow column for editorial information.

9. In the first column of the second page, key the name of the newsletter in 14-point bold and the current date and Page 2 in 12-point bold.

10. Insert a mailbox symbol from Wingdings for the Mail from Employees column.

11. Compose an article to fill the space left in the last column of the second page. You may choose your own topic or use one of the following:
   - The value of participating in community service activities (write from the perspective of both the employee and the company).
   - Invite employees to participate in an activity such as an investment club, an exercise group, a club sport, or some other area of interest. Share benefits of being involved and provide information about the activity.
   - Tips for keeping physically fit and why it is important to do so.
   - Tips for traveling on a tight budget.
   - Tips for managing time effectively.

12. Use an appropriate title for your article, and add your name and title **Production Associate** at the end of your article.

13. Save the document as **56e-d1** and print a copy.

9d v and ' (apostrophe)

Key each line once; repeat.

v Reach *down* with *left first* finger.

' Reach to ' with *right fourth* finger.

Apostrophe: The apostrophe shows (1) omission (as Rob't for Robert or it's for it is) or (2) possession when used with nouns (as Joe's hat).

v

20 v vf vf vie vie via via vim vat vow vile vale vote
21 vf vf ave vet ova eve vie dive five live have lave
22 cove dove over aver vivas hive volt five java jive

' (apostrophe)

23 '; '; it's it's Rod's; it's Bo's hat; we'll do it.
24 We don't know if it's Lee's pen or Norma's pencil.
25 It's ten o'clock; I won't tell him that he's late.

all reaches learned

26 It's Viv's turn to drive Iva's van to Ava's house.
27 Qua, not Vi, took the jet; so did Cal. Didn't he?
28 Wasn't Fae Baxter a judge at the post garden show?

Skillbuilding

9e Reinforcement

1. Follow the standard Open Screen directions on page 8.
2. Key each line twice; DS between groups. Strive to increase speed.

v/?

29 Viola said she has moved six times in five months.
30 Does Dave live on Vine Street? Must he leave now?

q/?

31 Did Viv vote? Can Paque move it? Could Val dive?
32 Didn't Raquel quit Carl Quent after their quarrel?

direct reach

33 Fred told Brice that the junior class must depart.
34 June and Hunt decided to go to that great musical.

double letter

35 Harriette will cook dinner for the swimming teams.
36 Bill's committee meets in an accounting classroom.

9f Speed Check

Take two 1' writings on the paragraph. Save the timings as **xx-9e-t1** and **xx-9e-t2**, substituting your initials for *xx*.
Goal: 14 wam

```
                  •           4           •           8           •
We must be able to express our thoughts with ease
          12          •           16          •           20
if we desire to find success in the business world.
      •           24          •           28
It is there that sound ideas earn cash.
```

New Functions
56d

help keywords
sections

Sections

Often long documents such as reports and newsletters are formatted in **sections** so that different formats may be applied on the same page or on different pages using section breaks. *Word* provides several different types of breaks. Page breaks, column breaks, and text wrapping breaks can all occur in the same section of a document.

> *Page break:* To move to the next page of a document.
>
> *Column break:* To move to the next column of text.
>
> *Text wrapping break:* To move text to the next line.

Section breaks differ from the breaks just described in that they divide a document into sections. Each section can have its own format and page numbering scheme.

To enter a section break:

1. Select **Break** from the Insert menu.

2. Click the type of Section break desired, and then click **OK**.

   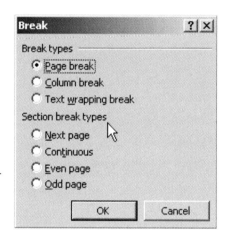

   Next page: Begins a new page at the point the section break is entered.

   Continuous: Begins a new section on the same page.

   Even page: Begins a new section on the next even-numbered page.

   Odd page: Begins a new section on the next odd-numbered page

In Normal View, section breaks appear as a dotted line with the type of break indicated. *Word* displays the current section number on the status bar. To copy the format of one section to a different section, select the section break and copy it to the new location.

```
Section 1, page 1
..................................................................Section Break (Continuous)..........
Section 2, page 1
..................................................................Section Break (Next Page)..........
Section 3, page 2
..................................................................Section Break (Even Page)..........
Section 4, page 4
..................................................................Section Break (Odd Page)..........
Section 5, page 5
```

D r i l l 1 │ **NEXT PAGE BREAKS**

1. Open **Time** from the data files.

2. Format the title using WordArt of your choice; leave two or three blank lines after the WordArt.

3. At the beginning of the text, insert a Continuous section break. Format the text as two equal columns.

4. At the end of the text, insert a Next Page section break.

5. Drag the pie chart to the approximate center of the page if it is not centered.

6. Save the document as **56d-drill1**, and print a copy. Leave the document open for the next activity.

LESSON 10   Z, Y, Quotation Mark, Tab

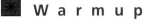

Warmup

10a
Key each line twice.

all letters	1	Quill owed those back taxes after moving to Japan.
spacing	2	Didn't Vi, Sue, and Paul go? Someone did; I know.
q/v/m	3	Marv was quite quick to remove that mauve lacquer.
easy	4	Lana is a neighbor; she owns a lake and an island.

New Keys

10b z and y
Key each line once; repeat.

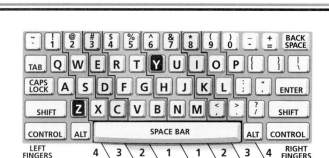

z Reach *down* with *left fourth* finger.

y Reach *up* with *right first* finger.

z

5 za za zap zap zing zig zag zoo zed zip zap zig zed

6 doze zeal zero haze jazz zone zinc zing size ozone

7 ooze maze doze zoom zarf zebus daze gaze faze adze

y

8 y yj yj jay jay hay hay lay nay say days eyes ayes

9 yj ye yet yen yes cry dry you rye sty your fry wry

10 ye yen bye yea coy yew dye yaw lye yap yak yon any

all reaches learned

11 Did you say Liz saw any yaks or zebus at your zoo?

12 Relax; Jake wouldn't acquire any favorable rights.

13 Has Mazie departed? Tex, Lu, and I will go alone.

10c **Reach Review**
Key each line once. DS between groups. Repeat.

	14	Cecilia brings my jumbo umbrella to every concert.
direct reach	15	John and Kim recently brought us an old art piece.
	16	I built a gray brick border around my herb garden.
	17	sa ui hj gf mn vc ew uy re io as lk rt jk df op yu
adjacent reach	18	In Ms. Lopez' opinion, the opera was really great.
	19	Polly and I were joining Walker at the open house.

LESSON 56 | Sections and Newsletters

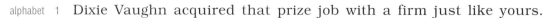

Skillbuilding

56a
Warmup
Key each line twice SS; DS between 2-line groups.

alphabet	1	Dixie Vaughn acquired that prize job with a firm just like yours.
figures	2	By May 15 do this: Call Ext. 4390; order 472 clips and 168 pens.
easy/figures	3	The 29 girls kept 38 bushels of corn and 59 bushels of rich yams.
easy	4	The members paid half of the endowment, and their firm paid half.

| 1 | 2 | 3 | 4 | 5 | 6 | 7 | 8 | 9 | 10 | 11 | 12 | 13 |

56b
Technique Builder
Key each set of lines three times; DS between 9-line groups; work at a controlled rate.

adjacent reaches	5	Is assessing potential important in a traditional career program?
	6	I saw her at an airport at a tropical resort leaving on a cruise.
direct reach	7	Fred kicked a goal in every college soccer game in June and July.
	8	Ned used their sled on cold days and my kite on warm summer days.
double letters	9	Bobby Lott feels that the meeting at noon will be cancelled soon.
	10	Pattie and Tripp meet at the swimming pool after football drills.

56c
Timed Writings
Key a 3' or a 5' timing at your control rate.

A all letters

gwam 3' | 5'

	3'	5'
You may be familiar with the expression that we live in an	4	2
information age now. People interpret this expression in a host of	8	5
diverse ways, but most people agree on two key things. The first	13	8
thing is that a huge amount of information exists today; some even	17	10
think we suffer from information overload. The second thing is that	22	13
technology has changed the way we access that huge pool of data.	26	16
Some people are quick to point out that a big difference exists	30	18
between the quantity and the quality of information. It is very	35	21
critical to recognize that anyone who has access can simply post	39	23
information on the Internet. No test exists to screen for junk	43	26
before something is posted. Some of the data may be helpful and	48	29
valid. However, much of it must be analyzed quite carefully to	52	31
judge if it is valid.	53	32
Just how do you judge if the data you have accessed is valid?	58	35
Some of the same techniques that can be used with print media can be	62	37
applied with electronic media. A good way to assess material is to	67	40
examine its source carefully. What do you know about the people who	71	42
provided this information? Is the provider ethical and qualified	75	45
to post that information? If you cannot unearth the answer to this	80	48
question, you should be wary of trusting it.	83	50

3'	1	2	3	4
5'	1	2	3	

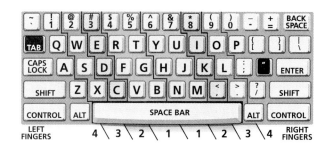

10d  " (quotation mark)
and TAB
Key each line once; repeat.

" Shift; then reach to " with *right fourth* finger.

TAB Reach up with *left fourth* finger.

" (quotation mark)

20 "; "; " " "lingo" "bugs" "tennies"   I like "malts."

21 "I am not," she said, "going."   I just said, "Oh?"

tab key

22   The tab key is used for indenting paragraphs and aligning columns.

23   Tabs that are set by the software are called default tabs, which are usually a half inch.

all reaches learned

24   The expression "I give you my word," or put another

25 way, "Take my word for it," is just a way I can say, "I

26 prize my name; it clearly stands in back of my words."

27 I offer "honor" as collateral.

Skillbuilding

10e Reinforcement
Follow the standard directions on page 8. Key each line twice; DS between groups.

10f Speed Check
Take two 1' writings of paragraph 2 in the Open Screen. Save as **xx-10e-t1** and **xx-10e-t2**.
Goal: 15 *wam*

tab 28   Strike the tab key and begin the line without a pause to maintain fluency.

29   She said that this is the lot to be sent; I agreed with her.

30   Strike Tab before starting to key a timed writing so that the first line is indented.

gwam 1'

Tab → All of us work for progress, but it is not   8
always easy to analyze "progress." We work hard   18
for it; but, in spite of some really good efforts, 28
we may fail to receive just exactly the response we 39
want.   40
Tab → When this happens, as it does to all of us,   9
it is time to cease whatever we are doing, have   18
a quiet talk with ourselves, and face up to the   28
questions about our limited progress. How can we   38
do better?   40
| 1 | 2 | 3 | 4 | 5 | 6 | 7 | 8 | 9 | 10 |

Arena Update

Get Your Shovels Ready!

The architects have put the final touches on the arena plans and the groundbreaking has been scheduled for March 18. Put the date on your calendar and plan to be a part of this exciting time. The Groundbreaking Ceremony will begin at 5:00 at the new arena site. After the ceremony, you will join the architects in the practice facility for refreshments and an exciting visual presentation of the new arena. The party ends when we all join the Western Cougars as they take on the Central Lions for the final conference game.

Cornerstone Club Named

Robbie Holiday of the Cougars Club submitted the winning name for the new premium seating and club area of the new arena. Thanks to all of you who submitted suggestions for naming the new club. For his suggestion, which was selected from over 300 names submitted, Robbie has won season tickets for next year and the opportunity to make his seat selection first. The Cornerstone Club name was selected because members of our premium clubs play a crucial role in making our new arena a reality. Without the financial support of this group, we could not lay the first cornerstone of the arena.

Cornerstone Club members have first priority in selecting their seats for both basketball and hockey in a specially designated section of the new arena. This section provides outstanding seats for both basketball games and hockey matches. Club members also have access to the Cornerstone Club before the game, during halftime, and after the game. They also receive a parking pass for the lot immediately adjacent to the arena. If you would like more information about the Cornerstone Club and how you can become a charter member of the club, call the Cougars Club office during regular business hours.

What View Would You Like?

Most of us would like to sit in our seats and try them out before we select them rather than look at a diagram of the seating in the new arena. Former Cougar players make it easy for you to select the  perfect angle to watch the ball go in the basket. Mark McKay and Jeff Dunlap, using their patented Real View visualization software, make it possible for you to experience the exact view you will have from the seats you select. In fact, they encourage you to try several different views. Most of the early testers of the new seat selection software reported that they came in with their minds  completely made up about the best seats in the house. However, after experiencing several different views with the Real View software, they changed their original seat location request.

LESSON 11 | Review

✳ W a r m u p

11a
Key each line twice SS
(slowly, then faster).

alphabet	1	Zeb had Jewel quickly give him five or six points.
" (quote)	2	Can you spell "chaos," "bias," "bye," and "their"?
y	3	Ty Clay may envy you for any zany plays you write.
easy	4	Did he bid on the bicycle, or did he bid on a map?

| 1 | 2 | 3 | 4 | 5 | 6 | 7 | 8 | 9 | 10 |

▣ Skillbuilding

**11b Keyboard
Reinforcement**
Key each line once; repeat the
drill to increase fluency.

5 za za zap az az maze zoo zip razz zed zax zoa zone
6 Liz Zahl saw Zoe feed the zebra in an Arizona zoo.

7 yj yj jy jy joy lay yaw say yes any yet my try you
8 Why do you say that today, Thursday, is my payday?

9 xs xs sax ox box fix hex ax lax fox taxi lox sixes
10 Roxy, you may ask Jay to fix any tax sets for you.

11 qa qa aqua quail quit quake quid equal quiet quart
12 Did Enrique quietly but quickly quell the quarrel?

13 fv fv five lives vow ova van eve avid vex vim void
14 Has Vivi, Vada, or Eva visited Vista Valley Farms?

TECHNIQUE **TIP**
Work for smoothness,
not for speed.

11c Speed Builders
Key each balanced-hand
line twice, as quickly as
you can.

15 is to for do an may work so it but an with them am
16 am yam map aid zig yams ivy via vie quay cob amend

17 to do is for an may work so it but am an with them
18 for it|for it|to the|to the|do they|do they|do it

19 Pamela may go to the farm with Jan and a neighbor.
20 Rod and Ty may go by the lake if they go downtown.

| 1 | 2 | 3 | 4 | 5 | 6 | 7 | 8 | 9 | 10 |

Applications

54–55b-d1
Newsletter with
WordArt

1. Open **Training** from the data files. Save it as **54–55b-d1**.
2. Format the document in two equal columns.
3. Select the main heading **Productivity Enhancement Program**, and format it as a banner heading that spans across both columns. Double-space after the heading.
4. Format the main heading in WordArt. Use the style from column 2, row 2 of the WordArt Gallery. Adjust the size to 24 points, and center-align it.
5. Save again and preview to check the document's appearance. Print when satisfied.

54–55b-d2
Newsletter with
Graphic

1. Open **Productivity** from the data files. Save as **54–55b-d2**. Format the document following steps 2–4 in **54–55b-d1**.
2. Go to the end of the document. Drag the graphic from the second page, and position it before the paragraph that begins with *Integration*. Work patiently.
3. Wrap the text around the graphic using square wrapping and center alignment.
   a. Right-click the graphic. Select **Format picture**.
   b. Click the **Layout** tab, and select **Square** wrapping and **Center** alignment.
4. If the graphic moves to the left column, drag it back so it is positioned above the *Integration* paragraph.
5. Add a dark blue, ½-point page border (**Format** menu, **Borders and Shading**, **Page** tab).
6. Add extra hard returns above column 2 to align with column 1. Save again.
7. Go to Normal view; find the Page break and delete it. Return to Print Layout view. Preview and print when you are satisfied.

54–55b-d3
Revise Column
Structure

1. Open **54–55b-d2** and save it as **54–55b-d3**. Change the format to three equal columns with .3" space between columns and with a line between columns.
2. Resize the graphic to fit within a column. Position it attractively in column 2.
3. Balance the columns so that they will end at approximately the same point on the page (**Insert** menu, **Break**, **Continuous**, **OK**). Save, preview, and print.

54–55b-d4
Newsletter
Challenge

1. Key the newsletter illustrated on the next page. Use .5" left and right margins, and apply what you have learned.
2. Use the WordArt shown or select another style for the banner.
3. The clip art files used are: **shovel—J0286330** from Clip Art folder 3, **basketball goals—J0282556** from Clip Art folder 3, and **J0238275** from Clip Art folder 2. You may substitute any appropriate clip art you find. Wrap the text around the graphics.
4. Use 18-point bold type for the internal headings in the newsletter.
5. Save the document as **54–55b-d4** and print.

54-55b-d5
Newsletter
Challenge

1. Reformat document **54–55d-d4** as a three-column newsletter. Change the font size for all text except the headings to 11 point to fit all of the text on one page. Change the headings to 14-point font size.
2. Reposition and size the graphics so they are the same width as the columns. Balance the columns if the last column is shorter than other columns.
3. Save the document as **54–55b-d5** and print.

11d Technique Builder
Key each line once; DS between groups.

enter: key smoothly without looking at fingers

21 Make the return snappily
22 and with assurance; keep
23 your eyes on your source
24 data; maintain a smooth,
25 constant pace as you key.

space bar: use down-and-in motion

26 us me it of he an by do go to us if or so am ah el
27 Have you a pen? If so, print "Free to any guest."

caps lock: press to toggle it on or off

28 Use ALL CAPS for items such as TO: FROM: SUBJECT.
29 Did Kristin mean Kansas City, MISSOURI, or KANSAS?

11e Speed Check

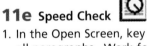

1. In the Open Screen, key all paragraphs. Work for smooth, continuous stroking, not speed.
2. Save as **xx-lle**. Substitute your initals for *xx*.
3. Take a 2' writing on all paragraphs.

Goal: 16 *gwam*

To determine gross-words-a-minute (*gwam*) rate for 2':
Follow these steps if you are *not* using the Timer in the Open Screen.

1. Note the figure at the end of the last line completed.

2. For a partial line, note the figure on the scale direcly below the point at which you stopped keying.

3. Add these two figures to determine the total gross words a minute (*gwam*) you keyed.

---

                                                                    gwam 2'

        •   4   •   8
Have we thought of communication as a kind   4 |31
 •   12   •   16
of war that we wage through each day?   8 |35
        •   4   •   8
When we think of it that way, good language   12 |39
 •   12   •   16   •
would seem to become our major line of attack.   17 |44
        •   4   •   8
Words become muscle; in a normal exchange or in   22 |49
 •   12   •   16   •   20
a quarrel, we do well to realize the power of words.   27 |54

11f Enrichment

1. Go to the Skillbuilding Workshop 1, Drill 1, page 31. Choose 6 letters that cause you difficulty. Key each line twice. Put a checkmark beside the lines in the book so that you know you have practiced them.

2. Save the drill as **xx-llf**. Substitute your initials for xx.

To create columns of unequal width:

1. Select **Columns** from the Format menu to display the Columns dialog box.

2. Choose one of the Preset options, or click in the **Number of columns** box and key the number of columns.

3. *Word's* default is columns of equal width. To vary the column widths, click the box to remove the check mark.

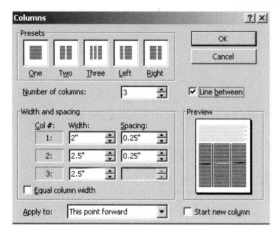

4. If you plan to vary the column widths, key the necessary information into the appropriate sections of the Width and spacing boxes.

5. If you want a vertical line between columns, click the **Line between** checkbox.

6. Click the down arrow beside the Apply to box, and choose one of the options. You can apply columns to the whole document, to one section, to selected sections, or from a particular point forward.

7. Use the Preview box to see what your layout will look like. In the dialog box shown here, the top portion of the document was formatted as a single column. At the end of that section, three unequal-width columns separated by lines were created. Note that in the Apply to box, **This point forward** has been selected.

To balance columns:

To balance columns so that all columns end at the same point on the page, position the insertion point at the end of the text to be balanced and insert a **Continuous section break (Insert, Break, Continuous, OK)**.

Drill 2 | COLUMNS OF VARYING LENGTHS

1. Open **Training** from the data files, and save as **54–55a-drill2**.

2. Use the Columns dialog box to create three columns of equal width. Click in the box Line between to add lines.

3. View the document.

4. Select the main heading, and use the Columns button to make a banner heading. Format it in 24-point bold. Double-space below the heading. Save again and print.

5. Click in the body of the document. Display the Columns dialog box. Format the document in two columns. Decrease column 1 width to 1"; increase space between columns to 1". View the document, but do not save.

Wrap Text Around Graphics

When graphic elements are included in documents such as newsletters, text usually wraps around the graphic.

To wrap text around graphics:

1. Insert the graphic; then place the insertion point over the graphic and right-click.

2. Select **Format picture** to display the Format Picture dialog box.

3. Click the **Layout** tab, and select the desired wrapping style (**Square**).

4. Click the desired alignment (**Right**), and then click **OK**.

LESSON 12 | Review

Warmup

12a

Key each line twice SS
(slowly, then faster).

alphabet 1 Jack won five quiz games; Brad will play him next.
q 2 Quin Racq quickly and quietly quelled the quarrel.
z 3 Zaret zipped along sizzling, zigzag Arizona roads.
easy 4 Did he hang the sign by the big bush at the lake?
| 1 | 2 | 3 | 4 | 5 | 6 | 7 | 8 | 9 | 10 |

Skillbuilding

12b New Key Review

Key each line once; DS
between groups; work for
smoothness, not for speed.

b/f 5 bf bf fab fab ball bib rf rf rib rib fibs bums bee
6 Did Buffy remember that he is a brass band member?

z/y 7 za za zag zig zip yj yj jay eye day lazy hazy zest
8 Liz amazed us with the zesty pizza on a lazy trip.

q/u 9 qa qa quo qt. quit quay quad quarm que uj jug quay
10 Where is Quito? Qatar? Boqueirao? Quebec? Quilmes?

v/m 11 vf vf valve five value mj mj ham mad mull mass vim
12 Vito, enter the words vim, vivace, and avar; save.

all 13 I faced defeat; only reserves saved my best crews.
14 In my opinion, I need to rest in my reserved seat.

all 15 Holly created a red poppy and deserves art awards.
16 My pump averages a faster rate; we get better oil.

12c Reach Review

Key each line once; work
for smooth, unhurried
keying.

de/ed 17 ed fed led deed dell dead deal sled desk need seed
18 Dell dealt with the deed before the dire deadline.

ol/lo 19 old tolls doll solo look sole lost love cold stole
20 Old Ole looked for the long lost olive oil lotion.

op/po 21 pop top post rope pout port stop opal opera report
22 Stop to read the top opera opinion report to Opal.

TECHNIQUE TIP

Keep fingers curved
and body aligned
properly.

we/ew 23 we few wet were went wears weather skews stew blew
24 Working women wear sweaters when weather dictates.

LESSONS 54–55 | Columns and Newsletters

New Functions

54-55a

help keywords
columns; newspaper columns

Columns

Text may be formatted in multiple columns on a page to make it easier to read. A newsletter, for example, is usually formatted in columns. Typically, newsletters are written in an informal, conversational style and are formatted with **banners** (text that spans multiple columns), newspaper columns, graphic elements, and other text enhancements. In newspaper columns, text flows down one column and then to the top of the next column. A simple, uncluttered design with a significant amount of white space is recommended to enhance the readability of newsletters.

To create columns of equal width:

1. Click the **Columns** button on the Standard toolbar.

2. Drag to select the number of columns.

3. Using this method to create columns will format the entire document with columns of equal widths.

Column format may be applied before or after keying text. If columns are set before text is keyed, use Print Layout View to check the appearance of the text. Generally, column formats are easier to apply after text has been keyed.

Columns

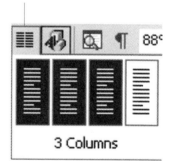

3 Columns

Occasionally, you may want certain text (such as a banner or headline) to span more than one column.

To format a banner:

1. Select the text to be included in the banner.

2. Click the **Columns** button, and drag the number of columns to one.

Drill 1 | SIMPLE COLUMNS

1. Open **Training** from the data files. Save it as **54–55a-drill1**.
2. Click **Columns** and format the document in three even columns. Preview to see how it looks.
3. Format the same document in two columns. Preview to check the appearance.

4. Select the heading **Productivity Enhancement Program**; click **Columns** and select one column. Apply 24 point. Center-align the heading. Add a hard return before column 1 to align the columns. Save again and close.

12d Speed Builder

1. Practice each line as fast as possible to build stroking speed.
2. Save as **xx-L12**. (Substitute your initials for *xx*.)

TECHNIQUE **TIP**

Keep hands quiet; keep fingers curved and upright.

12e Speed Check

1. In the Open Screen, key both paragraphs using wordwrap. Work for smooth, continuous stroking, not speed.
2. Save as **xx-12e**. Substitute your initials for *xx*.
3. Take a 1' writing on paragraph 1. Save as **xx-12e-t1**.
4. Repeat step 3 using paragraph 2. Save as **xx-12e-t2**.
5. Set the Timer for 2'. Take a 2' writing on both paragraphs. Save as **xx-12e-t3**.

 all letters

Goal: 16 *wam*

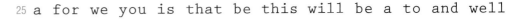

25 a for we you is that be this will be a to and well
26 as our with I or a to by your form which all would
27 new year no order they so new but now year who may

28 This is Lyn's only date to visit their great city.
29 I can send it to your office at any time you wish.
30 She kept the fox, owls, and fowl down by the lake.

31 Harriette will cook dinner for the swimming teams.
32 Annette will call at noon to give us her comments.
33 Johnny was good at running and passing a football.
| 1 | 2 | 3 | 4 | 5 | 6 | 7 | 8 | 9 | 10 |

Copy Difficulty

What factors determine whether copy is difficult or easy? Research shows that difficulty is influenced by syllables per word, characters per word, and percent of familiar words. Carefully controlling these three factors ensures that speed and accuracy scores are reliable—that is, increased scores reflect increased skill.

In Level 1, all timings are easy. Note "E" inside the triangle at left of the timing. Easy timings contain an average of 1.2 syllables per word, 5.1 characters per word, and 90 percent familiar words. Easy copy is suitable for the beginner who is mastering the keyboard.

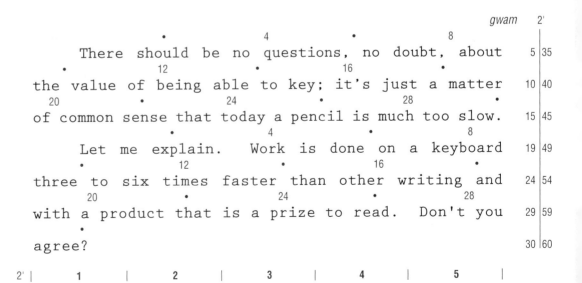

gwam 2'

                                    •   4   •   8
    There should be no questions, no doubt, about   5 |35
      •   12   •   16   •
the value of being able to key; it's just a matter   10 |40
    20   •   24   •   28   •
of common sense that today a pencil is much too slow. 15 |45
                    •   4   •   8
    Let me explain. Work is done on a keyboard   19 |49
      •   12   •   16   •
three to six times faster than other writing and   24 |54
    20   •   24   •   28
with a product that is a prize to read. Don't you   29 |59
      •
agree?   30 |60

2' | 1 | 2 | 3 | 4 | 5 |

Drill 5 | LINE CHART

1. Open **53c-drill3**, and save it as **53c-drill5**.
2. Double-click on the chart to open it.
3. Click **Chart**, then **Chart Type**, and select **Line Chart**.
4. In the Chart Sub-Type box, select the first option in row 2, Line with markers displayed at each data value.

5. Click **Chart**, and then click **Chart Options**.
6. Click the **Title** tab, and then click in the Title box, and key **Sales Trends for 2001**.
7. Click the **Legend** tab; then click **Show Legend** and select **Right**. Click outside the chart. Save again and print.

Applications

53d-d1
Radial Diagram

1. Prepare a radial diagram for a report you are writing.
2. Key **Critical Success Skills** in the center core element circle.
3. Add one additional circle to the three shown around the center.
4. Key **Reading**, **Writing**, **Listening**, and **Speaking** in the four circles.
5. Bold and center the text in each circle.
6. Save the document as **53d-d1** and print.

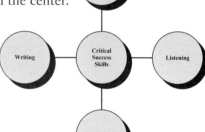

53d-d2
Pie Chart

1. Create a pie chart using the following data:
   Headings for Pie Slices: **Listening**, **Speaking**, **Reading**, and **Writing**
   Data: Listening **54**, Speaking **36**, Reading **19**, and Writing **11**
   Chart Title: **Communication Time**
   Legend: Show Legend at Bottom
   Data Labels: **Percentage** and **Legend Key**
2. Save the file as **53d-d2chart**.
3. Use the Elegant memo template, and key the following memo to **Customer Service Representatives** from you. Use the current date.
4. Use **Report from Consultants** as the subject. Send a copy to **Roger Massaro**.

Communication Time

The consultants sent me the results of the initial phase of their study of our customer service operation. One of the interesting findings was the average distribution of communication time of our customer service representatives.

The approach the consultants used was to observe each representative for 120 minutes over a two-week period. Ten-minute observations were randomly scheduled during this period. The following chart shows how our customer representatives spend their communication time.

Use paste special to insert the Communication Time chart (53d-d2chart) you created here. Position the chart at the center of the page.

These findings clearly support the need for our new Listening Skills Training Program.

LESSON 13 | Review

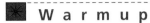

✳ Warmup

13a

Key each line twice SS
(slowly, then faster).

alphabet 1 Bev quickly hid two Japanese frogs in Mitzi's box.

shift 2 Jay Nadler, a Rotary Club member, wrote Mr. Coles.

, (comma) 3 Jay, Ed, and I paid for plates, knives, and forks.

easy 4 Did the amendment name a city auditor to the firm?

| 1 | 2 | 3 | 4 | 5 | 6 | 7 | 8 | 9 | 10 |

▣ Skillbuilding

13b Rhythm Builders
Key each line once SS.

word-level response: key short, familiar words as units

5 is to for do an may work so it but an with them am

6 Did they mend the torn right half of their ensign?

7 Hand me the ivory tusk on the mantle by the bugle.

letter-level response: key more difficult words letter by letter

8 only state jolly zest oil verve join rate mop card

9 After defeat, look up; gaze in joy at a few stars.

10 We gazed at a plump beaver as it waded in my pool.

combination response: use variable speed; your fingers will let you feel the difference

11 it up so at for you may was but him work were they

12 It is up to you to get the best rate; do it right.

13 This is Lyn's only date to visit their great city.

| 1 | 2 | 3 | 4 | 5 | 6 | 7 | 8 | 9 | 10 |

13c Keyboard
Reinforcement

Key each line once; fingers
well curved, wrists low;
avoid punching keys with
3rd and 4th fingers.

p 14 Pat appears happy to pay for any supper I prepare.

x 15 Knox can relax; Alex gets a box of flax next week.

v 16 Vi, Ava, and Viv move ivy vines, leaves, or stems.

' 17 It's a question of whether they can't or won't go.

? 18 Did Jan go? Did she see Ray? Who paid? Did she?

. 19 Ms. E. K. Nu and Lt. B. A. Walz had the a.m. duty.

" 20 "Who are you?" he asked. "I am," I said, "Marie."

; 21 Find a car; try it; like it; work a price; buy it.

To modify a chart:

1. Click on the chart to display the datasheet or grid that is similar to an *Excel* spreadsheet. New information in the form of labels (words) and data (figures) can be either keyed in the data sheet or imported from a spreadsheet.

2. Select and edit the data as desired.

3. Click outside the chart area when you have finished.

Document2 - Datasheet		A	B	C	D
		1st Qtr	2nd Qtr	3rd Qtr	4th Qtr
1	East	20.4	27.4	90	20.4
2	West	30.6	38.6	34.6	31.6
3	North	45.9	46.9	45	43.9
4					

Drill 3 | COLUMN CHART

1. Create the column chart illustrated on the previous page using the data chart below.

2. Click **Picture** on the Insert menu, and then click **Chart** to display the default column chart along with the data sheet. The *Microsoft Graph* commands become available on the menu bar and toolbars.

3. Click in the datasheet cell below *North* and key **South**. Note that the software adds a unique color for the columns displaying the data for the South region.

4. Click in each cell in columns A–D, and key the data shown below for the four quarters.

5. On the menu, click **Chart** and then **Chart Options**.

6. Click the **Titles** tab and then click in the Title box and key **Sales by Region**.

7. Click the **Legend** tab, and click the **Show Legend** box if it is not already checked. Click the **Right** button, and then click **OK**.

8. Click outside the chart area.

9. Save the document as **53c-drill3** and print.

C:\Mod 8 CK15\Mod 8 Sol\53... - Datasheet		A	B	C	D	E
		1st Qtr	2nd Qtr	3rd Qtr	4th Qtr	
1	East	257	265	340	250	
2	West	321	302	420	325	
3	North	402	340	320	245	
4	South	385	380	460	205	

Drill 4 | PIE CHART

1. Create a pie chart to show the percentage of the total fourth quarter sales each region had.

2. Click **Picture** on the Insert menu, and then click **Chart**.

3. On the Chart menu, click **Chart Type**, and select **Pie** from the list.

4. In the Chart Sub-Type box, select the second chart, **Pie with 3-D Visual Effect**.

5. Select the datasheet, and select and replace the labels and data with information shown below. The data for a pie

chart is formatted in a row. Each heading represents a slice of the pie.

6. Click **Chart**; then **Chart Options**. Click the **Title** tab and key **Fourth Quarter Sales** in the Title box.

7. Click the **Legend** tab, and show the legend at the right.

8. Click the **Data Labels** tab, and then click **Percentage** and **Legend Key**.

9. Click outside the chart.

10. Save the document as **53c-drill4** and print.

C:\Mod 8 CK15\Mod 8 Sol\53... - Datasheet		A	B	C	D	E	F
		East	West	North	South		
1	3-D Pie 1	250	325	245	205		
2							
3							

13d Troublesome Pairs

Key each line once; repeat if time permits.

t 22 at fat hat sat to tip the that they fast last slat

r 23 or red try ran run air era fair rid ride trip trap

t/r 24 A trainer sprained an arm trying to tame the bear.

m 25 am me my mine jam man more most dome month minimum

n 26 no an now nine once net knee name ninth know never

m/n 27 Many men and women are important company managers.

o 28 on or to not now one oil toil over only solo today

i 29 it is in tie did fix his sit like with insist will

o/i 30 Joni will consider obtaining options to buy coins.

a 31 at an as art has and any case data haze tart smart

s 32 us as so say sat slap lass class just sassy simple

a/s 33 Disaster was averted as the steamer sailed to sea.

e 34 we he ear the key her hear chef desire where there

i 35 it is in tie did fix his sit like with insist will

e/i 36 An expression of gratitude for service is desired.

13e Speed Check

1. In the Open Screen, key the paragraphs once SS.
2. Save as **xx-13e**.
3. Take a 1' writing on paragraph 1. Save as **xx-13e-t1**.
4. Take a 1' writing on paragraph 2. Save as **xx-13e-t2**.
5. Print the better 1' writing.
6. Take a 2' writing on both paragraphs. Start over if time permits.

  all letters

Goal: 16 *gwam*

gwam 2"

• 4 • 8

The questions of time use are vital ones; we   5

• 12 • 16

miss so much just because we don't plan.   9

• 4 • 8

When we organize our days, we save time for   13

• 12 • 16

those extra premium things we long to do.   17

2' | 1 | 2 | 3 | 4 | 5 |

1. Save **53c-drill1** as **53c-drill2**, and change the page setup to **Landscape**.
2. Select the box with your name, and add **Mason McGee, Administrative Assistant** as an assistant (Insert Shape, Assistant).
3. Add **Marcus Clements, Division Head** as a subordinate to the Executive Vice President (select box; Insert Shape; Left Hanging Layout).
4. Add **Angela Westin, Division Head** as a subordinate to the Vice President for Finance (select box; Insert Shape; Standard Layout).

5. Add **Lynn Watson, Division Head** as a subordinate to the Vice President for Marketing (select box; Insert Shape; Right Hanging Layout).
6. Select and drag the Canvas to the approximate center of the page.
7. Save the document again and print one copy.

Optional: Insert several of the other diagrams from the Drawing toolbar, and discover how to add elements to each and to format them.

Microsoft Graph

help keywords
chart, graph

Different types of charts can be created using *Microsoft Graph*. The most common are bar charts, column charts, line charts, and pie charts. Bar and column charts compare values over categories—the length of the bar or the height of the column is used to show the differences. Line charts show trends over time. Pie charts show percentages of a whole. Study the parts of a chart that are labeled on the column chart below.

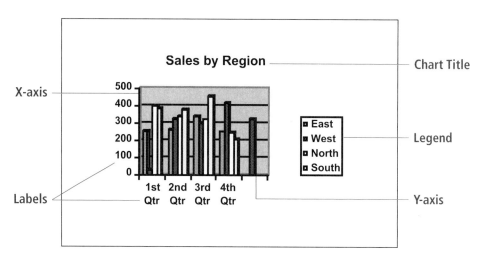

To create a chart:

1. Click **Picture** on the Insert menu, and then click **Chart** to display the default chart.
2. To choose another type of chart, click **Chart** on the menu; then click **Chart Type** to display the list of chart types.
3. Select the type of chart desired, and key or modify the data in the datasheet.
4. Click **Chart**, and then click **Chart Options**.
5. Click in the Title box, and key the title.
6. Click **Legend**, click the **Show Legend** box, and click a position, such as **Right**.
7. Click outside the chart area when you have completed the chart.

> **MOUS TIP**
>
> Another option for inserting a chart is to click **Insert; Object**. Then click **Create New tab** and select **Microsoft Graph Chart**.

SKILL BUILDERS I

 Use the Open Screen for Skill Builders 1. Save each drill as a separate file.

Drill 1

Goal: reinforce key locations
Key each line at a comfortable, constant rate; check lines that need more practice; repeat those lines.

Keep
- your eyes on source copy
- your fingers curved, upright
- your wrists low, but not touching
- your elbows hanging loosely
- your feet flat on the floor

A We saw that Alan had an alabaster vase in Alabama.

B My rubber boat bobbed about in the bubbling brook.

C Ceci gave cups of cold cocoa to Rebecca and Rocco.

D Don's dad added a second deck to his old building.

E Even as Ellen edited her document, she ate dinner.

F Our firm in Buffalo has a staff of forty or fifty.

G Ginger is giving Greg the eggs she got from Helga.

H Hugh has eighty high, harsh lights he might flash.

I Irik's lack of initiative is irritating his coach.

J Judge J. J. Jore rejected Jeane and Jack's jargon.

K As a lark, Kirk kicked back a rock at Kim's kayak.

L Lucille is silly; she still likes lemon lollipops.

M Milt Mumm hammered a homer in the Miami home game.

N Ken Linn has gone hunting; Stan can begin canning.

O Jon Soto rode off to Otsego in an old Morgan auto.

P Philip helped pay the prize as my puppy hopped up.

Q Quiet Raquel quit quoting at an exquisite marquee.

R As Mrs. Kerr's motor roared, her red horse reared.

S Sissie lives in Mississippi; Lissa lives in Tulsa.

T Nat told Betty not to tattle on her little sister.

U Ula has a unique but prudish idea on unused units.

V Eva visited every vivid event for twelve evenings.

W We watched as wayworn wasps swarmed by the willow.

X Tex Cox waxed the next box for Xenia and Rex Knox.

Y Ty says you may stay with Fay for only sixty days.

Z Hazel is puzzled about the azure haze; Zack dozes.

alphabet Jacky and Max quickly fought over a sizable prawn.

alphabet Just by maximizing liquids, Chick Prew avoids flu.

| 1 | 2 | 3 | 4 | 5 | 6 | 7 | 8 | 9 | 10 |

Diagrams

The **Insert Diagram or Chart** button is located on the Drawing toolbar and is used to access the Diagram Gallery. The Diagram Gallery at the right illustrates the six types of diagrams that are available. A good way to learn about each of the diagrams is to click on the diagram and read the description explaining its use.

To create a diagram:

1. Click the **Diagram** button on the Drawing toolbar. (*Option:* Click **Diagram** on the Insert menu.)

2. Select the desired diagram and click **OK** to display the diagram and the Diagram toolbar.

3. Click each box in the diagram to add text; format the text as desired. If text does not fit in the boxes, click **Layout** and then **Scale Organization Chart**. Drag the outside border of the chart to resize the boxes. Then, if necessary to fit the chart on a page, click **Layout** again and then **Fit Organization Chart to Contents**.

4. To add additional boxes, click **Insert Shape** on the Organization Chart toolbar.

5. To change the layout, click **Layout** on the Organization Chart toolbar.

(*Note:* Each diagram has its own toolbar. The toolbars are very similar and accomplish the same purposes.)

D r i l l 1 | ORGANIZATIONAL CHART

1. Create the organizational chart shown below.

2. If text does not fit in a box, click **Layout** and then **Scale Organization Chart**. Drag the outside border of the chart to increase the size of the boxes. Then, if necessary, click **Layout** again and then **Fit Organization Chart to Contents**.

3. Save the document as **53c-drill1** and print. Leave the document open for the next activity.

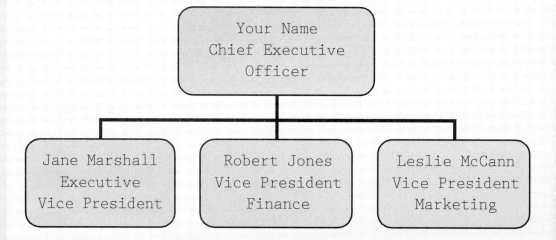

Drill 2

Goal: strengthen up and down reaches

Keep hands and wrists quiet; fingers well curved in home position; stretch fingers up from home or pull them palmward as needed.

home position
1 Hall left for Dallas; he is glad Jake fed his dog.
2 Ada had a glass flask; Jake had a sad jello salad.
3 Lana Hask had a sale; Gala shall add half a glass.

down reaches
4 Did my banker, Mr. Mavann, analyze my tax account?
5 Do they, Mr. Zack, expect a number of brave women?
6 Zach, check the menu; next, beckon the lazy valet.

up reaches
7 Prue truly lost the quote we wrote for our report.
8 Teresa quietly put her whole heart into her words.
9 There were two hilarious jokes in your quiet talk.

Drill 3

Goal: strengthen individual finger reaches

Rekey troublesome lines.

first finger
1 Bob Mugho hunted for five minutes for your number.
2 Juan hit the bright green turf with his five iron.
3 The frigates and gunboats fought mightily in Java.

second finger
4 Dick said the ice on the creek had surely cracked.
5 Even as we picnicked, I decided we needed to diet.
6 Kim, not Mickey, had rice with chicken for dinner.

third/fourth finger
7 Pam saw Roz wax an aqua auto as Lex sipped a cola.
8 Wally will quickly spell Zeus, Apollo, and Xerxes.
9 Who saw Polly? Zoe Pax saw her; she is quiet now.

Drill 4

Goal: strengthen special reaches

Emphasize smooth stroking. Avoid pauses, but do not reach for speed.

adjacent reaches
1 Falk knew well that her opinions of art were good.
2 Theresa answered her question; order was restored.
3 We join there and walk north to the western point.

direct reaches
4 Barb Nunn must hunt for my checks; she is in debt.
5 In June and December, Irvin hunts in Bryce Canyon.
6 We decided to carve a number of funny human faces.

double letters
7 Anne stopped off at school to see Bill Wiggs cook.
8 Edd has planned a small cookout for all the troop.
9 Keep adding to my assets all fees that will apply.

| 1 | 2 | 3 | 4 | 5 | 6 | 7 | 8 | 9 | 10 |

LESSON 53 | Charts and Diagrams

Skillbuilding

53a
Warmup

Key each line twice SS; DS between 2-line groups.

alphabet 1 Jacky Few's strange, quiet behavior amazed and perplexed even us.

figures 2 Dial Extension 1480 or 2760 for a copy of the 3-page 95-cent book.

double letters 3 Ann will see that Edd accepts an assignment in the school office.

easy 4 If I burn the signs, the odor of enamel may make a toxic problem.

| 1 | 2 | 3 | 4 | 5 | 6 | 7 | 8 | 9 | 10 | 11 | 12 | 13 |

53b
Timed Writings

1. Take two 1' timings on each paragraph.
2. Key either a 3' or 5' timing.

 all letters

gwam 3' | 5'

Who is a professional? The word can be defined in many   4 | 2 32

ways. Some may think of a professional as someone who is in an   8 | 5 35

exempt job category in an organization. To others the word can   12 | 7 37

denote something quite different; being a professional denotes an   17 | 10 40

attitude that requires thinking of your position as a career, not   21 | 13 43

just a job. A professional exerts influence over her or his job   25 | 15 45

and takes pride in the work accomplished.   28 | 17 47

Many individuals who remain in the same positions for a long   32 | 19 49

time characterize themselves as being in dead-end positions.   36 | 22 52

Others who remain in positions for a long time consider them-   40 | 24 54

selves to be in a profession. A profession is a career to which   45 | 27 57

you are willing to devote a lifetime. How you view your pro-   49 | 29 59

fession is up to you.   50 | 30 60

3' | 1 | 2 | 3 | 4 |
5' | 1 | 2 | 3 |

New Functions

53c

help keywords
chart, diagram, graph

Create and Modify Diagrams and Charts

Diagrams and charts provide a meaningful way of illustrating data to make it easier for the reader to understand. Diagrams can be created using Drawing tools. Charts can be created using *Microsoft Graph* or other applications such as *Excel* spreadsheets. In this lesson, you will create diagrams with Drawing tools and charts using *Microsoft Graph*.

Drill 5

Goal: improve troublesome pairs

Use a controlled rate without pauses.

1 ad add did does dish down body dear dread dabs bad

d/k 2 kid ok kiss tuck wick risk rocks kayaks corks buck

3 Dirk asked Dick to kid Drake about the baked duck.

4 deed deal den led heed made needs delay he she her

e/i 5 kit kiss kiln kiwi kick kilt kind six ribs kill it

6 Abie had neither ice cream nor fried rice in Erie.

7 fib fob fab rib beg bug rob bad bar bed born table

b/v 8 vat vet gave five ever envy never visit weave ever

9 Did Harv key jibe or jive, TV or TB, robe or rove?

10 aft after lift gift sit tot the them tax tutu tyro

t/r 11 for far ere era risk rich rock rosy work were roof

12 In Toronto, Ruth told the truth about her artwork.

13 jug just jury judge juice unit hunt bonus quiz bug

u/y 14 jay joy lay you your only envy quay oily whey body

15 Willy usually does not buy your Yukon art in July.

Drill 6

Goal: build speed

Set the Timer for 1'.

Key each sentence for 1'. Try to complete each sentence twice (20 *gwam* or more). Ignore errors for now.

1 Dian may make cocoa for the girls when they visit.
2 Focus the lens for the right angle; fix the prism.
3 She may suspend work when she signs the torn form.
4 Augment their auto fuel in the keg by the autobus.
5 As usual, their robot did half turns to the right.
6 Pamela laughs as she signals to the big hairy dog.
7 Pay Vivian to fix the island for the eighty ducks.

| 1 | 2 | 3 | 4 | 5 | 6 | 7 | 8 | 9 | 10 |

Drill 7

Goal: build speed

From the columns at the right, choose a gwam goal that is two to three words higher than your best rate. Set the Timer for **Variable** and then either **20"** or **30"**. Try to reach your goal.

	words	30"	20"
1 Did she make this turkey dish?		12	18
2 Blake and Laurie may go to Dubuque.		14	21
3 Signal for the oak sleigh to turn right.		16	24
4 I blame Susie; did she quench the only flame?		18	27
5 She turns the panel dials to make this robot work.		20	30

| 1 | 2 | 3 | 4 | 5 | 6 | 7 | 8 | 9 | 10 |

Applications

52c-d1

Report with Graphics

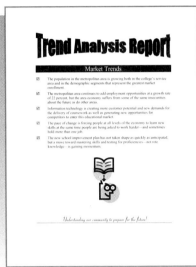

1. In a new document, format the main heading, **Trend Analysis Report**, using the fourth design in the first row of the WordArt Gallery; adjust the size to extend over the line of writing.
2. Create a subheading below the WordArt by keying **Market Trends** using 20-point font and adding black shading to the paragraph.
3. Insert the symbol ☑ from the Wingdings font to each of the items in the body of the report. Use hanging indent to format the paragraphs with 6-point spacing after each paragraph, and key the five paragraphs.
4. Search for clip art using the keyword **academic** and add an appropriate piece of clip art centered below the five paragraphs.
5. Add a horizontal line at the bottom of the page. Above the line, key in 18-point script font **Understanding our community to prepare for our future!**
6. Save the document as **52c-d1**, and print a copy.

Trend Analysis Report

Market Analysis

☑ The population in the metropolitan area is growing both in the college's service area and in the demographic segments that represent the greatest market enrollment.

☑ The metropolitan area continues to add employment opportunities at a growth rate of 22 percent, but the area economy suffers from some of the same insecurities about the future as do other areas.

☑ Information technology is creating more customer potential and new demands for the delivery of coursework as well as generating new opportunities for competitors to enter this educational market.

☑ The pace of change is forcing people at all levels of the economy to learn new skills at the same time people are being asked to work harder—and sometimes hold more than one job.

☑ The new school improvement plan has not taken shape as quickly as anticipated, but a move toward mastering skills and testing for proficiencies—not rote knowledge—is gaining momentum.

 52c-d2

Announcement

MOUS TIP

To position the clip art on the same line as the text, right-click the clip art and select **Format Picture**. On the Layout tab, click **Square** wrapping style and left alignment.

1. Open **Tour** from the data files.
2. Replace the heading, *Tour of Facilities*, with WordArt of your choice.
3. Add two clip art objects appropriate for the content of the document.
4. Format the document so that it will make a nice announcement that can be posted for guests to read.
5. Save the document as **52c-d2**, and print a copy.

D r i l l 8

Goal: build staying power

1. Key each paragraph as a 1' timing.
2. Key a 2' timing on both paragraphs.

Note: The dot above text represents two words.

 all letters

These writings may be used as Diagnostic Writings.

Writing 1: **18** *gwam*   *gwam* 2'

      •   4   •   8   •

Why spend weeks with some problem when just a few quiet   6

12   •   16   •

minutes can help us to resolve it.   9

      •   4   •   8   •

If we don't take time to think through a problem, it will   15

12   •   16   •

swiftly begin to expand in size.   18

Writing 2: **20** *gwam*

      •   4   •   8   •

We push very hard in our quest for growth, and we all   5

12   •   16   •   20

think that only excellent growth will pay off.   10

      •   4   •   8   •

Believe it or not, one can actually work much too hard,   16

12   •   16   •   20

be much too zealous, and just miss the mark.   20

Writing 3: **22** *gwam*

      •   4   •   8   •

A business friend once explained to me why he was often   6

12   •   16   •   20   •

quite eager to be given some new project to work with.   11

      •   4   •   8   •

My friend said that each new project means he has to   16

12   •   16   •   20   •

organize and use the best of his knowledge and his skill.   22

Writing 4: **24** *gwam*

      •   4   •   8   •

Don't let new words get away from you. Learn how to spell   6

12   •   16 •   20   •   24

and pronounce new words and when and how finally to use them.   12

      •   4   •   8   •

A new word is a friend, but frequently more. New words   18

12   •   16   •   20   •   24

must be used lavishly to extend the size of your own word power.   24

2' | 1 | 2 | 3 | 4 | 5 | 6 |

The WordArt Gallery provides a number of shapes and styles for WordArt. The first example shown below was created using the first design in the WordArt Gallery. The second example was created by adding a textured fill color and a 3-D effect to the first banner.

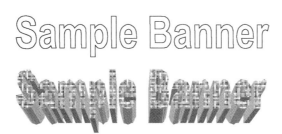

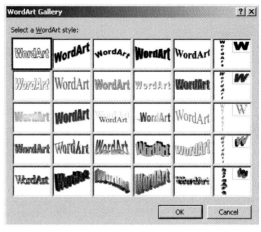

To use WordArt:

1. Display the Drawing toolbar, and click the **WordArt** button. The WordArt Gallery displays.

2. Select the desired style and click **OK** to display the Edit WordArt Text dialog box as shown at the right.

3. Key the text; change the font size or style in this textbox if desired. Click **OK**. Your text is now displayed as WordArt.

4. Select the text to display the WordArt toolbar. Format the WordArt text using the buttons on the WordArt toolbar. You may also use the buttons on the Drawing toolbar.

D r i l l   3 | WORDART

1. Open a new document and display the Drawing toolbar. Click the **Insert WordArt** button.

2. Select the first style from the second row of the WordArt Gallery.

3. Key the text **Happy Birthday to you!**

4. Select the text and click the **Format WordArt** button on the WordArt toolbar. Choose **Pale Blue** color and then **Patterned Lines**.

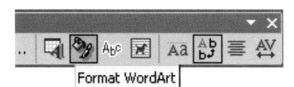

5. Apply the fifth patterned effect in the first column of patterns to the foreground.

6. Apply the first 3-D effect.

7. Save the document as **52b-drill3**.

These writings may be used as Diagnostic Writings.

Writing 5: 26 *gwam*

gwam 2'

        • 4 • 8 •
We usually get best results when we know where we are   5
12 • 16 • 20 •
going. Just setting a few goals will help us quietly see what   12
24 •
we are doing.   13

        • 4 • 8 •
Goals can help measure whether we are moving at a good   19
12 • 16 • 20 •
rate or dozing along. You can expect a goal to help you find   25
24 •
good results.   26

Writing 6: 28 *gwam*

        • 4 • 8 •
To win whatever prizes we want from life, we must plan to   6
12 • 16 • 20 •
move carefully from this goal to the next to get the maximum   12
24 • 28
result from our work.   14

        • 4 • 8 •
If we really want to become skilled in keying, we must   19
12 • 16 • 20 •
come to see that this desire will require of us just a little   26
24 • 28
patience and hard work.   28

Writing 7: 30 *gwam*

        • 4 • 8 •
Am I an individual person? I'm sure I am; still, in a   5
12 • 16 • 20 •
much, much bigger sense, other people have a major voice in   12
24 • 28 •
thoughts I think and actions I take.   15

        • 4 • 8 •
Although we are each a unique person, we all work and   21
12 • 16 • 20 •
play in organized groups of people who do not expect us to   26
24 • 28 •
dismiss their rules of law and order.   30

2' | 1 | 2 | 3 | 4 | 5 | 6 |

You will create the drawing objects shown below. The first five steps create the first drawing.

1. Click the **Rectangle** button, and draw a rectangle approximately 1.5" wide. Use the Horizontal Ruler as a guide.

2. Right-click on the rectangle, and key the text **Happy Holidays**. Change the font to Lucida Handwriting (or an alternate font) 16-point bold. Change font color to Gold, and center-align the text in the rectangle.

3. Use the Fill Color button to add Red fill to the rectangle and the text box.

4. Click the **3-D Effect** button , and select the third shape in the third row (Style 11).

5. Click the down arrow beside AutoShapes, select **Basic Shapes**, and add a smiley face below the rectangle. Change the line color to Blue and the fill to Yellow.

6. Draw an oval on the right side of the rectangle; use Tan fill and Brown line; add your name to the oval, and change the font color to Brown. Center your name in the oval.

7. Add the arrow as shown below the oval. Adjust the size so that it is as wide as the oval, and add Dark Red fill.

8. Group the four objects so that they can be moved as one object.

9. Select the group, select **Copy**, open a new document, and paste the group into the new document.

10. Save the new document as **52b-drill2**, and print it. Close the original document without saving your changes.

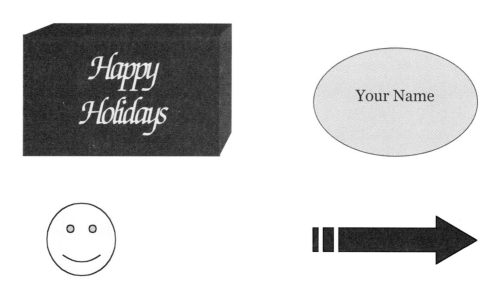

WordArt

WordArt provides an interesting way to add banners to documents that are formatted in columns, to format casual letterheads, or to add large print to documents such as announcements. Since WordArt is part of the Drawing program, it can be formatted using other drawing features such as colored or textured fills and 3-D effects.

module 2

Figure and Symbol Keys

OBJECTIVES

* Key the numeric keys by touch.
* Use symbol keys correctly.
* Build keying speed and accuracy.
* Apply correct number expression.
* Apply proofreaders' marks.
* Apply basic Internet skills.

LESSON 14 | 1 and 8

✳ W a r m u p

14a
Key each line twice SS.
Line 2: Space once after
a series of brief questions
within a sentence.

alphabet	1	Jessie Quick believed the campaign frenzy would be exciting.
space bar	2	Was it Mary? Helen? Pam? It was a woman; I saw one of them.
3d row	3	We were quietly prepped to write two letters to Portia York.
easy	4	Kale's neighbor works with a tutor when they visit downtown.

| 1 | 2 | 3 | 4 | 5 | 6 | 7 | 8 | 9 | 10 | 11 | 12 |

▥ Skillbuilding

14b High-Frequency Words
The words at the right are
from the 100 most used words.
Key each line once; work for
fluency.

Top 100

5 a an it been copy for his this more no office please service

6 our service than the they up was work all any many thank had

7 business from I know made more not me new of some to program

8 such these two with your about and have like department year

9 by at on but do had in letter most now one please you should

10 their order like also appreciate that there gentlemen letter

11 be can each had information letter may make now only so that

12 them time use which am other been send to enclosed have will

Drawing Tools

A variety of drawing tools are available in *Word.* These tools can be accessed from the Drawing toolbar (**View, Toolbars, Drawing**). An easy way to become familiar with all of the tools is to display the Drawing toolbar and hold the mouse pointer over each object on the toolbar to display its function. Click the down arrow on each object that has one to display the available options for the tool. A canvas will display when you click a drawing tool to help with the formatting of the object.

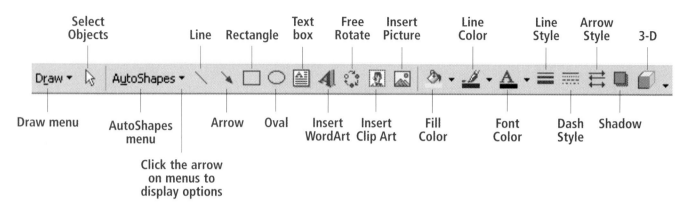

To insert a drawing tool object:

1. With the Drawing toolbar displayed, click on the desired object such as **Rectangle** or **AutoShapes**. If you choose AutoShapes, a list of various shapes displays. If a triangular arrow appears beside an object, click on it to display the available options.

2. When you choose the desired object, a "canvas" displays with the message "Create your drawing here." The mouse pointer turns into a crosshairs. Drag the mouse to create the object on the canvas.

3. Select the object and format it using the effects such as fill, lines, and 3-D that are available on the Drawing toolbar.

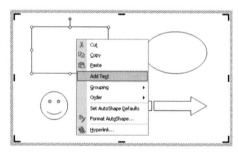

4. To add text to an object such as a rectangle or an oval, right-click the object and select **Add Text** from the drop-down menu. Then key your text.

Group Objects

Often multiple drawing objects are used together. The objects can be grouped so that all of them can be moved as one object. They also can be ungrouped so that you can change the formatting of individual objects.

To group objects:

1. Select the first object; then press CTRL and select each of the other objects to be grouped.

2. Click the down arrow on the Draw button Draw ▾ . Click **Group**.

3. To ungroup objects, select the objects, click the down arrow on the Draw button, and click **Ungroup**.

New Keys

14c 1 and 8

Key each line once SS.

Note: The digit "1" and the letter "l" have separate values on a computer keyboard. Do not interchange these characters.

1 Reach *up* with *left fourth* finger.

8 Reach *up* with *right second* finger.

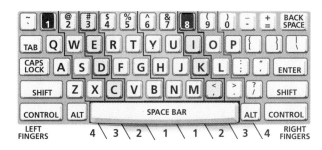

Abbreviations: Do not space after a period within an abbreviation, as in Ph.D., U.S., C.O.D., a.m.

1

13 1 1a a1 1 1; 1 and a 1; 1 add 1; 1 aunt; 1 ace; 1 arm; 1 aye
14 1 and 11 and 111; 11 eggs; 11 vats; Set 11A; May 11; Item 11
15 The 11 aces of the 111th Corps each rated a salute at 1 p.m.

8

16 8 8k k8 8 8; 8 kits; ask 8; 8 kites; kick 8; 8 keys; spark 8
17 OK 88; 8 bags; 8 or 88; the 88th; 88 kegs; ask 88; order 888
18 Eight of the 88 cars score 8 or better on our Form 8 rating.

all figures learned

19 She did live at 818 Park, not 181 Park; or was it 181 Clark?
20 Put 1 with 8 to form 18; put 8 with 1 to form 81. Use 1881.
21 On May 1 at 8 a.m., 18 men and 18 women left Gate 8 for Rio.

Skillbuilding

14d Reinforcement

Key each line once; DS between groups. Repeat. Key with accuracy.

figures

22 Our 188 trucks moved 1881 tons on August 18 and December 18.
23 Send Mary 181 No. 188 panes for her home at 8118 Oak Street.
24 The 188 men in 8 boats left Docks 1 and 18 at 1 p.m., May 1.

25 pop was lap pass slaw wool solo swap Apollo wasp load plaque
26 Was Polly acquainted with the equipped jazz player in Texas?
27 The computer is a useful tool; it helps you to perform well.

14e Speed Builder

Set the timer for 1'. Key each sentence as many times as possible.

Goal: to complete each sentence twice in one minute.

28 Did their form entitle them to the land?
29 Did the men in the field signal for us to go?
30 I may pay for the antique bowls when I go to town.
31 The auditor did the work right, so he risks no penalty.
32 The man by the big bush did signal us to turn down the lane.

| 1 | 2 | 3 | 4 | 5 | 6 | 7 | 8 | 9 | 10 | 11 | 12 |

To insert clip art:

1. Click **Insert** on the menu bar, click **Picture**, and then click **Clip Art**.

2. In the Task Pane Search text box, key the type of clip art to search for such as rabbit, baseball, or roses, then click **Search**.

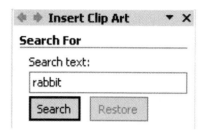

MOUS TIP

Another option for inserting clip art is to display the Drawing toolbar (View, Toolbars, Drawing), and click the Insert Clip Art button.

3. When the results are displayed, use the scroll bar to view the thumbnail sketches. When you find the desired clip art, point to the image to display a down arrow at the right of the image, click the down arrow, and then click **Insert**. (*Option:* Click the clip art image.)

4. To display a collection of clip art from various places, choose one of the options under Other Search Options on the Task Pane.

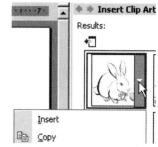

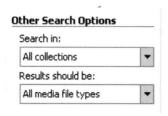

To move or size clip art:

1. Select the clip art.

2. To size the clip art, position the insertion point over one of the handles. When the pointer turns to a double-headed arrow, drag the lower-right handle down and to the right to increase the size; drag it up and to the left to make it smaller. Drag a corner handle to maintain the same proportion.

3. To move the clip art, hold down the left mouse button and drag the clip art to the desired position.

MOUS TIP

Graphics can be formatted by right-clicking the image and selecting **Format Picture**. Click on the various tabs to note the options available.

D r i l l 1 | CLIP ART

1. Open a new document.

2. Search for roses in the clip art gallery, and insert the clip art into the document.

3. Increase the size of the clip art to approximately double its size. Use the Horizontal and Vertical Rulers to guide you.

4. Move it to the center of the page near the top margin.

5. Create the folder **Module 8 Keys**, and save the document as **52b-drill1** in this folder. Save all exercises for Module 8 in this folder.

LESSON 15 | 5 and 0

Warmup
15a
Key each line twice SS.
For a series of capital letters, press CAPS LOCK with the left little finger. Press again to release.

alphabet 1 John Quigley packed the zinnias in twelve large, firm boxes.

1/8 2 Idle Motor 18 at 8 mph and Motor 81 at 8 mph; avoid Motor 1.

caps lock 3 Lily read BLITHE SPIRIT by Noel Coward. I read VANITY FAIR.

easy 4 Did they fix the problem of the torn panel and worn element?
| 1 | 2 | 3 | 4 | 5 | 6 | 7 | 8 | 9 | 10 | 11 | 12 |

15b Technique Reinforcement
Reach up or down without moving your hands. Key each line once; repeat drill.

adjacent reaches

5 as oil red ask wet opt mop try tree open shred operas treaty
6 were pore dirt stew ruin faster onion alumni dreary mnemonic
7 The opened red hydrants were powerful, fast, and very dirty.

outside reaches

8 pop zap cap zag wasp equip lazy zippers queue opinion quartz
9 zest waste paper exist parquet azalea acquaint apollo apathy
10 The lazy wasp passed the potted azalea on the parquet floor.

New Keys

15c 5 and 0
Key each line once SS.

5 Reach *up* with *left first* finger.

0 Reach *up* with *right fourth* finger.

5

11 5 5f f5 5 5; 5 fans; 5 feet; 5 figs; 5 fobs; 5 furs; 5 flaws
12 5 o'clock; 5 a.m.; 5 p.m.; is 55 or less; buy 55; 5 and 5 is
13 Call Line 555 if 5 fans or 5 bins arrive at Pier 5 by 5 p.m.

0

14 0 0; ;0 0 0; skip 0; plan 0; left 0; is below 0; I scored 0;
15 0 degrees; key 0 and 0; write 00 here; the total is 0 or 00;
16 She laughed at their 0 to 0 score; but ours was 0 to 0 also.

all figures learned

17 I keyed 550 pages for Invoice 05, or 50 more than we needed.
18 Pages 15 and 18 of the program listed 150, not 180, members.
19 On May 10, Rick drove 500 miles to New Mexico in car No. 08.

module 8

Newsletters and Electronic Communications

OBJECTIVES

* Enhance document format with graphics, charts, and diagrams.
* Create multicolumn newsletters.
* Create and send e-mails.
* Create simple Web pages.
* Collaborate with other writers.

LESSON 52 | Clip Art, Drawing Tools, and WordArt

Skillbuilding

52a

Warmup

Key each line twice SS; DS between 2-line groups.

New Functions

52b

help keywords
clip art

Clip art, pictures, AutoShapes, WordArt, charts, and other images are graphic elements that enhance documents such as announcements, invitations, reports, and newsletters. In this lesson, you will work with clip art, drawing tools, and WordArt.

Clip Art

Microsoft Word (and other applications such as *Excel*, *PowerPoint*, and *Publisher*) provides a collection of pictures, clip art, and sounds that can be added to documents. Additional clips are available online. You can also add your own clips to the collection. The clips are organized into different collections to simplify finding appropriate clip art. The Clip Organizer adds keywords to enable you to search for various types of clip art. You also have the option of selecting the collection and viewing thumbnail sketches (small pictures) of the various clip art available in each category. Once clip art has been inserted into a document, you can size it, copy and paste it, wrap text around it, or drag it to other locations.

 **Skillbuilding**

15d Keyboard Reinforcement

Key each line twice SS (slowly, then faster); DS between 2-line groups.

improve figures

20 Read pages 5 and 8; duplicate page 18; omit pages 50 and 51.
21 We have Model 80 with 10 meters or Model 180 with 15 meters.
22 After May 18, French 050 meets in room 15 at 10 a.m. daily.

improve long reaches

23 Barb Abver saw a vibrant version of her brave venture on TV.
24 Call a woman or a man who will manage Minerva Manor in Nome.
25 We were quick to squirt a quantity of water at Quin and West.

15e Tab Review

1. Read the instructions to clear and set tabs.
2. Set a left tab at 4".
3. Practice the lines; strike TAB without watching your keyboard.

STANDARD PLAN | for Setting and Clearing Tabs in the Open Screen

Preset or default tabs are displayed on the Ruler. If necessary, display the Ruler in the Open Screen. (Choose the **Show Ruler** option on the Format menu.) Sometimes you will want to remove or clear existing tabs before setting new ones.

To clear and set tabs:

1. On the menu bar, click **Format**, then **Clear All Tabs**.
2. To set tabs, select the type of tab you want to set (left, center, decimal, or right) shown at the lower-left side of the ruler.
3. Click the Ruler at the location where you want to set a tab.

Set tab 4"

⟶ Tab Keyboarding
has become ⟶ Tab the primary
means of ⟶ Tab written communication
in business and ⟶ Tab in our personal lives.
Keyboarding is ⟶ Tab used by persons
in every profession ⟶ Tab and most job levels.

15f Speed Check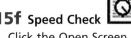

1. Click the Open Screen button.
2. Take two 1' writings on paragraph 2. Note your *gwam*.
3. Take two 1' writings on paragraph 1. Try to equal paragraph 2 rate.
4. Take one 2' writing on both paragraphs.

 all letters

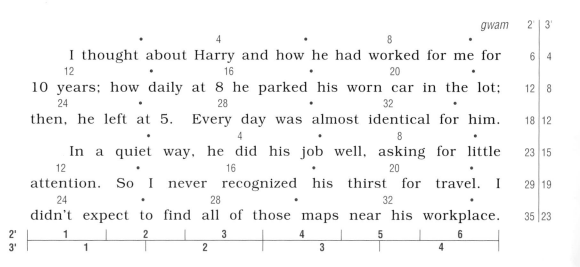

MODULE 7 Checkpoint

Objective Assessment
Answer the questions below to see if you have mastered the content of Module 7.

1. The _____ feature removes text or an image from a document and places it on the Clipboard.
2. To locate and replace existing text with new text in a document, click _____ on the Edit menu.
3. The_____ is a tool that allows you to look up words and replace them with a synonym.
4. To find the word *car* and replace it with *automobile* each time it occurs in a document, click the _____ button in the Find and Replace dialog box.
5. A master copy or a formatting guide for a particular type of document is called a(n) _____.
6. A(n) _____ uses templates and responses to questions to create different types of documents.
7. The two basic types of styles are character and _____ styles.
8. The character effect _____ positions small text above the line of writing.
9. The _____ command is used to copy an object into a document and maintain the ability to format that object.
10. The _____ feature allows you to apply a group of formats automatically to a document.

Performance Assessment

Document 1
Report with styles

1. Open **Sampling Plan** from the data files. Make the edits listed below.
2. Save the document as **checkpoint7-d1**.
   - Apply **Title** style to the report title.
   - Apply **Heading 1** style to the next two headings.
   - Apply **Heading 2** style to the last two headings.
   - Search for both *athlete* and *athletes* and replace with *student athlete* or *student athletes*.
   - Modify the footer to include your name rather than Student's Name.
   - Apply a paragraph border around the title. Use a 3-point, triple-line box border. Add dark red shading. Place a blank line before and after the title.

Document 2
Memo from wizard

1. Use the Memo Wizard to prepare a contemporary style memo. Save the document as **Checkpoint7-d2**.
2. Send the message To: **Student Athletes** From: **Jan Marks, Faculty Athletics Representative** Date: **Current** Subject: **Exit Interview**

In accordance with NCAA by-laws, the enclosed survey is sent to you as a student athlete who has completed your eligibility to compete in college athletics. This survey gives you an opportunity to share your opinions about your experience both as a student and as an athlete.

Please complete the survey and return it to me in the enclosed self-addressed envelope within two weeks. We urge you to be honest with your responses. The information is used to improve the athletics experience for future students. Your coach does not have access to this information, and your responses will be treated confidentially.

We appreciate your sharing your thoughts with us.

LESSON 16 | 2 and 7

✹ W a r m u p

16a
Key each line twice SS.

alphabet 1 Perry might know I feel jinxed because I have missed a quiz.

figures 2 Channels 5 and 8, on from 10 to 11, said Luisa's IQ was 150.

caps lock 3 Ella Hill will see Chekhov's THE CHERRY ORCHARD on Czech TV.

easy 4 The big dog by the bush kept the ducks and hen in the field.

| 1 | 2 | 3 | 4 | 5 | 6 | 7 | 8 | 9 | 10 | 11 | 12 |

⬚ New Keys

16b [2] and [7]
Key each line once SS.

2 Reach *up* with *left third* finger.

7 Reach *down* with *right first* finger.

2

5 2 2s s2 2 2; has 2 sons; is 2 sizes; was 2 sites; has 2 skis

6 add 2 and 2; 2 sets of 2; catch 22; as 2 of the 22; 222 Main

7 Exactly at 2 on August 22, the 22d Company left from Pier 2.

7

8 7 7j j7 7 7; 7 jets; 7 jeans; 7 jays; 7 jobs; 7 jars; 7 jaws

9 ask for 7; buy 7; 77 years; June 7; take any 7; deny 77 boys

10 From May 7 on, all 77 men will live at 777 East 77th Street.

all figures learned

11 I read 2 of the 72 books, Ellis read 7, and Han read all 72.

12 Tract 27 cites the date as 1850; Tract 170 says it was 1852.

13 You can take Flight 850 on January 12; I'll take Flight 705.

16c Number Reinforcement
Key each line twice SS (slowly, then faster); DS between 2-line groups.

8/1 14 line 8; Book 1; No. 88; Seat 11; June 18; Cart 81; date 1881

2/7 15 take 2; July 7; buy 22; sell 77; mark 27; adds 72; Memo 2772

5/0 16 feed 5; bats 0; age 50; Ext. 55; File 50; 55 bags; band 5005

all 17 I work 18 visual signs with 20 turns of the 57 lenses to 70.

all 18 Did 17 boys fix the gears for 50 bicycles in 28 racks or 10?

51c-d3
Memo

1. Use the Professional memo template to key the memo shown below.
2. Key **Community Park Site Committee** in the *Company Name Here* placeholder.
3. Drag the *Company Name Here* placeholder so that *Community Park Site Committee* is on one line.
4. Send the memo to the **Planning Commission** from the **Community Park Site Committee**. Use the current date, and send a copy of the memo to **Mayor Charles Morgan**.
5. Use the report title from document **51c-d1** as the subject of the memo. Save it as **51c-d3**.

The Community Park Site Committee has completed its assessment of the potential sites for the new park. Our report is attached.

The Committee unanimously recommends that the Westlake site be used for the new park. The Woodcreek site was considered acceptable, but it is not as desirable as the Westlake site. The Southside site was the least desirable of the three sites.

Please contact us if you have any questions.

51c-d4
Block Letter

1. Key the following letter in block format. Use the current date and sign your name.
2. Save it as **51c-d4**.

Ms. Margaret C. Worthington
4957 Mt. Elon Church Road
Hopkins, SC 29061-9837

Dear Ms. Worthington

The Planning Commission has authorized me to contact you to discuss the possible purchase of the 120-acre site that we discussed with you for the new Community Park. When we spoke with you yesterday, you indicated that you would be available to meet with us any afternoon next week. If it is still convenient, we would like to meet with you on Wednesday afternoon at 2:00 at the site.

Earlier you indicated that you had a recent survey and an appraisal of the property. We would appreciate it if you could have those documents available for the meeting.

If this time is not convenient, please call my office and leave a message so that I may reschedule the meeting. We look forward to working with you.

Sincerely

Skillbuilding

16d Reach Review

Key each line once; fingers curved and relaxed; wrists low.

3d/4th
19 pop was lap pass slaw wool solo swap apollo wasp load plaque
20 Al's quote was, "I was dazzled by the jazz, pizza, and pool."

1st/2d
21 bad fun nut kick dried night brick civic thick hutch believe
22 Kim may visit her friends in Germany if I give her a ticket.

3d/1st
23 cry tube wine quit very curb exit crime ebony mention excite
24 To be invited, petition the six executive committee members.

16e Rhythm Builder

Key each line twice; do not pause at the end of lines.

> **TECHNIQUE TIP**
> Think and key the words and phrases as units rather than letter by letter.

words: *think, say,* and *key* words

25 is do am lay cut pen dub may fob ale rap cot hay pay hem box
26 box wit man sir fish also hair giant rigor civic virus ivory
27 laugh sight flame audit formal social turkey bicycle problem

phrases: *think, say,* and *key* phrases

28 is it|is it|if it is|if it is|or by|or by|or me|or me|for us
29 and all|for pay|pay dues and|the pen|the pen box|the pen box
30 such forms|held both|work form|then wish|sign name|with them

easy sentences

31 The man is to do the work right; he then pays the neighbors.
32 Sign the forms to pay the eight men for the turkey and hams.
33 The antique ivory bicycle is a social problem for the chair.
| 1 | 2 | 3 | 4 | 5 | 6 | 7 | 8 | 9 | 10 | 11 | 12 |

16f Speed Check

1. Take two 1' writings on paragraph 1.
2. Take two 1' writings on paragraph 2.
3. Take one 2' writing on both paragraphs.

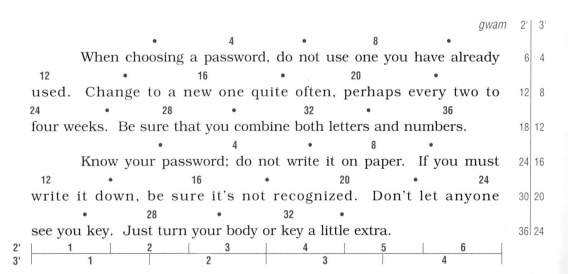

gwam 2'|3'

•   4   •   8   •
When choosing a password, do not use one you have already   6|4
12   •   16   •   20   •
used. Change to a new one quite often, perhaps every two to   12|8
24   •   28   •   32   •   36
four weeks. Be sure that you combine both letters and numbers.   18|12
•   4   •   8   •
Know your password; do not write it on paper. If you must   24|16
12   •   16   •   20   •   24
write it down, be sure it's not recognized. Don't let anyone   30|20
•   28   •   32   •
see you key. Just turn your body or key a little extra.   36|24
2'| 1 | 2 | 3 | 4 | 5 | 6 |
3'| 1 | 2 | 3 | 4 |

51c-d1
Report with Styles

1. Open **Site Assessment** from the data files, and make the following edits:
   - SS and use 6-point spacing after paragraphs.
   - Apply **Title** style to the title of the report.
   - Apply **Heading 1** style to all side headings.
   - Use **Paste Special** to add the chart from data file **Site Costs** at the end of the report.
   - Use Find and Replace to find *Theme*, and replace it with *Community* each time it occurs.
   - Add a blank line before and after the title of the report. Add a red triple-line box border with sky blue shading to the title.
   - Check the footer to ensure that *Theme* was replaced by *Community*. Change the date format to month/day/year in the footer.
2. Save it as **51c-d1**. Proofread and print.

51c-d2
Numbered Outline

1. Key the following outline that will be attached to **51c-d1**. Leave a 2" top margin.
2. Use **Title** style for the title.
3. Use the second outline numbered list for the document (1., 1.1, 1.1.1).
4. Save it as **51c-d2**.

Criteria for Evaluating Sites

1. Site Location
   1.1. The site must be located within ten miles of city center.
   1.2. The site must be easily accessed with good roads—preferably from an Interstate.
2. Site Size
   2.1. The site must be at least 100 acres.
   2.2. The county must not be required to buy more than 150 acres to obtain a site.
   2.3. The terrain must be such that it facilitates the building of the infrastructure needed for the park facilities.
3. Cost
   3.1. The cost of the site including the land and the estimated infrastructure costs must be less than $1,000,000.
4. Other Factors
   4.1. Aesthetic factors should be considered only if a site meets the first three criteria.
      4.1.1. A lake, pond, river, creek, or other body of water must be available.
      4.1.2. At least a portion of the land must be wooded.

LESSON 17 | 4 and 9

✱ Warmup

17a
Key each line twice.

alphabet 1 Bob realized very quickly that jumping was excellent for us.

figures 2 Has each of the 18 clerks now corrected Item 501 on page 27?

shift keys 3 L. K. Coe, M.D., hopes Dr. Lopez can leave for Maine in May.

easy 4 The men paid their own firms for the eight big enamel signs.

New Keys

17b [4] and [9]
Key each line once SS.

4 Reach *up* with *left first* finger.

9 Reach *up* with *right third* finger.

4

5 4 4f f4 4 4 4; if 4 furs; off 4 floors; gaff 4 fish; 4 flags

6 44th floor; half of 44; 4 walked 44 flights; 4 girls; 4 boys

7 I order exactly 44 bagels, 4 cakes, and 4 pies before 4 a.m.

9

8 9 9l l9 9 9 9; fill 9 lugs; call 9 lads; Bill 9 lost; dial 9

9 also 9 oaks; roll 9 loaves; 9.9 degrees; sell 9 oaks; Hall 9

10 Just 9 couples, 9 men and 9 women, left at 9 on our Tour 99.

all figures learned

11 Memo 94 says 9 pads, 4 pens, and 4 ribbons were sent July 9.

12 Study Item 17 and Item 28 on page 40 and Item 59 on page 49.

13 Within 17 months he drove 85 miles, walked 29, and flew 490.

Skillbuilding

17c Figure Keyreaches
Key each line twice; DS between 2-line groups.

14 My staff of *18* worked *11* hours a day from May *27* to June *12*.

15 There were *5* items tested by Inspector *7* at *4* p.m. on May *8*.

16 Please send her File *10* today at *8*; her access number is *97*.

17 Car *47* had its trial run. The qualifying speed was *198* mph.

18 The estimated score? *485*. Actual? *190*. Difference? *295*.

LESSON 51 | Assessment

Skillbuilding

51a
Warmup
Key each line twice SS.
DS between 2-line groups.

alphabet	1	Max Biqua watched jet planes flying in the azure sky over a cove.
figures	2	Send 105 No. 4 nails and 67 No. 8 brads for my home at 329 Annet.
3d row	3	We two were ready to type a report for our quiet trio of workers.
easy	4	Pamela owns a big bicycle; and, with it, she may visit the docks.

| 1 | 2 | 3 | 4 | 5 | 6 | 7 | 8 | 9 | 10 | 11 | 12 | 13 |

51b
Timed Writings
Take one 3' and one 5' timing on the paragraphs.

gwam 3' | 5'

Voting is a very important part of being a good citizen. 4 | 2
However, many young people who are eligible to vote choose not 8 | 5
to do so. When asked to explain or justify their decision, many 12 | 7
simply shrug their shoulders and reply that they have no particular 16 | 10
reason for not voting. The explanation others frequently give is 21 | 13
that they just did not get around to going to the voting polls. 25 | 15

A good question to consider concerns ways that we can motivate 29 | 18
young people to be good citizens and to go to the polls and to vote. 34 | 21
Some people approach this topic by trying to determine how satisfied 39 | 23
people are who do not vote with the performance of their elected 43 | 26
officials. Unfortunately, those who choose not to vote are just as 48 | 29
satisfied with their elected officials as are those who voted. 52 | 31

One interesting phenomenon concerning voting relates to the 56 | 34
job market. When the job market is strong, fewer young people vote 61 | 36
than when the job market is very bad. They also tend to be less 65 | 39
satisfied with their elected officials. Self-interest seems to 69 | 41
be a powerful motivator. Unfortunately, those who do not choose 74 | 44
to vote miss the point that it is in their best interest to be a 78 | 47
good citizen. 79 | 47

3' | 1 | 2 | 3 | 4 |
5' | 1 | 2 | 3 |

Assessment: Tables

51c
Timed production: 25'

Continue

Check

With CheckPro 2002: When you complete a document, proofread it, check the spelling, and preview for placement. When you are completely satisfied, click the **Continue** button to move to the next document. You will not be able to return and edit a document once you continue to the next document. Click the **Check** button when you are ready to error-check the test. Review and/or print the document analysis results.

Without CheckPro 2002: Key the documents in sequence. When time has been called, proofread all documents again; identify errors, and determine *g-pwam*.

$$g\text{-}pwam = \frac{\text{total words keyed}}{25}$$

17d Technique Reinforcement

Key smoothly; strike the keys at a brisk, steady pace.

first finger

19 buy them gray vent guy brunt buy brunch much give huge vying
20 Hagen, after her July triumph at tennis, may try volleyball.
21 Verna urges us to buy yet another of her beautiful rag rugs.

second finger

22 keen idea; kick it back; ice breaker; decide the issue; cite
23 Did Dick ask Cecelia, his sister, if she decided to like me?
24 Suddenly, Micki's bike skidded on the Cedar Street ice rink.

third/fourth finger

25 low slow lax solo wax zip zap quips quiz zipper prior icicle
26 Paula has always allowed us to relax at La Paz and at Quito.
27 Please ask Zale to explain who explores most aquatic slopes.

17e Speed Builder

1. Key each paragraph in the Open Screen for a 1' writing.
2. Set the Timer for 2'. Take two 2' writings on all paragraphs. Reach for a speed within two words of 1' gwam.
3. Take a 3' writing on all paragraphs. Reach for a speed within four words of 1' gwam. Print.

 all letters

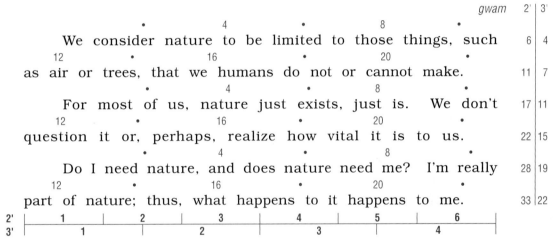

gwam   2' | 3'

We consider nature to be limited to those things, such   6 | 4
as air or trees, that we humans do not or cannot make.   11 | 7
For most of us, nature just exists, just is. We don't   17 | 11
question it or, perhaps, realize how vital it is to us.   22 | 15
Do I need nature, and does nature need me? I'm really   28 | 19
part of nature; thus, what happens to it happens to me.   33 | 22

17f Speed Builder

TECHNIQUE TIP

Keep hands quiet and fingers well curved over the keys. Do not allow your fingers to bounce.

1. In the Open screen, key the information below at the left margin.

Your name   ENTER
Current date   ENTER
Skillbuilders 1, Drill 2   ENTER ENTER

2. Key Drill 2, page 32 from your textbook. Concentrate as you practice on your own, working for good control.

Midlands Properties *Heading style 1*

The Midlands portfolio of property consists of more than sixty individual parcels of land. Approximately 60 percent of the land was purchased and 40 percent was received as gifts. The land is valued at $12,650,000.

The Wheeler Tract *Heading style 2*

A decision has been made to sell this property. Currently, the property is being surveyed and a new appraisal has been ordered. The property will be ~~put~~ placed on the market as soon as the survey and appraisal have been completed.

The Blossom Tract *Heading style 2*

The Foundation contracted to have infrastructure work completed before turning the tract over to Midlands University for development.

Modify the footer to read—
Master Plan Prepared by (your name).
Current date

50c-d2
Report with Styles

1. Open **Meade2** from the data files and save it as **50c-d2**.
2. Select the entire document, and change the spacing to single with 6-point spacing after paragraphs.
3. Delete the tab from the first line of all paragraphs.
4. Change all paragraph headings to side headings, and apply the style **Heading 3**.
5. Delete the period and spaces after the heading, position the insertion point at the beginning of the sentence, press ENTER to bring the text back to the margin, and capitalize the main words in each heading. (*Hint:* Format Painter can be used to copy formats.)
6. Check to ensure that all paragraphs begin at left margin, that heading styles are used on all headings, and that there are no widows and orphans.
7. Print the document, and save again.

MOUS TIP

Microsoft Word does not recognize a paragraph heading as a heading style. A heading is a paragraph and must have a paragraph marker at the end of it.

50c-d3
Title Page

1. Create a title page for the report you edited in **50c-d2**, **Expansion of Meade Outpatient Center**. Be creative and use either a page border or horizontal lines.
2. This report was prepared for the Strategic Planning Committee by you.
3. Use today's date.
4. Print the document, and save it as **50c-d3**.

LESSON 18 | 3 and 6

Warmup

18a
Key each line twice SS.

alphabet 1 Jim Kable won a second prize for his very quixotic drawings.

figures 2 If 57 of the 105 boys go on July 29, 48 of them will remain.

easy 3 With the usual bid, I paid for a quantity of big world maps.

| 1 | 2 | 3 | 4 | 5 | 6 | 7 | 8 | 9 | 10 | 11 | 12 |

New Keys

18b 3 and 6
Key each line once SS.

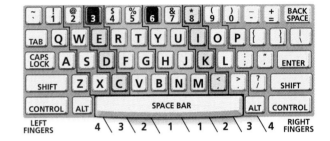

3 Reach *up* with *left second* finger.

6 Reach *up* with *right first* finger.

3

4 3 3d d3 3 3; had 3 days; did 3 dives; led 3 dogs; add 3 dips

5 we 3 ride 3 cars; take 33 dials; read 3 copies; save 33 days

6 On July 3, 33 lights lit 33 stands holding 33 prize winners.

6

7 6 6j 6j 6 6; 6 jays; 6 jams; 6 jigs; 6 jibs; 6 jots; 6 jokes

8 only 6 high; on 66 units; reach 66 numbers; 6 yams or 6 jams

9 On May 6, Car 66 delivered 66 tons of No. 6 shale to Pier 6.

all figures learned

10 At 6 p.m., Channel 3 reported the August 6 score was 6 to 3.

11 Jean, do Items 28 and 6; Mika, 59 and 10; Kyle, 3, 4, and 7.

12 Cars 56 and 34 used Aisle 9; Cars 2 and 87 can use Aisle 10.

Skillbuilding

18c Keyboard Reinforcement
Key each line once; DS between groups of three.

long reaches

13 ce cede cedar wreck nu nu nut punt nuisance my my amy mystic

14 ny ny any many company mu mu mull lumber mulch br br furbish

15 The absence of receiving my umbrella disturbed the musician.

number review

16 set 0; push 4; Car 00; score 44; jot 04; age 40; Billet 4004

17 April 5; lock 5; set 66; fill 55; hit 65; pick 56; adds 5665

18 Her grades are 93, 87, and 100; his included 82, 96, and 54.

> **TECHNIQUE TIP**
> Make the long reaches without returning to the home row between reaches.

for future development and use by Midlands University. Usually, properties in the other two categories are held only if they are likely to appreciate significantly; otherwise, they are sold and the proceeds are used to support various University needs. Currently, no out-of-state property is being held.

Insert Prop Location from the data files here.

Use Paste Special

The total value of the property currently held is $34,815,000. The property values are based on the appraisal price.

Coastal Properties   *Heading style 1*

Highlight in yellow

seven

Currently the Foundation owns a number of different tracts of land in the Coastal Region valued at $18,325,000. Decisions on the future use of five of the tracts are pending. The master plan contains specific plans for only two of the tracts the Marshall tract and the Richardson tract.

em dash

The Marshall Tract   *Heading style 2*

The Marshall tract consists of over 1,200 acres of environmentally sensitive coastal property. Approximately one-half of the tract consists of wetlands with a conservation and preservation easement one the property. A portion of the remaining property has endangered species, including the red cockaded woodpecker. An eagle nest has also been spotted on the property.

Insert

The master plan calls for the retention of the property because of its potential for research and environmental education. The short-term plans call for the establishment of a system of nature trails and boardwalks and the development of a parking area for visitors. Long-term plans specify the design and construction of a research and learning center.

The Richardson Tract   *Heading style 2*

The Richardson tract consists of an entire barrier island that is used for research purposes. The property currently has a very basic research and education center. The gift agreement severely restricts development of facilities on the island; therefore, it is not likely to be highly developed at any point in the future.

18d Rhythm Builder

Key each line twice SS; DS between 2-line groups; repeat.

word response: *think* and *key* words

19 he el id is go us it an me of he of to if ah or bye do so am

20 Did she enamel emblems on a big panel for the downtown sign?

stroke response: *think* and *key* each stroke

21 kin are hip read lymph was pop saw ink art oil gas up as mop

22 Barbara started the union wage earners tax in Texas in July.

combination response: vary speed but maintain rhythm

23 upon than eve lion when burley with they only them loin were

24 It was the opinion of my neighbor that we may work as usual.

18e Diagnostic Writing

Return to the Numeric Lesson menu. Click the **Diagnostic Writings** button. Key the paragraph as a 3' Diagnostic Writing.

Goals: 1', 17–23 *gwam*
2', 15–21 *gwam*
3', 14–20 *gwam*

  all letters

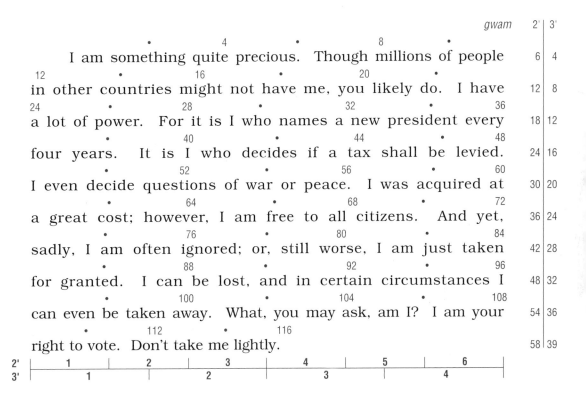

	gwam	2'	3'

I am something quite precious. Though millions of people — 6 | 4

in other countries might not have me, you likely do. I have — 12 | 8

a lot of power. For it is I who names a new president every — 18 | 12

four years. It is I who decides if a tax shall be levied. — 24 | 16

I even decide questions of war or peace. I was acquired at — 30 | 20

a great cost; however, I am free to all citizens. And yet, — 36 | 24

sadly, I am often ignored; or, still worse, I am just taken — 42 | 28

for granted. I can be lost, and in certain circumstances I — 48 | 32

can even be taken away. What, you may ask, am I? I am your — 54 | 36

right to vote. Don't take me lightly. — 58 | 39

Communication

18f Composition

1. Go to the Open Screen.

2. Introduce yourself to your instructor by composing two paragraphs, each containing about three sentences. Use proper grammatical structure. Do not worry about keying errors at this time.

3. Save the document as **xx-profile**. It is not necessary to print the document. You will open and print it in a later lesson.

Modify Headers and Footers

help keywords
change headers or footers

Reports often include headers or footers or both. A header consists of text that appears at the top of the pages of a document, and a footer consists of text that appears at the bottom of the pages of the document. Changing the header or footer on one page changes it throughout the document.

To modify a header or footer:

1. Click **Header and Footer** on the View menu.

2. Click the **Switch Between Header and Footer** button to move to either a header or footer and the **Previous** or **Next** button to view the desired header or footer if the document has more than one header or footer.

3. Make the desired changes; then click **Close**.

D r i l l   5 | MODIFY HEADERS AND FOOTERS

1. Open **Proposed Guides** from the data files.

2. Change the header to **Revised Guidelines** (**View, Header and Footer**).

3. Switch to the footer, change it to **Internal Approval**, and add the date in the right position (click the **Switch Between** button, edit the text; then click the **Date** button).

4. Print the document, and save it as **50b-drill5**.

Applications

50c-d1
Report with Styles

1. Open **Master Plan** from the data files. Save as **50c-d1**.

2. Increase the spacing after all paragraphs to 6 points.

3. Make the edits shown below. Some of the edits are corrections to the data file. Add text that is in script to the file. Notice that you will be inserting a data file using Paste Special.

4. Add a ½-point black, single-line border and 10% gray shading to all handwritten paragraphs that have been inserted so they can be reviewed carefully.

5. When you finish editing the document, save again. Proofread carefully. Check that you have followed all instructions. Print when you are satisfied.

Master Plan for Foundation Properties

The Midlands University Foundation properties are categorized into four classifications: Coastal Property, Midlands Property, other in-state property, and out-of-state property. The Foundation acquires property by purchasing it or by accepting gifts from donors desiring to support Midlands University.

Insert → *Generally, the Foundation retains coastal properties for research and environmental education purposes and properties in the Midlands area*

LESSON 19 | $ and - (hyphen), Number Expression

✳ Warmup

19a

Key each line twice SS.

alphabet 1 Why did the judge quiz poor Victor about his blank tax form?

figures 2 J. Boyd, Ph.D., changed Items 10, 57, 36, and 48 on page 92.

3d row 3 To try the tea, we hope to tour the port prior to the party.

easy 4 Did he signal the authentic robot to do a turn to the right?

| 1 | 2 | 3 | 4 | 5 | 6 | 7 | 8 | 9 | 10 | 11 | 12 |

⌐ New Keys

19b $ and -

Key each line once SS;
DS between 2-line groups.

- = hyphen
-- = dash
Do not space before or after a hyphen or a dash.

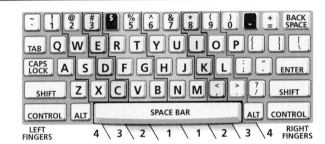

$ Shift; then reach up with *left first* finger.

- (hyphen) Reach up with *right fourth* finger.

$

5 $ $f f$ $ $; if $4; half $4; off $4; of $4; $4 fur; $4 flats

6 for $8; cost $9; log $3; grab $10; give Rolf $2; give Viv $4

7 Since she paid $45 for the item priced at $54, she saved $9.

- (hyphen)

8 - -; ;- - - -; up-to-date; co-op; father-in-law; four-square

9 pop-up foul; big-time job; snap-on bit; one- or two-hour ski

10 You need 6 signatures--half of the members--on the petition.

all symbols learned

11 I paid $10 for the low-cost disk; high-priced ones cost $40.

12 Le-An spent $20 for travel, $95 for books, and $38 for food.

13 Mr. Loft-Smit sold his boat for $467; he bought it for $176.

⌐ Skillbuilding

19c Keyboard Reinforcement

Key each line once; repeat the drill.

e/d 14 Edie discreetly decided to deduct expenses in making a deed.

w/e 15 Working women wear warm wool sweaters when weather dictates.

r/e 16 We heard very rude remarks regarding her recent termination.

s/d 17 This seal's sudden misdeeds destroyed several goods on land.

v/b 18 Beverley voted by giving a bold beverage to every brave boy.

help keywords
document map

Document Map

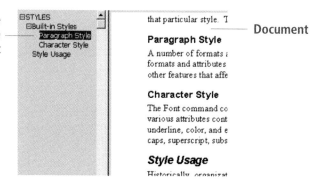

The document map provides a list of headings within a document. It displays in a separate pane usually at the left side of the document window. The document map provides an effective means for navigating through a document that has been formatted using heading styles. Headings in the document map act as **hyperlinks**—text that you click to go to a specific location. To move to a heading in the document, click on the heading in the document map.

To display and use the document map, click the **View** menu and then **Document Map**, or the **Document Map** button on the Standard toolbar. Click on the desired heading to move to that point in the document.

Click on the headings in the Document Map to navigate through the document

---

Drill 3 | **DOCUMENT MAP**

1. Open **50b-drill2** and display the document map.
2. Click on the heading **Character Style** in the document map.

3. In the last sentence of the paragraph under *Character Style*, apply the character effects to the words listed, i.e., format the word *subscript* as a subscript.
4. Print the document, and save it as **50b-drill3**.

---

help keywords
paragraph spacing

Space After Paragraphs

Double-spaced documents do not need additional space between paragraphs. However, to make single-spaced documents more readable, add additional space after each paragraph. You can add additional space automatically by setting the space after paragraphs to 6 points, the equivalent of one line. Each time you press ENTER, an additional line is added.

To set spacing after paragraphs:

1. Click **Paragraph** on the Format menu.
2. Select the **Indents and Spacing** tab.
3. In the Spacing section of the dialog box, increase spacing *After* from 0 to 6 pt. Click **OK**.

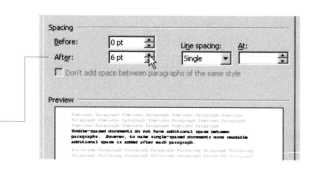

Drill 4 | **PARAGRAPH SPACING**

1. Open **Preview** from the data files.
2. Select all of the single-spaced paragraphs.

3. Increase the space after the paragraphs to 6 points.
4. Save it as **50b-drill4** and print.

19d Speed Builder

Key each line once, working for fluid, consistent stroking. Repeat at a faster speed.

TECHNIQUE TIP

- Key the easy words as "words" rather than stroke by stroke.
- Key each phrase (marked by a vertical line) without pauses between words.

easy words

19 am it go bus dye jam irk six sod tic yam ugh spa vow aid dug
20 he or by air big elf dog end fit and lay sue toe wit own got
21 six foe pen firm also body auto form down city kept make fog.

easy phrases

22 it is|if the|and also|to me|the end|to us|if it|it is|to the
23 if it is|to the end|do you wish|to go to|for the end|to make
24 lay down|he or she|make me|by air|end of |by me|kept it|of me

easy sentences

25 Did the chap work to mend the torn right half of the ensign?
26 Blame me for their penchant for the antique chair and panel.
27 She bid by proxy for eighty bushels of a corn and rye blend.

Communication

19e Number Expression

1. Study the rules and examples at the right.
2. In the Open Screen, key the information below at the left margin. Press ENTER as shown.

   Your name ENTER

   Current date ENTER

   Skillbuilders 1, Drill 6

   ENTER ENTER

3. Key the sample sentences 28–33. Backspace to correct errors.
4. Change figures to words as needed in sentences 34–36.
5. Save the file as **xx-19e**.

Spell out numbers:

1. **First word in a sentence.** Key numbers ten and lower as words unless they are part of a series of related numbers, any of which are over ten.

   Three of the four members were present.

   She wrote 12 stories and 2 plays in five years.

2. The **smaller of two adjacent numbers** as words.

   SolVir shipped six 24-ton engines.

3. **Isolated fractions and approximate numbers.** Key as words **large round numbers that can be expressed as one or two words**. Hyphenate fractions expressed as words.

   She completed one-fourth of the experiments.

   Val sent out three hundred invitations.

4. **Preceding "o'clock".**

   John's due at four o'clock. Pick him up at 4:15 p.m.

28 **Six** or **seven** older players were cut from the **37**-member team.
29 I have **2** of **14** coins I need to start my set.   Kristen has **9**.
30 Of **nine 24**-ton engines ordered, we shipped **six** last Tuesday.
31 Shelly has read just **one-half** of about **forty-five** documents.
32 The **six** boys sent well over **two hundred** printed invitations.
33 **One** or **two** of us will be on duty from **two** until **six** o'clock.
34 The meeting begins promptly at 9.   We plan 4 sessions.
35 The 3-person crew cleaned 6 stands, 12 tables, and 13 desks.
36 The 3d meeting is at 3 o'clock on Friday, February 2.

Drill 1 | STYLES

1. Open a new document. Display the styles list box. Notice the default styles that are available.

2. Key your name on one line and your address below it. Select your name and apply Heading 1 style. Select your address and apply Heading 2 style.

3. Select your name again and apply Normal. Then select your name and italicize it. Display the styles list. Notice that Italic has been added as a character style.

4. Close the document without saving.

5. Open **Body Text** from the data files.

6. Apply the style **Body Text** to the document. Since there is only one paragraph, simply click anywhere within the paragraph and apply the style. The entire paragraph changes to the new style.

7. Save the document as **50b-drill1**.

Drill 2 | STYLES

1. Open **Styles** from the data files.

2. Select the first heading (**Styles**), apply the style **Heading 1**. Then center align the heading.

3. Select the next heading (**Built-in Styles**), and apply the style **Heading 2**.

4. Apply the style **Heading 3** to the next two headings (**Paragraph Style** and **Character Style**).

5. Apply the style **Heading 2** to the last heading (**Style Usage**).

6. Save it as **50b-drill2**. Your document should be similar to the one shown below. Print the report. Leave the document open for Drill 3.

STYLES   Heading 1 (centered)

An overall document format can be applied to one document or to many different documents. A document is usually formatted manually if the format style is applied to a single document. However, many documents produced in offices are formatted using the same style.

Built-in Styles   Heading 2

Consistency is very important if documents are to have a professional appearance. One way to ensure consistency is to use one of the built-in styles contained in *Microsoft Word* software. Many organizations, however, prefer to use customized formats. The way they can ensure consistency is to create the specific style that they want to use in their documents, name the style, and apply it to all documents that they wish to format with that particular style. Two types of styles are used for automatic formatting of text.

Paragraph Style   Heading 3

A number of formats and attributes may comprise the total style of a paragraph. These formats and attributes include font, size, spacing, tab stops, alignment, bullets, and any other features that affect the appearance of the paragraph.

Character Style   Heading 3

The Font command contains a number of formats that can be applied to characters. The various attributes contained on the Font dialog box tab (such as font, font style, size, underline, color, and effects) make up character style. Character effects include small caps, superscript, subscript, strikethrough, outline, and shadow.

Style Usage   Heading 2

Historically, organizations ensured consistency of style by preparing a procedures manual that contained style guides and model documents. Today, they often rely on the built-in styles or on customized styles they created and stored in the word processing software. These customized styles can then be applied to their documents in the same manner as the built-in styles.

Styles can be modified or copied very easily. For example, the paragraph style, Heading 1, is aligned at the left margin. The heading could be centered by clicking the Center button on the Formatting toolbar. This change would affect only the current heading. However, if the style were modified, the centered format would be applied each time the Heading 1 style is used.

Using the Styles feature has benefits that extend beyond helping to format documents. It helps to simplify other document processing tasks such as a table of contents with headings, leaders, and page numbers. The table of contents can be generated automatically.

LESSON 20 | # and /

Warmup
20a
Key each line twice SS
(slowly, then faster).

alphabet 1 Freda Jencks will have money to buy six quite large topazes.

symbols 2 I bought 10 ribbons and 45 disks from Cable-Han Co. for $78.

home row 3 Dallas sold jade flasks; Sal has a glass flask full of salt.

easy 4 He may cycle down to the field by the giant oak and cut hay.

New Keys

20b # and /
Key each line once SS.

> # = number sign, pounds
>
> / = diagonal, slash

Shift; then reach *up* with *left second* finger.

/ Reach *down* with *right fourth* finger.

#

5 # #e e# # # #; had #3 dial; did #3 drop; set #3 down; Bid #3

6 leave #82; sold #20; Lyric #16; bale #34; load #53; Optic #7

7 Notice #333 says to load Car #33 with 33# of #3 grade shale.

/

8 / /; ;/ / / /; 1/2; 1/3; Mr./Mrs.; 1/5/94; 22 11/12; and/or;

9 to/from; /s/ William Smit; 2/10, n/30; his/her towels; 6 1/2

10 The numerals 1 5/8, 3 1/4, and 60 7/9 are "mixed fractions."

all symbols learned

11 Invoice #737 cites 15 2/3# of rye was shipped C.O.D. 4/6/95.

12 B-O-A Company's Check #50/5 for $87 paid for 15# of #3 wire.

13 Our Co-op List #20 states $40 for 16 1/2 crates of tomatoes.

Skillbuilding

gwam 30"

20c Keyboard Reinforcement

Key each line once; work for fluency.

Option: In the Open Screen, key 30" writings on both lines of a pair. Work to avoid pauses.

14 She did the key work at the height of the problem. 20

15 Form #726 is the title to the island; she owns it. 20

16 The rock is a form of fuel; he did enrich it with coal. 22

17 The corn-and-turkey dish is a blend of turkey and corn. 22

18 It is right to work to end the social problems of the world. 24

19 If I sign it on 3/19, the form can aid us to pay the 40 men. 24

LESSON 50 | **Edit Reports**

 Skillbuilding

50a
Warmup
Key each line twice SS;
DS between 2-line
groups.

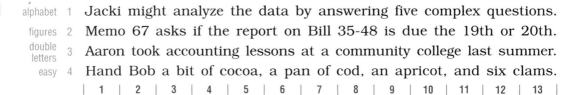

alphabet 1 Jacki might analyze the data by answering five complex questions.
figures 2 Memo 67 asks if the report on Bill 35-48 is due the 19th or 20th.
double letters 3 Aaron took accounting lessons at a community college last summer.
easy 4 Hand Bob a bit of cocoa, a pan of cod, an apricot, and six clams.
| 1 | 2 | 3 | 4 | 5 | 6 | 7 | 8 | 9 | 10 | 11 | 12 | 13 |

 New Functions

50b

help keywords
format using styles

MOUS TIP
To display
the styles of
a document
in the Task
Pane, click the **Styles and Formatting** button
on the Formatting tool-
bar, or click **Styles and Formatting** on the
Format menu.

Styles

The **Styles** feature enables you to apply a group of formats automatically to a document. The memo and fax templates that you worked with in Lesson 47 had styles attached to them. A new *Word* document opens with the following styles attached to it: Normal, Heading 1, Heading 2, and Heading 3. Normal is the default style of 12-point Times New Roman, left alignment, single spacing, and no indent. Text that you key is formatted in the Normal style unless you apply another style.

Styles include both character and paragraph styles. The attributes listed in the Font dialog box make up the character styles. **Character styles** apply to a single character or characters that are selected. To apply character styles using the Formatting toolbar, select the characters to be formatted and apply the desired font.

| Helvetica | 12 |

Paragraph styles include both the character styles and other formats that affect paragraph appearance such as line spacing, bullets, numbering, and tab stops. The illustration below shows a list of styles that have been applied within a particular document. Character styles are listed; paragraph styles are indicated with the paragraph marker.

To apply paragraph styles using the Formatting toolbar:

1. Select the text to which you want to apply a style.
2. Click the down arrow on the Style box on the Formatting toolbar.
3. Select the desired style.

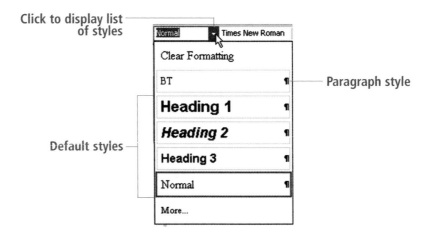

Communication

20d Number Usage Review

DS; decide whether the circled numbers should be keyed as figures or as words and make needed changes. Check your finished work with 19e, page 47.

20 Six or ⑦ *seven* older players were cut from the ㊲ -member team.

21 I have ② *two* of 14 coins I need to start my set.   Kristen has ⑨.

22 Of ⑨ *nine* 24-ton engines ordered, we shipped ⑥ *six* last Tuesday.

23 Shelly has read just ① *one* half of about ㊺ *forty-five* documents.

24 The ⑥ *six* boys sent well over ㉜ *two hundred,* 200 printed invitations.

25 ① *one* or ② *two* of us will be on duty from ② *two* until ⑥ *six* o'clock.

Skillbuilding

20e Speed Builder

1. Go to the Open Screen.
2. Follow the procedures at the right for increasing your speed by taking guided writings.
3. Take a 3' writing without the guide on the complete writing.

 all letters

STANDARD PLAN | **for Guided Writing Procedures**

1. In the Open Screen, take a 1' writing on paragraph 1. Note your *gwam*.
2. Add four words to your 1' *gwam* to determine your goal rate.
3. Set the Timer for 1'. Set the Timer option to beep every 15''.
4. From the table below, select from Column 4 the speed nearest your goal rate. Note the ¼' point at the left of that speed. Place a light check mark within the paragraphs at the ¼' points.
5. Take two 1' guided writings on paragraphs 1 and 2.   Do not save.
6. Turn the beeper off.

		gwam	
1/4'	1/2'	3/4'	1'
4	8	12	16
5	10	15	20
6	12	18	24
7	14	21	28
8	16	24	32
9	18	27	36
10	20	30	40

	gwam	2'	3'
Some of us think that the best way to get attention is	6	4	35
to try a new style, or to look quixotic, or to be different	12	8	39
somehow. Perhaps we are looking for nothing much more than	18	12	43
acceptance from others of ourselves just the way we now are.	24	16	47
There is no question about it; we all want to look our	29	19	50
best to impress other people. How we achieve this may mean	35	23	54
trying some of this and that; but our basic objective is to	41	27	58
take our raw materials, you and me, and build up from there.	47	31	62

2' | 1 | 2 | 3 | 4 | 5 | 6 |
3' | 1 | 2 | 3 | 4 |

---

help keywords
go to

Go To

The **Go To** function is used to move quickly to various points within a document, such as a specific page, section, line, footnote, table, graphic, or other location.

To use Go To:

1. From the Edit menu, choose **Go To**. (*Shortcut:* CTRL + G) If Go To is not listed on the menu, click the double down arrows at the bottom of the menu to display more options.

2. In the Go to what box, click the type of item (such as **Page**) you wish to access.

3. Enter the appropriate number in the text box.

4. Click **Go To**; then **Close**.

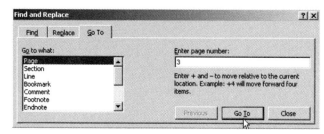

Drill 5 | GO TO

1. Open **Meade** from the data files.

2. Go to line 14. The status line should read Page 1, Sec 1, 1/5, At 5.1, Ln 14.

3. Go to page 3. The status line should read Page 3, Sec 1, 3/5, At 1".

4. Go to heading 4. The Heading should read *Development of the Business Plan*.

5. Keep the document open to use in the application activity that follows.

Applications

49d-d1

Report

Follow these steps using the Go To function to facilitate editing a report:

1. Be sure the **Meade** data file is open, and go to page 2.

2. Remove the highlighting from *years*, and key this citation: **(Snyder, 2000, 6)**.

3. Remove the highlighting from *Metro Analysis Feasibility Study*, and key this citation: **(Emerson, 2000, 8)**.

4. Go to page 3, remove the highlighting from *expenses*, and key this citation: **(Maxey, 2000, 36)**.

5. Go to the top of page 3, and key the table below. Save as **49d-d1** and print.

TABLE 1. BED CAPACITY AND UTILIZATION

Capacity	Roxy	Central	Meade
Number of beds	165	184	385
Hospital utilization average daily census	136	94	326
Medicare utilization average daily census	60	53	104
Full-time equivalent	615	364	1,682

LESSON 21 | % and !

✳ W a r m u p
21a
Key each line twice SS.

alphabet 1 Merry will have picked out a dozen quarts of jam for boxing.

fig/sym 2 Jane-Ann bought 16 7/8 yards of #240 cotton at $3.59 a yard.

1st row 3 Can't brave, zany Cave Club men/women next climb Mt. Zamban?

easy 4 Did she rush to cut six bushels of corn for the civic corps?

🔲 New Keys

21b % and !
Key each line once SS.

% Shift; then reach up with *left first* finger.

> % = percent sign: Use % with business forms or where space is restricted; otherwise, use the word "percent." Space twice after the exclamation point!

%

5 % %f f% % %; off 5%; if 5%; of 5% fund; half 5%; taxes of 5%

6 7% rent; 3% tariff; 9% F.O.B.; 15% greater; 28% base; up 46%

7 Give discounts of 5% on rods, 50% on lures, and 75% on line.

! reach *up* with the *left fourth* finger

8 ! !a a! ! ! !; Eureka! Ha! No! Pull 10! Extra! America!

9 Listen to the call! Now! Ready! Get set! Go! Good show!

10 I want it now, not next week! I am sure to lose 50% or $19.

all symbols

11 The ad offers a 10% discount, but this notice says 15% less!

12 He got the job! With Clark's Supermarket! Please call Mom!

13 Bill #92-44 arrived very late from Zyclone; it was paid 7/4.

21c Keyboard Reinforcement
Key each line once; work for fluency.

> **SPACING TIP**
> ■ Do not space between a figure and the % or $ signs.
> ■ Do not space before or after the dash.

all symbols

14 As of 6/28, Jeri owes $31 for dinner and $27 for cab fare.

15 Invoice #20--it was dated 3/4--billed $17 less 15% discount.

16 He deducted 2% instead of 6%, a clear saving of 6% vs. 7%.

combination response

17 Look at my dismal grade in English; but I guess I earned it.

18 Kris started to blend a cocoa beverage for a shaken cowhand.

19 Jan may make a big profit if she owns the title to the land.

---

1. Key the report shown below with double spacing (do not key the pie chart).

2. Open **Prop Location** (the source document) from the data files.

3. Click on the pie chart to select it, and click **Copy** on the Edit menu.

4. Switch back to the report and use Paste Special (**Edit, Paste Special**) to embed the pie chart into your report (the destination document) where shown below.

5. Click on the pie chart to select it; then drag it into the correct position.

6. Save the document as **49c-drill4**.

The Foundation owns both in-state and out-of-state property. However, the bulk of the property is located within the state. In-state property is divided into three regions—Coastal, Midlands, and Other. The following chart shows the distribution of the property by region:

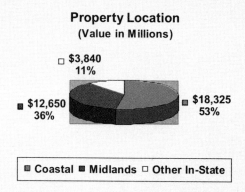

The total value of the property is $34,815,000. More than half of the property is located in the Coastal region. The next largest concentration is in the Midlands region.

The property values are based on the appraisal price at the time of acquisition. Properties are acquired by gift or purchase. Current market value of the property is significantly higher than the value at the time of acquisition.

Skillbuilding

21d Reach Mastery

Key each set of lines SS;
DS between each group;
fingers curved, hands quiet.
Repeat if time permits.

1st finger

20 by bar get fun van for inn art from gray hymn July true verb
21 brag human bring unfold hominy mighty report verify puny joy
22 You are brave to try bringing home the van in the bad storm.

2d finger

23 ace ink did cad keyed deep seed kind Dick died kink like kid
24 cease decease decades kick secret check decide kidney evaded
25 Dedre likes the idea of ending dinner with cake for dessert.

3d finger

26 oil sow six vex wax axe low old lox pool west loss wool slow
27 swallow swamp saw sew wood sax sexes loom stew excess school
28 Wes waxes floors and washes windows at low costs to schools.

4th finger

29 zap zip craze pop pup pan daze quote queen quiz pizza puzzle
30 zoo graze zipper panzer zebra quip partizan patronize appear
31 Czar Zane appears to be dazzled by the apple pizza and jazz.

21e Speed Runs with Numbers

Take 1' writings; the last
number you key when you stop
is your approximate *gwam*.

1 and 2 and 3 and 4 and 5 and 6 and 7 and 8 and 9 and 10 and
11 and 12 and 13 and 14 and 15 and 16 and 17 and 18 and 19
and 20 and 21 and 22 and 23 and 24 and 25 and 26 and 27 and

21f Speed Check

Key a 1' and 3' writing.

all letters

	gwam	1'	2'
Teams are the basic unit of performance for a firm.		11	5 42
They are not the solution to all of the organizational needs.		23	12 48
They will not solve all of the problems, but it is known		35	17 54
that a team can perform at a higher rate than other groups.		47	23 60
It is one of the best ways to support the changes needed for		59	30 66
a firm. The team must have time in order to make		71	36 72
a quality working plan.		74	37 74

To apply shading:

1. Click in the paragraph or select the text to be shaded.
2. Click **Borders and Shading** on the Format menu, and then click the **Shading** tab.
3. Select the fill and pattern, and then apply them to the paragraph.

D r i l l   2 | **BORDERS AND SHADING**

Key the paragraph at the right. Then apply a ½-point red, double-line box border and pale blue shading to the paragraph. Save as **49c-drill2**.

> This paragraph is formatted with a ½-point red, double-line box border and pale blue shading.

help keywords
highlight

Highlight

 Text can be highlighted in a variety of colors to call attention to it.

To highlight text:

1. Click the **Highlight** button on the Formatting toolbar.
2. Click the down arrow and select the desired color.
3. Select the text to be highlighted; then click the **Highlight** button to turn off Highlight.
4. To remove the highlight, select the highlighted text and click **None** on the Highlight drop-down menu.

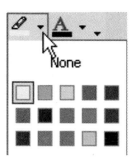

D r i l l   3 | **HIGHLIGHT TEXT**

Key the sentence that follows. Highlight the words in yellow and blue as shown: Save as **49c-drill3**.

> This text illustrates the use of yellow and blue highlights.

help keywords
paste special

Paste Special

An advantage of using a software suite, such as *Microsoft Office*, is that you can create an object in one application and use it in other applications. For example, a chart you create in *PowerPoint* using *Microsoft Graph* could also be used in a *Word* document. The **Paste Special** command enables you to copy an **object** (chart, graphic image, clip art, or worksheet) from one document, called the **source document**, and embed it in another document, called the **destination document**. The Paste Special feature is used rather than the Copy feature because it enables you to modify the object that was created in another software application.

To embed an object in a document:

1. Open the file containing the object to be embedded.
2. Select the object and click **Copy**.
3. Click in the destination document.
4. On the Edit menu, click **Paste Special**.
5. Click the **Paste** radio button in the Paste Special dialog box.
6. Select the format from the As: list such as Microsoft Graph Chart Object; then click **OK**.

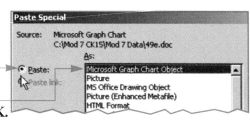

LESSON 22 | (and) and Backspace Key

■ Warmup

22a

Key each line twice SS.

alphabet	1	Avoid lazy punches; expert fighters jab with a quick motion.
fig/sym	2	Be-Low's Bill #483/7 was $96.90, not $102--they took 5% off.
caps lock	3	Report titles may be shown in ALL CAPS; as, BOLD WORD POWER.
easy	4	Do they blame me for their dismal social and civic problems?

| 1 | 2 | 3 | 4 | 5 | 6 | 7 | 8 | 9 | 10 | 11 | 12 |

▣ New Keys

22b (and)
(parentheses)

Key each line once SS.

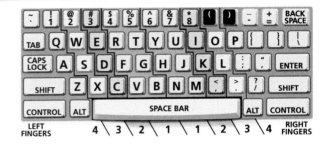

( ) = parentheses
Parentheses indicate offhand, aside, or explanatory messages.

(Shift; then reach up with the *right third* finger.

) Shift; then reach up with the *right fourth* finger.

5 ((l l((; (; Reach from l for the left parenthesis; as, ((.

6)); ;))); Reach from ; for the right parenthesis; as,)).

( )

7 Learn to use parentheses (plural) or parenthesis (singular).

8 The red (No. 34) and blue (No. 78) cars both won here (Rio).

9 We (Galen and I) dined (bagels) in our penthouse (the dorm).

all symbols learned

10 The jacket was $35 (thirty-five dollars)--the tie was extra.

11 Starting 10/29, you can sell Model #49 at a discount of 25%.

12 My size 8 1/2 shoe--a blue pump--was soiled (but not badly).

22c Number and Symbol Reinforcement

Key each line twice, keeping eyes on copy. DS between pairs.

13 Jana has one hard-to-get copy of her hot-off-the-press book.

14 An invoice said that "We give discounts of 10%, 5%, and 3%."

15 The company paid Bill 3/18 on 5/2/97 and Bill 3/1 on 3/6/97.

16 The catalog lists as out of stock Items #230, #710, and #13.

17 Elyn had $8; Sean, $9; and Cal, $7. The cash total was $24.

D r i l l   1 | OUTLINE

1. Key the outline that follows. Use a 2" top margin; center and bold the title.
2. Format the outline using the first option on the Outline Numbered tab in the Bullets and Numbering dialog box

(Format, Bullets and Numbering, Outline Numbering tab).

3. Save as **49c-drill1** and print.

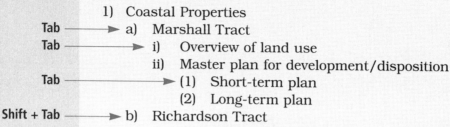

Master Plan for Foundation Properties

1) Coastal Properties

Tab ────────▶ a) Marshall Tract

Tab ────────▶ i)   Overview of land use

ii) Master plan for development/disposition

Tab ────────▶ (1) Short-term plan

(2) Long-term plan

Shift + Tab ────▶ b) Richardson Tract

i)   Overview of land use

ii) Master plan for development/disposition

(1) Short-term plan

(2) Long-term plan

2) Midlands Properties

a) Wheeler Tract

i)   Overview of land use

ii) Master plan for development/disposition

(1) Short-term plan

(2) Long-term plan

b) Blossom Tract

i)   Overview of land use

ii) Master plan for development/disposition

Note: The report you prepare in Lesson 50 (**50d-d1**) will be based on this outline.

---

help keywords
borders and shading

Paragraph Borders and Shading

Borders and shading can be added to paragraphs, pages, or selected text. Various line styles, weights, and colors can be applied to borders. Shading can be applied in a variety of colors and patterns.

> This paragraph illustrates a block border with a 1-point black line. The shading for the paragraph is 10% gray fill.

MOUS TIP

Borders option available on Formatting Toolbar.

To apply a paragraph border:

1. Click in the paragraph or select the text to be formatted with a border.
2. Click **Borders and Shading** on the Format menu, and then click the **Borders** tab.
3. Select the type of border, line style, color, and width; then click **Apply to Paragraph** and **OK**.

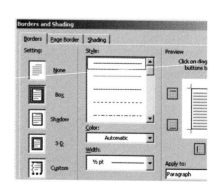

Skillbuilding

22d Backspace Key

Practice reaching to the Backspace key with your left little finger. Key the sentences, using the backspace key to correct errors.

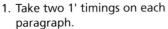

22e Speed Check

1. Take two 1' timings on each paragraph.
2. Take a 3' timing on all paragraphs. Determine *gwam*.

Goal: 17 *gwam*

   all letters

18 You should be interested in the special items on sale today.
19 If she is going with us, why don't we plan to leave now?
20 Do you desire to continue working on the memo in the future?
21 Did the firm or their neighbors own the autos with problems?
22 Juni, Vec, and Zeb had perfect grades on weekly query exams.
23 Jewel quickly explained to me the big fire hazards involved.

	gwam	1'	3'
Most people will agree that we owe it to our children	10	4	28
to pass the planet on to them in better condition than we	22	7	32
found it. We must take extra steps just to make the quality	34	12	36
of living better.	38	13	37
If we do not change our ways quickly and stop damaging	11	16	41
our world, it will not be a good place to live. We can save	12	21	45
the ozone and wildlife and stop polluting the air and water.	35	25	49

1'	1	2	3	4	5	6	7	8	9	10	11	12
3'		1		2		3			4			

Communication

22f Number Expression

1. Study the rules and examples at the right.
2. In the Open Screen, key the information below at the left margin. Press ENTER as shown.

   Your name ENTER

   Current date ENTER

   Skillbuilders 1, Drill 6

   ENTER ENTER

3. Key the sample sentences 24–28. Backspace to correct errors.
4. Save the file as **xx-22f**.

Express as figures

1. **Money amounts** and **percentages, even when appoximate.** Spell out cents and percent except in statistical copy.

   The 16 percent discount saved me $145; Bill, 95 cents.

2. **Round numbers expressed in millions or higher with their word modifier.**

   Ms. Ti contributed $3 million.

3. **House numbers** (Except house number One) and street names over ten. If a street name is a number, separate it from the house number with a dash.

   1510 Easy Street   One West Ninth Avenue   1592-11th Street

4. **Date followed by a month.** A date preceding the month or standing alone is expressed in figures followed by "d" or "th."

   June 9, 2001   4th of July   March 3d

5. **Numbers used with nouns.**

   Volume 1   Chapter 6

24 Ask **Group 1** to read **Chapter 6** of **Book 11** (**Shelf 19, Room 5**).
25 All **six** of us live at **One Bay Road**, not at **126--56th Street**.
26 At **9 a.m.** the owners decided to close from **12 noon** to **1 p.m.**
27 Ms. Vik leaves **June 9**; she returns the **14th or 15th of July.**
28 The **16 percent** discount saves **$115**. A stamp costs **35 cents.**

LESSON 49 | Edit Reports

Skillbuilding

49a
Warmup
Key each line twice SS;
DS between 2-line
groups.

1 When Jorg moves away, quickly place five dozen gloves in the box.
2 Flight 372 leaves at 10:46 a.m. and arrives in Omaha at 9:58 p.m.
3 I obtain unusual services from a number of celebrated decorators.
4 She may sign an authentic name and title to amend this endowment.

| 1 | 2 | 3 | 4 | 5 | 6 | 7 | 8 | 9 | 10 | 11 | 12 | 13 |

49b
Timed Writings
1. Key one 3' timing.
2. Key one 5' writing.
   Strive for control.

 all letters

	gwam	3'	5'

Subtle differences exist among role models, mentors, and | 4 | 2 | 32
sponsors.   A role model is a person you can emulate, or one who | 8 | 5 | 35
provides a good example to follow.   A mentor is one who will | 12 | 7 | 37
advise, coach, or guide you when you need information about your | 16 | 10 | 40
job or your organization.   A sponsor is a person who will support | 21 | 12 | 42
you or recommend you for a position or a new responsibility. | 25 | 15 | 45

One person may fill all three roles, or several people may | 30 | 18 | 48
serve as role models, mentors, or sponsors.   These individuals | 34 | 20 | 50
usually have higher ranks than you do, which means they will be | 38 | 23 | 53
able to get information that you and your peers may not have. | 42 | 25 | 55
Frequently, a mentor will share information with you that will | 46 | 28 | 58
enable you to make good decisions about your career. | 50 | 30 | 60

3' | 1 | 2 | 3 | 4 |
5' | 1 | 2 | 3 |

New Functions

49c

Create Outlines

An **outline** is a document formatted in different hierarchical levels. Good writers often use outlines to structure long documents such as reports before writing so that they will be organized effectively. An outline numbered list can have up to nine levels.

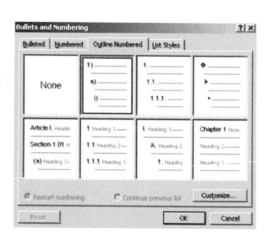

To create an outline numbered list:

1. Click **Format** on the menu; then click **Bullets and Numbering**.
2. Click the **Outline Numbered** tab, and select the desired style.
3. Key each line of the outline; press ENTER after each item.
4. To demote an item to a lower level, click **Increase Indent** (or press TAB). To promote an item to a higher level, click **Decrease Indent** (or press SHIFT + TAB).

LESSON 23 | & and : (colon), Proofreaders' Marks

✳ **Warmup**
23a
Key each line twice SS.

alphabet 1 Roxy waved as she did quick flying jumps on the trapeze bar.

symbols 2 Ryan's--with an A-1 rating--sold Item #146 (for $10) on 2/7.

space bar 3 Mr. Fyn may go to Cape Cod on the bus, or he may go by auto.

easy 4 Susie is busy; may she halt the social work for the auditor?

| 1 | 2 | 3 | 4 | 5 | 6 | 7 | 8 | 9 | 10 | 11 | 12 |

New Keys

23b **&** and **:** (colon)
Key each line once SS.

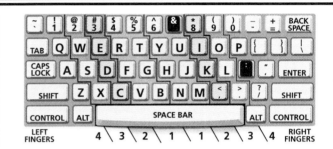

& = ampersand: The ampersand is used only as part of company names.
Colon: Space twice after a colon except when used within a number for time.

& Shift; then reach up with *right first* finger.

: (colon) Left shift; then press key with *right fourth* finger.

& (ampersand)

5 & &j j& & & &; J & J; Haraj & Jay; Moroj & Jax; Torj & Jones
6 Nehru & Unger; Mumm & Just; Mann & Hart; Arch & Jones; M & J
7 Rhye & Knox represent us; Steb & Doy, Firm A; R & J, Firm B.

: (colon)

8 : :; ;: : : :; as: for example: notice: To: From: Date:
9 in stock: 8:30; 7:45; Age: Experience: Read: Send: See:
10 Space twice after a colon, thus: To: No.: Time: Carload:

all symbols learned

11 Consider these companies: J & R, Brand & Kay, Uper & Davis.
12 Memo #88-89 reads as follows: "Deduct 15% of $300, or $45."
13 Bill 32(5)--it got here quite late--from M & N was paid 7/3.

23c Keyboard
Reinforcement

Key each line twice; work for fluency.

double letters

14 Di Bennett was puzzled by drivers exceeding the speed limit.
15 Bill needs the office address; he will cut the grass at ten.
16 Todd saw the green car veer off the street near a tall tree.

figures and symbols

17 Invoice #84 for $672.91, plus $4.38 tax, was due on 5/19/02.
18 Do read Section 4, pages 60-74 and Section 9, pages 198-225.
19 Enter the following: (a) name, (b) address, and (c) tax ID.

Applications

48b-d1

Memo

Create the following memo using the Professional style memo (do not use the Memo Wizard). Add the company name **Ocean Springs, Inc.** Add your reference initials. Save as **48b-d1**.

To: Richard M. Taylor | From: Dianne Gibson | CC: Bruce Diamond | Date: Current date | Re: Trail Design

Last week, Madilyn signed the contract for the trail design for Phase 1 of our Georgetown property. NatureLink was selected as the contractor. This firm was chosen because of its extensive experience in selecting interpretative sites, designing trails, and installing boardwalks to protect wetlands and environmentally sensitive areas.

The first onsite meeting is scheduled for November 10. We plan to meet at the main entrance at 10:30 a.m. to tour the property and review the procedures that NatureLink plans to use in designing the trails near the red cockaded woodpecker (RCW) habitat. Since the RCW is an endangered species, we want to balance the desires of ecotourists to observe these birds and the need to protect them.

Please let me know if you plan to participate in the initial meeting with NatureLink.

48b-d2

Fax Cover Sheet

1. Use the Professional fax template to create a fax cover sheet for the memo you created in document **48b-d1**. Use the address and telephone numbers shown here:

   Ocean Springs, Inc., 2948 Toms Creek Road, Hopkins, SC 29061-5387
   Telephone: 803-555-0197 Fax: 803-555-0146
   Richard M. Taylor: Fax: 846-555-0172   Telephone: 846-555-0139

2. Change the number of pages to 2 and the telephone number at the bottom of the cover sheet. Save the document as **48b-d2**.

48b-d3

Attach New Template

1. Open **48b-d1**. Save it as **48b-d3**.

✳ 2. A template can be attached to an existing document or a different template can be applied to an existing template. You have formatted **48b-d1** using the Professional style memo. Attach the Elegant template to this document. Save the file again. Check that the format of the document is satisfactory.

Note: You will learn to attach a template to a document that is not formatted as a template in a later lesson.

To attach a template to a document: Click **Format** menu, **Theme**, and then the **Style Gallery** button. Scroll to find the desired template theme, select it; then click **OK**.

Skillbuilding

23d Speed Builder

Key each line twice; work for fluency.

20 *Jane may work with an auditing firm if she is paid to do so.*
21 *Pam and eight girls may go to the lake to work with the dog.*
22 *Clancy and Claudia did all the work to fix the sign problem.*
23 *Did Lea visit the Orlando land of enchantment or a neighbor?*
24 *Ana and Blanche made a map for a neighbor to go to the city.*
25 *Sidney may go to the lake to fish with worms from the docks.*
26 *Did the firm or the neighbors own the auto with the problem?*

| 1 | 2 | 3 | 4 | 5 | 6 | 7 | 8 | 9 | 10 | 11 | 12 |

 23e Speed Check

Key two 1' timed writings on each paragraph; then two 3' writings on both paragraphs; compute *gwam*.

Goals: 1', 20–27 *gwam*
　　　　 3', 17–24 *gwam*

 all letters

gwam 1' | 3'

Is how you judge my work important? It is, of course; |11| 4 |26
I hope you recognize some basic merit in it. We all expect |23| 8 |30
to get credit for good work that we conclude. |32|11 |33

I want approval for stands I take, things I write, and |11|14 |36
work I complete. My efforts, by my work, show a picture of |23|18 |41
me; thus, through my work, I am my own unique creation. |34|22 |44

1' | 1 | 2 | 3 | 4 | 5 | 6 | 7 | 8 | 9 | 10 | 11 | 12 |
3' | 1 | | 2 | | 3 | | 4 |

 # Communication

23f Edit Text

1. Read the information about proofreaders' marks.
2. In the Open Screen, key your name, class, and 23f at the left margin. Then key lines 27–32, making the revisions as you key. Use the Backspace key to correct errors.
3. Save as **xx-23f** and print.

Proofreaders' marks are used to identify mistakes in typed or printed text. Learn to apply these commonly used standard proofreaders' marks.

Symbol	Meaning	Symbol	Meaning
～～～	Bold	¶	Paragraph
Cap or ＝	Capitalize	#	Add horizontal space
∧	Insert	/ or *lc*	Lowercase letters
✓	Delete	◡	Close up space
☐	Move to left	～	Transpose
☐	Move to right	*stet*	Leave as originally written

27 We miss 50% in life's rewards by refusing to new try things.

28 do it now--today--then tomorrow's load will be 100% lighter.

29 Satisfying work-- whether it pays $40 or $400-is the pay off.

30 Avoid mistakes: confusing a #3 has cost thousands.

31 Pleased most with a first-rate job is the person who did it.

32 My wife and/or me mother will except the certificate for me.

Wizards

Wizards enable you to enter information into different document templates by responding to questions. Wizards are located in the Templates dialog box. For example, the Memo Wizard is the third item on the Memo tab of the Templates dialog box.

To create a new document using a wizard:

1. Click **New** on the File menu.
2. Select **General Templates** in the Task Pane.
3. Click on the appropriate tab for the desired type of document (**Letters & Faxes, Memos**).
4. Double-click the Wizard icon for the type of document you desire.
5. Follow the directions in the Wizard to add the appropriate information.

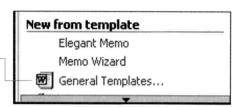

New from template
Elegant Memo
Memo Wizard
General Templates...

Drill 2 | MEMO WIZARD

1. Use the Memo Wizard to create the same memo you did in Drill 1.

2. Click the **Next** button to move through the various screens to key the necessary information.

3. Leave those fields for which you have no information blank or deselect them. Enter **dg** as the writer's initials (Dianne Gibson) and your initials as the typist.

4. Click the **Finish** button to view the memo.

5. Save the memo as **48a-drill2**, and print one copy.

Editing Templates

Templates can be edited or customized and saved as document templates so that you do not need to insert repetitive information such as the company name each time you use the template. Customized document templates are stored under the General Templates tab of the Templates dialog box.

To use the template, click **File** menu, **New**. Under New from Template, click **General Templates**, select the **General** tab, and double-click the appropriate template icon.

Drill 3 | CUSTOMIZE A TEMPLATE

1. Click **New** on the File menu. Select **General Templates** in the task pane.

2. Click the **Letters and Faxes** tab, and under Create New, click **Template**; then select **Professional Fax**.

Create New
○ Document   ● Template

Fill in the company information at the top of the template with the following:

Ocean Springs, Inc.
2948 Toms Creek Road, Hopkins, SC 29061-5387
Telephone: 803-555-0197 Fax: 803-555-0199

3. Save as **48a-drill3**, and print. Close the document.

4. Click the **General** tab in the Template dialog box. Notice that the file you created, **48a-drill3**, is saved as a template. It can be opened and a message added.

2948 Toms Creek Road, Hopkins, SC 29061-5387
Telephone: 803-555-0197 Fax: 803-555-0199

Ocean Springs, Inc.

LESSON 24 | Other Symbols

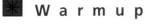

Warmup
24a
Key each line twice SS.

alphabet | 1 Pfc. Jim Kings covered each of the lazy boxers with a quilt.
figures | 2 Do problems 6 to 29 on page 175 before class at 8:30, May 4.
" | 3 They read the poems "September Rain" and "The Lower Branch."
easy | 4 When did the busy girls fix the tight cowl of the ruby gown?

| 1 | 2 | 3 | 4 | 5 | 6 | 7 | 8 | 9 | 10 | 11 | 12 |

New Keys

24b

Key each pair of lines once SS;
DS between 2-line groups.

Become familiar with
these symbols:

@   at
<   less than
>   greater than
*   asterisk
+   plus sign (use a
     hyphen for minus
     and x for "times")
=   equals
[ ]   left and right
     bracket

@   shift; reach *up* with *left third* finger to @
5 @ @s s@ @ @; 24 @ .15; 22 @ .35; sold 2 @ .87; were 12 @ .95
6 You may contact Luke @: LJP@rx.com or fax @ (602) 555-0101.

<   shift; reach *down* with *right second* finger to <
>   shift; reach *down* with *right third* finger to >
7 Can you prove "a > b"? If 28 > 5, then 5a < x. Is a < > b?
8 E-mail Al ajj@crewl.com and Matt mrw10@scxs.com by 9:30 p.m.

*   shift; reach *up* with *right second* finger to *
9 * *k k8* * *; aurelis*; May 7*; both sides*; 250 km.**; aka*
10 Note each *; one * refers to page 29; ** refers to page 307.

+   shift; reach *up* with *right fourth* finger to +
11 + ;+ +; + + +; 2 + 2; A+ or B+; 70+ F. degrees; +xy over +y;
12 The question was 8 + 7 + 51; it should have been 8 + 7 + 15.

=   reach *up* with *right fourth* finger to =
13 = =; = = =; = 4; If 14x = 28, x = 2; if 8x = 16, then x = 2.
14 Change this solution (where it says "= by") to = bx or = BX.

[ ]   reach *up* with *right fourth* finger to [and]
15 Mr. Wing was named. [That's John J. Wing, ex-senator. Ed.]
16 We [Joseph and I] will be in Suite #349; call us @ 555-0102.

LESSON 48 | Edit Memos

New Functions

48a

help keywords
templates

Templates

A **template** is a master copy of a set of predefined styles for a particular type of document. Templates are available for formatting documents such as a memo, fax, or letter. A template can be used exactly as it exists, or it can be modified or customized and saved as a new template. The tabs on the Templates dialog box indicate the variety of templates that *Word* has available. You can also attach a template to a document.

To use an existing template:

1. Click **New** on the File menu.

2. In the New Document pane, under New from template, click **General Templates**.

3. In the Templates dialog box, click the desired tab, such as **Memos**.

4. Select the desired memo style, such as **Contemporary, Elegant,** or **Professional**.

5. If necessary, click **Document** under Create New.

6. Click **OK**. Follow the directions on the template to key the desired document.

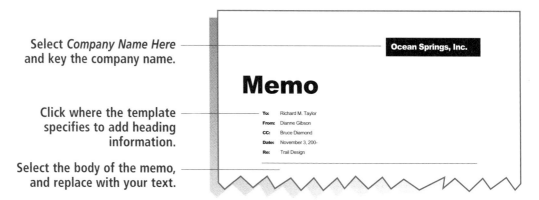

Select *Company Name Here* and key the company name.

Click where the template specifies to add heading information.

Select the body of the memo, and replace with your text.

Drill 1 | MEMO TEMPLATE

1. Create a new document using the Professional memo template.

2. Select **Company Name Here**; key **Ocean Springs, Inc.**

3. Read the instructions on the memo template, and then key the heading information provided in the next column. The date is automatically inserted.

To:	Richard M. Taylor
From:	Dianne Gibson
CC:	Bruce Diamond
Date:	Current
Re:	Trail Design

4. Save the document as **48a-drill1,** and print one copy.

5. Check the folder where your file is saved. The file has the extension *.doc* since it was created as a document.

Skillbuilding

24c Rhythm Builder

In the Open Screen, key each line twice; DS between two-line groups.

double letters	17 feel pass mill good miss seem moons cliffs pools green spell
	18 Assets are being offered in a stuffy room to two associates.
balanced hand	19 is if of to it go do to is do so if to to the it sign vie to
	20 Pamela Fox may wish to go to town with Blanche if she works.
one hand	21 date face ere bat lip sew lion rear brag fact join eggs ever
	22 get fewer on; after we look; as we agree; add debt; act fast
combination	23 was for|in the case of|they were|to down|mend it|but pony is
	24 They were to be down in the fastest sleigh if you are right.

| 1 | 2 | 3 | 4 | 5 | 6 | 7 | 8 | 9 | 10 | 11 | 12 |

24d Edited Copy

1. Key each line, making the corrections marked with proofreaders' marks.
2. Correct errors using the Backspace key.
3. Save as **xx-24d**.

25 Ask Group 1 to read Chater 6 of Book 11 (Shelf 19, Room 5).

26 All 6 of us live at One Bay road, not at 126-56th Street. *(six)*

27 At 9 a.m. the owners decided to close from 12 noon to 1 p.m.

28 Ms. Vik leaves June 9; she returns the 14th or 15th of July.

29 The 16 percent discount saves $115. A stamp costs 35 cents.

30 Elin gave $300,000,000; our gift was only 75 cents. *($3 million to charity)*

24e Speed Check

1. Key a 1' writing on each paragraph.
2. Key two 3' writings on both paragraphs. Save the timings if desired (**xx24e-t1** and **xx24e-t2**).

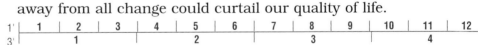

	gwam	1'	3'

Why don't we like change very much? Do you think that   11 | 4 26
just maybe we want to be lazy; to dodge new things; and, as   23 | 8 30
much as possible, not to make hard decisions?   32 | 11 33
    We know change can and does extend new areas for us to   11 | 14 36
enjoy, areas we might never have known existed; and to stay   24 | 18 40
away from all change could curtail our quality of life.   34 | 22 44

1' | 1 | 2 | 3 | 4 | 5 | 6 | 7 | 8 | 9 | 10 | 11 | 12 |
3' | 1 | 2 | 3 | 4 |

Communication

24f Composition Revision

1. In the Open Screen, open the file **xx-profile** that you created in Lesson 18.
2. Position the insertion point at the end of the last paragraph. Press ENTER twice.
3. Key an additional paragraph that begins with the following sentence:
   Thank you for allowing me to introduce myself.
4. Finish the paragraph by adding two or more sentences that describe your progress and satisfaction with keyboarding.
5. Correct any mistakes you have made. Click **Save** to resave the document. Print.
6. Mark any mistakes you missed with proofreaders' marks. Revise the document, save, and reprint. Submit to your instructor.

Applications

47d-d1
Letter

1. Open **Brady** from the data files. Save it as **47d-d1**. Make the following edits:
   - Revise the letter so that it will be formatted correctly as a modified-block letter.
   - Search for the name *Debauche*; each time it appears, replace it with *DeBauche*.
   - Use the Thesaurus to find a synonym for *statistics*. Replace *statistics* with the second synonym listed.
   - Make the following correction in the first sentence of paragraph 2:
     Brad Swinton, our new vice president of Marketing, indicated. . .
   - Cut the following sentence from paragraph 2:
     I hope this will not be a problem for you.
2. Save the document again, and print it.

 **47d-d2**
Letter

1. Open document **47d-d1** that you completed in the previous activity.
2. Reformat the document as a block-style letter.
3. Save it as **47d-d2** and print.

 **47d-d3**
Letter

1. Open document **47d-d2**, and open a new blank document. Keep both documents open.
2. Copy Ms. DeBauche's address and the salutation from **47d-d2** to the new document.
3. Key the letter below in the block-style format.
4. Copy and paste the closing lines from **47d-d2**, except the enclosure notation.
5. Search for *section*, and replace it each time it appears with *phase*.
6. Use the Thesaurus to find a synonym for *prolific*. Select the first option.
7. Save it as **47d-d3** and print.

October 11, 200-

Our team completed its preliminary review of your proposal today. Overall, we are very pleased with the approach you have taken.

Please plan to provide the following information at our meeting on October 18:

1. Please provide a more detailed pricing plan. We would like to have each section of the project priced separately specifying hourly rate and expenses rather than the one total sum quoted.

2. How many hours do you estimate will be necessary to complete each section of the project? When would your firm be able to begin the project?

We look forward to a very prolific meeting on October 18.

LESSON 25 | Assessment

Warmup

25a
Key each line twice SS.

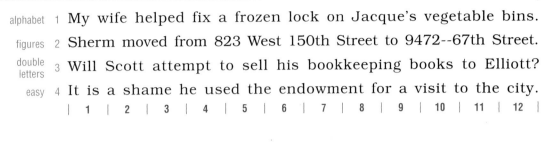

alphabet 1 My wife helped fix a frozen lock on Jacque's vegetable bins.

figures 2 Sherm moved from 823 West 150th Street to 9472--67th Street.

double letters 3 Will Scott attempt to sell his bookkeeping books to Elliott?

easy 4 It is a shame he used the endowment for a visit to the city.

| 1 | 2 | 3 | 4 | 5 | 6 | 7 | 8 | 9 | 10 | 11 | 12 |

25b Reach Review
Key each line once; repeat.

> **TECHNIQUE TIP**
> Keep arms and hands quiet as you practice the long reaches.

n/y
5 deny many canny tiny nymph puny any puny zany penny pony yen
6 Jenny Nyles saw many, many tiny nymphs flying near her pony.

b/r
7 bran barb brim curb brat garb bray verb brag garb bribe herb
8 Barb Barber can bring a bit of bran and herbs for her bread.

c/e
9 cede neck nice deck dice heck rice peck vice erect mice echo
10 Can Cecil erect a decent cedar deck? He erects nice condos.

n/u
11 nun gnu bun nut pun numb sun nude tuna nub fun null unit gun
12 Eunice had enough ground nuts at lunch; Uncle Launce is fun.

25c Speed Check
Key two 3' writings.
Strive for accuracy.
Goal: 3', 19–27 *gwam*

all letters

gwam 3'

The term careers can mean many different things to   3 | 51
different people. As you know, a career is much more than a   8 | 55
job. It is the kind of work that a person has through life. 12 | 59
It includes the jobs a person has over time. It also involves 16 | 63
how the work life affects the other parts of our life. There 20 | 67
are as many types of careers as there are people.   23 | 71

Almost all people have a career of some kind. A career   27 | 74
can help us to reach unique goals, such as to make a living   31 | 79
or to help others. The kind of career you have will affect   35 | 83
your life in many ways. For example, it can determine where 39 | 87
you live, the money you make, and how you feel about yourself. 44 | 91
A good choice can thus help you realize the life you want.   47 | 95

3' | 1 | 2 | 3 | 4 |

To replace text:

1. Click **Edit** on the menu bar; then click **Replace**.

2. Enter the text you wish to locate in the Find what box.

3. Key the replacement text in the Replace with box.

4. Click **Find Next** to find the first occurrence of the text.

5. Click **Replace** to replace one occurrence, or click **Replace All** to replace all occurrences of the text.

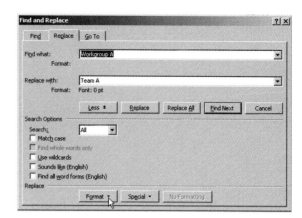

✳ **DISCOVER**

Click the **Format** and **Special** buttons in the extended Find and Replace dialog box to learn about search options for formats and other elements.

Drill 1 | FIND AND REPLACE

1. Open **Restructure** from the data files.
2. Find the word *restructuring* the first place it appears.
3. Find the second and third occurrences of *restructuring*.
4. Find *Workgroup A* and replace it with *Team A*.
5. Edit the document so that the letter is formatted correctly as a block-style letter.

6. Save the document as **47c-drill1**.
✳ 7. Open **Meade** from the data files. Search the document for text formatted in Arial. In the Find and Replace dialog box, click **Format, Font**, and then select **Arial**. Search again to find all occurrences of highlighting; then close the document without saving any changes.

Thesaurus

The Thesaurus is a tool that enables you to look up words and replace them with synonyms, antonyms, or related words.

To use the Thesaurus:

1. Position the insertion point in the word you wish to replace.

2. Click **Tools** on the menu, click **Language**, and then click **Thesaurus**.

3. If more than one meaning appears, select the appropriate meaning.

4. Select the desired synonym or antonym, and click **Replace**.

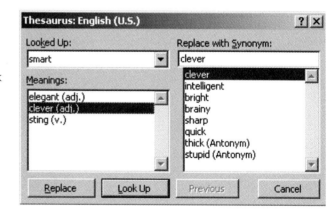

MOUS TIP

An alternative way to use the Thesaurus is to position the insertion point in a word and right-click the mouse. Select **Synonyms** and then the desired word or **Thesaurus** for more information.

Drill 2 | THESAURUS

1. Key the following words on separate lines:
   generous   data   smart   profit
2. Replace *generous* and *data* with synonyms.
3. Replace *smart* (meaning clever) with a synonym.

4. Key **smart** again (meaning elegant), and replace it with an antonym.
5. Replace *profit* with an antonym.
6. Save the document as **47c-drill2**.

Skillbuilding

25d Rhythm Builder

Key each line once; DS between groups; repeat.

Key with precision and without hesitation.

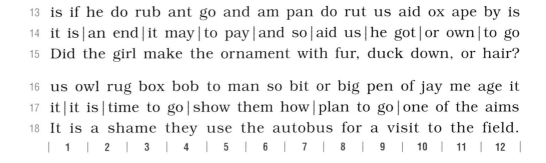

13 is if he do rub ant go and am pan do rut us aid ox ape by is

14 it is|an end|it may|to pay|and so|aid us|he got|or own|to go

15 Did the girl make the ornament with fur, duck down, or hair?

16 us owl rug box bob to man so bit or big pen of jay me age it

17 it|it is|time to go|show them how|plan to go|one of the aims

18 It is a shame they use the autobus for a visit to the field.

| 1 | 2 | 3 | 4 | 5 | 6 | 7 | 8 | 9 | 10 | 11 | 12 |

25e Figure Check

In the Open Screen, key two 1' writings and two 3' writings at a controlled speed.

all letters/figures

Goal: 3', 16–24 gwam

		gwam	3'
Do I read the stock market pages in the news? Yes; and		4	35
at about 9 or 10 a.m. each morning, I know lots of excited		8	39
people are quick to join me. In fact, many of us zip right		12	43
to the 3d or 4th part of the paper to see if the prices of		16	47
our stocks have gone up or down. Now, those of us who are		19	51
"speculators" like to "buy at 52 and sell at 60"; while the		23	55
"investors" among us are more interested in a dividend we		27	59
may get, say 7 or 8 percent, than in the price of a stock.		31	62

3' | 1 | 2 | 3 | 4 |

Communication

25f Edited Copy

1. Key the paragraphs and make the corrections marked with proofreaders' marks. Use the Backspace key to correct errors.
2. Check all number expressions and correct any mistakes that may exist.
3. Save as **xx-25f**.

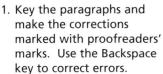

Last week the healthy heart foundation released the findings of a *significant* study that showed exercise diet and ~~if individuals don't~~ smoke are the major controllable factors that led to a healthy heart. Factors such as heredity can not be controlled. The study included 25 to 65 year-old males as well as females *aged* *both* *and* *women especially benefited from*

The study also showed that just taking a walk ~~benefits our health~~. Those who walked an average of 2 to 3 hours a week were more then 30% less likely to have problems than those who did no exercise.

LESSON 47 | Edit Letters

Skillbuilding

47a
Warmup
Key each line twice SS; DS between 2-line groups.

 alphabet 1 Jakob will save the money required for your next big cash prizes.
fig/sym 2 I saw Vera buy 13 7/8 yards of #240 cotton denim at $6.96 a yard.
3d/4th 3 Zone 12 is impassable; quickly rope it off. Did you wax Zone 90?
 easy 4 Did an auditor handle the formal audit of the firms for a profit?

| 1 | 2 | 3 | 4 | 5 | 6 | 7 | 8 | 9 | 10 | 11 | 12 | 13 |

47b
Timed Writings
1. Take two 1' timings; key as rapidly as you can.
2. Take one 2' timing. Try to maintain your 1' rate.

 all letters

	gwam	1'	2'
The value of an education has been a topic discussed many	12	6	48
times with a great deal of zest. The value is often measured in	25	12	54
terms of costs and benefits to the taxpayer. It is also judged	37	19	61
in terms of changes in the individuals taking part in the	49	24	67
educational process. Gains in the level of knowledge, the	61	30	72
development and refinement of attitudes, and the acquiring of	73	36	79
skills are believed to be crucial parts of an education.	84	42	84

1' | 1 | 2 | 3 | 4 | 5 | 6 | 7 | 8 | 9 | 10 | 11 | 12 | 13 |
2' | 1 | 2 | 3 | 4 | 5 | 6 |

New Functions

47c

help keywords
find, replace

Find and Replace

Find is used to locate text, formatting, footnotes, graphics, or other items within a document. **Replace** is used to find text, formatting, or other items within a document and replace them with different text, formatting, or items.

Clicking the More button on the Find or Replace tab displays a list of search options such as *Match case* or *Find whole words only*, as shown in the illustration at the right. The Format and Special buttons in the extended dialog box provide options for searching for formatting features or for special elements.

To find text:
1. Click **Edit** on the menu bar; then click **Find**.
2. Enter the text you wish to locate in the Find what box.
3. Click **Find Next** to find the next occurrence of the text.

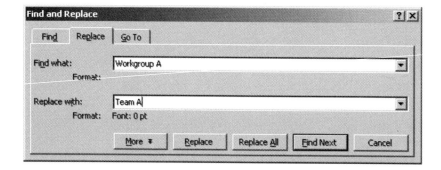

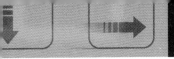

Skill Builders 2

 Use the Open Screen for Skill Builders 2. Save each drill as a separate file.

Drill 1

OPPOSITE HAND REACHES

Key at a controlled rate; concentrate on the reaches.

i/e
1 ik is fit it sit laid site like insist still wise coil light
2 ed he ear the fed egg led elf lake jade heat feet hear where
3 lie kite item five aide either quite linear imagine brighter
4 Imagine the aide eating the pears before the grieving tiger.

w/o
5 ws we way was few went wit law with weed were week gnaw when
6 ol on go hot old lot joy odd comb open tool upon money union
7 bow owl word wood worm worse tower brown toward wrote weapon
8 The workers lowered the brown swords toward the wood weapon.

y/t
9 yj my say may yes rye yarn eye lye yap any relay young berry
10 tf at it let the vat tap item town toast right little attire
11 yet toy yogurt typical youth tycoon yacht tympani typewriter
12 Yesterday a young youth typed a cat story on the typewriter.

b/n
13 bf but job fibs orb bow able bear habit boast rabbit brother
14 nj not and one now fun next pony month notice runner quicken
15 bin bran knob born cabin number botany nibble blank neighbor
16 A number of neighbors banked on bunking in the brown cabins.

g/h
17 gag go gee god rig gun log gong cog gig agog gage going gang
18 huh oh hen the hex ash her hash ah hush shah hutch hand ache
19 ugh high ghoul rough ghosts cough night laugh ghee bough ghi
20 Hush; Greg hears rough sounds. Has Hugh laughed or coughed?

r/u
21 row or rid air rap par rye rear ark jar rip nor are right or
22 cut us auk out tutu sun husk but fun cub gun nut mud tug hug
23 rut aura run your rub cure rum our rue cur rug urn true pure
24 Ryan is sure you should pour your food from an urn or cruet.
| 1 | 2 | 3 | 4 | 5 | 6 | 7 | 8 | 9 | 10 | 11 | 12 |

Drill 2

NUMBER SPEED

Take 1' writings; the last number you key when you stop is your approximate *gwam*.

1 and 2 and 3 and 4 and 5 and 6 and 7 and 8 and 9 and 10 and
11 and 12 and 13 and 14 and 15 and 16 and 17 and 18 and 19
and 20 and 21 and 22 and 23 and 24 and 25 and 26 and 27 and

D r i l l 5 | CHARACTER EFFECTS

1. Key the text at the right, applying the character effects shown.

2. Add the text effect Marching Red Ants to the text in small caps in line 1. Add the text effect Shimmer to the second line.

3. Save it as **46b-drill5** and print it.

Apply SMALL CAPS to this text.

The symbol for water, H_2O, contains a subscript.

Math formulas often use superscripts, such as $X^2 + Y^3$.

~~Strikethrough~~ is a useful effect in editing text.

Outline and shadow change the appearance of text.

 ## Applications

46c-d1

Report

Convert Case
To change the case of text, select it. Then click **Format** menu, **Change Case**.

1. Open **Punctuality** from the data files, and save it as **46c-d1**. Edit as follows:
   a. Select the main heading. Change the font to 14-point bold. Apply the **Shadow** character effect. Convert the heading to uppercase.
   b. In the sentence *Punctuality-Not Performance-Determines Outcome!*, change hyphens to em dashes. In the sentence that follows, replace the commas around *and by all accounts one who was unbeatable and assured to repeat the title*, with em dashes.
   c. Select **Punctuality—Not Performance—Determines Outline!** in paragraph 1, and apply italic format and blinking background.
   d. Select paragraph 3, and move it between paragraphs 1 and 2.
   e. Change the spacing of paragraph 1 to 1.5, and indent the paragraph using TAB. Use **Format Painter** to apply this format to the next two paragraphs.
   f. Select the last sentence, bold it, and change the font to blue.
   g. Change the side margins to 1.5" and center the text vertically on the page.
   h. Add a header to the document. Key your name at the left, and insert the filename at the right edge of the header.

2. Save the document again, and print a copy.

COURTESY OF © PHOTODISC, INC.

N E W S | on punctuality—
does it really matter?

Just how important is punctuality? What difference does a few minutes one way or the other make? A local newspaper sports headline recently read, "Punctuality—Not Performance Determines Outcome!" A defending champion hurdler—and by all accounts one who was unbeatable and assured to repeat the title—was a few minutes late for the championship meet because of traffic problems and missed the 110-meter hurdle event. At least this young athlete learned the cost of being late early in life.

What message does tardiness convey to others? This question perhaps is the most important one. The message conveyed to most people is that you think your time is more important than their time. It conveys rudeness and lack of care about others. It also conveys that you are not organized and can't get things done in a timely manner. Punctuality really does matter!

Drill 3

TECHNIQUE BUILDERS

Key each line once; DS between groups; repeat.

TECHNIQUE TIP

Concentrate on keeping quiet hands and fingers. Reach directly from the top to bottom rows.

adjacent keys

1 I saw her at an airport at a tropical resort leaving on a cruise.

2 Is assessing potential important in a traditional career program?

3 The boisterous boys were playing on a trampoline near an airport.

4 Three policemen were cruising down that street in Freeport today.

long, direct reach

5 The brave driver swerved to avoid the RV and the boy on the curb.

6 The umpire must check the Brums for number of pitches in one day.

7 The happy bride and groom decided on nuptials preceded by brunch.

8 The nervous mother decided she must keep Marv at a small nursery.

| 1 | 2 | 3 | 4 | 5 | 6 | 7 | 8 | 9 | 10 | 11 | 12 | 13 |

Drill 4

REACH FOR NEW GOALS

1. From the second or third column at the right, choose a goal 2–3 *gwam* higher than your best rate on either straight or statistical copy.

2. Take 1' writings on that sentence; try to finish it the number of times shown at the top of the goal list.

3. If you reach your goal, take 1' writings on the next line. If you don't reach your goal, use the preceding line.

	words	1' timing 6 times gwam	1' timing 5 times gwam
Do they blame me for the goal?	6	36	30
The 2 men may enamel 17 oboes.	6	36	30
The auditor may handle the problem.	7	42	35
Did the 4 chaps focus the #75 lens?	7	42	35
She did vow to fight for the right name.	8	48	40
He paid 10 men to fix a pen for 3 ducks.	8	48	40
The girl may cycle down to the dormant field.	9	54	45
The 27 girls paid their $9 to go to the lake.	9	54	45
The ensign works with vigor to dismantle the auto.	10	60	50
Bob may work problems 8 and 9; Sid did problem 40.	10	60	50
The form may entitle a visitor to pay for such a kayak.	11	66	55
They kept 7 panels and 48 ivory emblems for 29 chapels.	11	66	55

| 1 | 2 | 3 | 4 | 5 | 6 | 7 | 8 | 9 | 10 | 11 |

Drill 5

IMPROVE CONCENTRATION

Set a right tab at 5.5" for the addresses. Key the Internet addresses in column 2 exactly as they are listed. Accuracy is critical.

The paperless guide to New York City	http://www.mediabridge.com/nyc
A trip to outer space	http://spacelink.msfc.nasa.gov
Search engine	http://webcrawler.com
Government printing office access	http://www.access.gpo.gov/index.html
MarketPlace--corporate information	http://www.mktplace.com
Touchstone's PC-cillin virus scan	http://www.antivirus.com

Drag-and-Drop Editing

Another way to edit text is to use the mouse. With **drag and drop**, you can move or copy text using the mouse. To move copy, you must first select the text, then hold down the left mouse button, and drag the text to the desired location. The mouse pointer displays a rectangle indicating that copy is being moved. Release the mouse button to "drop" the text into the desired location.

Follow a similar procedure to copy (or duplicate) text. Hold down the left mouse button and the CTRL key, and drag the text to the desired location. A plus sign indicates the text is being copied.

Copy and Paste Between Documents

Multiple documents can be opened at the same time. Each document is displayed in its own window. To move from one document to another, click **Window** on the menu; then click the document name. You may also just click the document name on the Windows taskbar. Text can then be copied and pasted between documents.

 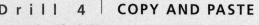
Character and Text Effects

Character effects include a number of special attributes that enhance the appearance of text. Commonly used character effects include superscript, subscript, small caps, strikethrough, shadow, and outline. Character effects are available on the Font dialog box (**Format menu, Font**).

help keywords
font

Text Effects include various animations such as a blinking background or a shimmer. Text effects are appropriate for documents that are to be read on screen or online. To access these animations, select the **Text Effects** tab in the Font dialog box.

Drill 6

ASSESS SKILL GROWTH: STRAIGHT COPY

1. Key 1' writings on each paragraph of a timing. Note that paragraphs within a timing increase by two words.

   Goal: to complete each paragraph.

2. Key a 3' timing on the entire writing.

 all letters

To access writings on *MicroPace Pro*, key **W** and the timing number. For example, key **W8** for *Writing 8*.

Timings are also available as Diagnostic Writings in *Keyboarding Pro*.

Writing 8

Any of us whose target is to achieve success in our professional	13	4
lives will understand that we must learn how to work in harmony	26	8
with others whose paths may cross ours daily.	35	12
We will, unquestionably, work for, with, and beside people, just	13	16
as they will work for, with, and beside us. We will judge them,	26	20
as most certainly they are going to be judging us.	38	24
A lot of people realize the need for solid working relations and	13	28
have a rule that treats others as they, themselves, expect to be	26	33
treated. This seems to be a sound, practical idea for them.	40	37

Writing 9

I spoke with one company visitor recently; and she was very much	13	4
impressed, she said, with the large amount of work she had noted	26	9
being finished by one of our front office workers.	36	12
I told her how we had just last week recognized this very person	13	16
for what he had done, for output, naturally, but also because of	26	21
its excellence. We know this person has that "magic touch."	38	25
This "magic touch" is the ability to do a fair amount of work in	13	29
a fair amount of time. It involves a desire to become ever more	26	34
efficient without losing quality--the "touch" all workers should	39	38
have.	40	38

Writing 10

Isn't it great just to untangle and relax after you have keyed a	13	4
completed document? Complete, or just done? No document is	25	8
quite complete until it has left you and passed to the next step.	38	13
There are desirable things that must happen to a document before	13	17
you surrender it. It must be read carefully, first of all, for	26	22
meaning to find words that look right but aren't. Read word for	39	26
word.	40	26
Check all figures and exact data, like a date or time, with your	13	31
principal copy. Make sure format details are right. Only then,	26	35
print or remove the work and scrutinize to see how it might look	39	39
to a recipient.	42	40

1' | 1 | 2 | 3 | 4 | 5 | 6 | 7 | 8 | 9 | 10 | 11 | 12 | 13 |
3' | | 1 | | 2 | | 3 | | 4 |

D r i l l   1 | CUT AND PASTE

1. Open **Cut and Paste** from the data files.

2. Select **Cut and** in the first heading and cut it so the heading is **Paste**.

3. Select the heading **Paste** and the paragraph that follows it.

4. Move the selected copy below the last paragraph.

5. Key a line across the page.

6. Copy both paragraphs, and paste them below the line.

7. Create the folder **Module 7 Keys** and save the document as **46b-drill1** in this folder. Save all documents for Module 7 in this folder.

---

help keywords
clipboard

Office Clipboard

The **Clipboard** can store up to 24 items that have been cut or copied. The Clipboard displays in the side pane. If it is not displayed, click **Edit** on the menu bar and then **Office Clipboard** to display it. Note that each item on the Clipboard is displayed for easy reference. All items on the Clipboard can be pasted at once by clicking **Paste All**. A single item can be pasted by clicking on the item and selecting **Paste** from the drop-down menu.

All items on the Clipboard can be removed by clicking the **Clear All** button. A single item can be removed by clicking the item and selecting **Delete** from the drop-down menu.

When an item is pasted into a document, the Paste button smart tag provides options for formatting the text that has been pasted.

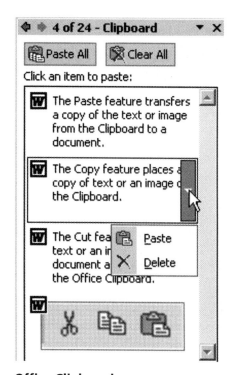

Office Clipboard

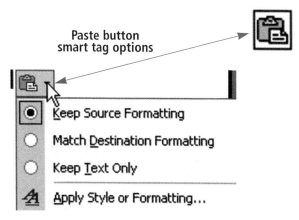

Paste button smart tag options

To format the text using the same format as the new document, click **Match Destination Formatting**. To format the text using the same format as the document from which the text was copied, click **Keep Source Formatting**.

Key as 1' guided writings, working for either speed or control.

Optional: Key as a 3' writing.

🕐 To access writings on *MicroPace Pro*, key **W** and the timing number. For example, key **W11** for Writing 11.

Writing 11

gwam 3'

	•	4	•	8	•	12	

Anyone who expects some day to find an excellent job should   4 | 34

begin now to learn the value of accuracy. To be worth anything,   8 | 38

completed work must be correct, without question. Naturally, we   13 | 43

realize that the human aspect of the work equation always raises   17 | 47

the prospect of errors; but we should understand that those same   20 | 51

errors can be found and fixed. Every completed job should carry   26 | 56

at least one stamp; the stamp of pride in work that is exemplary.   30 | 60

Writing 12

No question about it: Many personal problems we face today   4 | 34

arise from the fact that we earthlings have never been very wise   8 | 38

consumers. We haven't consumed our natural resources well; as a   13 | 43

result, we have jeopardized much of our environment. We excused   17 | 47

our behavior because we thought that our stock of most resources   20 | 51

had no limit. So, finally, we are beginning to realize just how   26 | 56

indiscreet we were; and we are taking steps to rebuild our world.   30 | 60

Writing 13

When I see people in top jobs, I know I'm seeing people who   4 | 34

sell. I'm not just referring to employees who labor in a retail   8 | 38

outlet; I mean those people who put extra effort into convincing   13 | 43

others to recognize their best qualities. They, themselves, are   17 | 47

the commodity they sell; and their optimum tools are appearance,   20 | 51

language, and personality. They look great, they talk and write   26 | 56

well; and, with candid self-confidence, they meet you eye to eye.   30 | 60

3' | 1 | 2 | 3 | 4 |

module 7

Edit Business Documents

OBJECTIVES

* Edit business letters.
* Use and edit memo templates.
* Create outlines and edit reports.
* Format reports with styles and embedded objects.
* Build keying skills.

LESSON 46 | Edit Text

 Skillbuilding

46a
Warmup
Key each line twice SS;
DS between 2-line
groups.

alphabet | 1 | Jim Daley gave us in that box the prize he won for his quick car.
figures | 2 | At 7 a.m., I open Rooms 18, 29, and 30; I lock Rooms 4, 5, and 6.
adjacent reaches | 3 | As Louis said, few questioned the points asserted by the porters.
easy | 4 | Did he vow to fight for the right to work as the Orlando auditor?

| 1 | 2 | 3 | 4 | 5 | 6 | 7 | 8 | 9 | 10 | 11 | 12 | 13 |

New Functions

46b

help keywords
*move or copy text; cut;
copy; paste*

Cut, Copy, and Paste

 The **Cut** feature removes text or an image from a document and places it on the Office Clipboard. The **Copy** feature places a copy of text or an image from a document on the Clipboard. The **Paste** feature transfers a copy of the text or image from the Clipboard to a document.

To move text to a new location:
1. Select the text to be copied. Click **Cut** on the Standard toolbar.
2. Move the insertion point to the new location. Click **Paste**.

To copy text to a new location:
1. Select the text to be copied. Click **Copy** on the Standard toolbar.
2. Move the insertion point to the new location. Click **Paste**.

Writing 14

What do you expect when you travel to a foreign country? 12 4
Quite a few people realize that one of the real joys of 23 8
traveling is to get a brief glimpse of how others think, work, 36 12
and live. 40 12

The best way to enjoy a different culture is to learn as 11 16
much about it as you can before you leave home. Then you can 24 20
concentrate on being a good guest rather than trying to find 36 24
local people who can meet your needs. 44 27

Writing 15

gwam
1' 3'

What do you enjoy doing in your free time? Health experts 12 4
tell us that far too many people choose to be lazy rather than 24 8
to be active. The result of that decision shows up in our 36 12
weight. 37 13

Working to control what we weigh is not easy, and seldom 12 16
can it be done quickly. However, it is quite important if our 24 21
weight exceeds what it should be. Part of the problem results 37 25
from the amount and type of food we eat. 44 27

If we want to look fit, we should include exercise as a 11 31
substantial part of our weight loss plan. Walking at least 23 35
thirty minutes each day at a very fast rate can make a big 35 39
difference both in our appearance and in the way we feel. 47 42

Writing 16

gwam
1' 3'

Doing what we like to do is quite important; however, 10 4
liking what we have to do is equally important. As you ponder 23 8
both of these concepts, you may feel that they are the same, 36 12
but they are not the same. 41 14

If we could do only those things that we prefer to do, the 12 18
chances are that we would do them exceptionally well. Generally, 25 22
we will take more pride in doing those things we like doing, 37 26
and we will not quit until we get them done right. 47 29

We realize, though, that we cannot restrict the things 11 33
that we must do just to those that we want to do. Therefore, 23 37
we need to build an interest in and an appreciation of all the 36 41
tasks that we must do in our positions. 44 44

1'	1	2	3	4	5	6	7	8	9	10	11	12
3'		1			2			3			4	

Activity 5

Map a trip

Determining the route to your destination city is most important in ensuring a pleasant journey. The printed atlas is a valuable tool for mapping a trip; however, with today's technology, we can map our trips electronically using the Maps hyperlinks provided by several search engines. This invaluable site will search for the specific route you identify and provide you an overview map and turn-by-turn maps with text.

D r i l l

1. Click the **Search** button in your Web browser. Browse the search engines to locate the hyperlinks for *Maps*; click to open.

2. Your destination city is Asheville, North Carolina. Enter your city and state as the starting point. Search for a turn-by-turn map with text. Print the directions.

   What is the total distance? _____ What is the estimated time? _____

3. You are having a party and need to give several guests directions to your home. Using the Excite search engine, go to *Maps* and choose *Map a U.S. Address* to search for directions to your home. Enter your street address, city, state, and ZIP. Print and trim the map to fit in your party invitation.

4. Use *Maps* from the AltaVista search engine to create a map of your city. Use the *Fancy Features* and enter your phone number. Print the map.

Activity 6

Use a comprehensive search engine

Using a comprehensive search engine can be very helpful in locating various information quickly. The All-in-One Web site (http://www.AllOneSearch.com) is a compilation of various search tools found on the Internet. Search tools include various categories, such as *People*, *News/Weather*, *Desk Reference*, and *Other Interesting Searches/Services*.

D r i l l

1. Open the All-in-One Web site (http://www.AllOneSearch.com). Browse the various categories and the many search tools within the categories.

2. From the *People* category:

   a. Use BigFoot to find the e-mail address for (*provide a name*).

   b. Use Ahoy! to find the home page for (*provide a name*).

3. From the *News/Weather* category:

   a. Use Pathfinder Weather Now to find your current weather.

   b. Use one of the news searches to find news articles about (*provide current event*).

4. From the *Desk Reference* category:

   a. Find the area code for Jackson, Mississippi _____; Cincinnati, Ohio _____.

   b. Find a quotation from *Bartlett's Quotations* about (*provide the topic*).

5. From the *Other Interesting Searches/Services* category:

   a. Convert the U.S. dollar to Canadian dollar. _____

   b. Locate a recipe for red velvet cake (*or your recipe choice*).

6. Choose a category and determine a search. List category, question, and answer.

Writing 17

gwam 1' 3'

Many people like to say just how lucky a person is when 11 4 29
he or she succeeds in doing something well. Does luck play a 24 8 33
large role in success? In some cases, it might have a small 36 12 37
effect. 37 13 38

Being in the right place at the right time may help, but 11 16 41
hard work may help far more than luck. Those who just wait for 24 20 46
luck should not expect quick results and should realize luck 36 24 50
may never come. 39 26 51

1' | 1 | 2 | 3 | 4 | 5 | 6 | 7 | 8 | 9 | 10 | 11 | 12 |
3' | 1 | 2 | 3 | 4 |

Writing 18

gwam 1' 3'

New golfers must learn to zero in on just a few social 11 4 39
rules. Do not talk, stand close, or move around when another 23 8 44
person is hitting. Be ready to play when it is your turn. 35 12 47

Take practice swings in an area away from other people. 11 15 51
Let the group behind you play through if your group is slow. 24 20 55
Do not rest on your club on the green when waiting your turn. 36 23 59

Set your other clubs down off the green. Leave the green 12 27 63
quickly when done; update your card on the next tee. Be sure 24 31 67
to leave the course in good condition. Always have a good time. 37 36 72

1' | 1 | 2 | 3 | 4 | 5 | 6 | 7 | 8 | 9 | 10 | 11 | 12 |
3' | 1 | 2 | 3 | 4 |

Writing 19

gwam 1' 3'

Do you know how to use time wisely? If you do, then its 11 4 51
proper use can help you organize and run a business better. 24 8 55
If you find that your daily problems tend to keep you from 35 12 59
planning properly, then perhaps you are not using time well. 48 16 63
You may find that you spend too much time on tasks that are 60 20 67
not important. Plan your work to save valuable time. 70 24 70

A firm that does not plan is liable to run into trouble. 12 27 74
A small firm may have trouble planning. It is important 23 31 78
to know just where the firm is headed. A firm may have a 35 35 82
fear of learning things it would rather not know. To say 46 39 86
that planning is easy would be absurd. It requires lots of 58 43 90
thinking and planning to meet the expected needs of the firm. 70 47 94

1' | 1 | 2 | 3 | 4 | 5 | 6 | 7 | 8 | 9 | 10 | 11 | 12 |
3' | 1 | 2 | 3 | 4 |

INTERNET ACTIVITIES 2

 Activity 3   **Explore search engines**

To find information on the World Wide Web (WWW), the best place to start is often a search engine. Search engines are used to locate specific information. Just a few examples of search engines are AltaVista, Excite, Google, AskJeeves, Lycos, and Yahoo.

 To go to a search engine, click on the **Search** button on your Web browser. (Browsers vary.)

D r i l l

1. Go to the search engines on your browser. Click on the first search engine. Browse the hyperlinks available such as Maps, People Finder, News, Weather, Stock Quotes, Sports, Games, etc. Click each search engine and explore the hyperlinks.

2. Conduct the following search using Dogpile, a multithreaded search engine that searches multiple databases;

   a. Open the Web site for Dogpile (http://www.dogpile.com).

   b. In the Search entry box, key the keywords **American Psychological Association** publications; click **Fetch**.

3. Pick two of the following topics and search for each using three of your browser's search engines. Look over the first ten results you get from each search. Which search engine gave you the greatest number of promising results for each topic?

aerobics	antivirus software	career change
censorship	college financing	teaching tolerance

 Activity 4   **Search Yellow Pages**

Searching the Yellow Pages for information on businesses and services is commonplace, both in business and at home. Let your computer do the searching for you the next time. Several search engines provide a convenient hyperlink to the Yellow Pages.

D r i l l

1. Click the **Search** button in your Web browser. Browse the search engines to locate the hyperlinks for the Yellow Pages; click to open this valuable site.

2. Determine a city that you would like to visit. Assume you will need overnight accommodations. Use the Yellow Pages to find a listing of hotels in this city.

3. Your best friend lives in (*you provide the city*); you want to send him/her flowers. Find a listing of florists in this city.

4. You create a third scenario and find listings.

INTERNET ACTIVITIES I

 **Activity 1**

Open Web Browser

Know your Browser

Knowing your browser includes opening the browser, opening a Web site, and getting familiar with the browser toolbar. You will also learn to set a bookmark at a favorite Web site.

Word users can quickly access the Internet while in *Word* by using the Web toolbar.

1. Display the Web toolbar by right-clicking on any toolbar and then choosing **Web** from the list of choices.

2. Open your Web browser by clicking the **Start Page** button on the Web toolbar. The Web page you have designated as your Home or Start Page displays.

Start Page

D r i l l 1

1. Begin a new *Word* document.
2. Display the Web toolbar.
3. Click the **Start Page** button to open your Web browser.

Open Web Site

With the Web browser open, click **Open** or **Open Page** from the **File** menu (or click the **Open** button if it is available on your browser's toolbar). Key the Web address (e.g., http://www.weather.com) and click **Open**. The Web site displays.

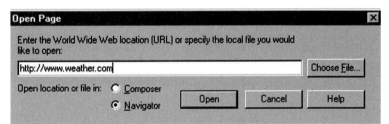

Shortcut: Click inside the Location or Address entry box, key the web address, and press ENTER.

A **Web address** or site—commonly called the *URL* or *Uniform Resource Locator*—is composed of one or more domains separated by periods: http://www.house.gov/.

As you move from left to right in the address, each domain is larger than the previous one. In the Web address above, *gov* (United State government) is larger than *house* (House of Representatives). Other domains include educational institutions (.edu), commercial organizations (.com), military sites (.mil), and other organizations (.org).

A Web address may also include a directory path and filenames separated by slashes. In the address below, the Web document named *news* resides at this site. http://ur.mstate.edu/news/

Drill 2

Key the sentences, correcting the errors in pronoun case. Save as pronoun-drill2.

1. Marie and me have volunteered to work on the committee.
2. Give the assignment to George and I.
3. It is she who received the free airline ticket.
4. It was not me who sent in the request.
5. She has more time available than me for handling this project.
6. Did you see Cheryl and he at the opening session?

Drill 3

Key the sentences, correcting the errors in pronoun and antecedent agreement. Save as pronoun-drill3.

1. Each student must have their own data disk.
2. Several students have his or her own computer.
3. Some of the employees were happy with their raises.
4. The company has not decided whether they will make profit sharing available.
5. All candidates must submit his or her résumé. (*To key the acute accent mark, press* CTRL + *apostrophe; then key* **e**.)
6. Napoleon organized their armies.

 Apostrophe Guides

Apostrophes

1. Add 's to a singular noun not ending in *s*.

2. Add 's to a singular noun not ending in *s* or *z* sound if the ending *s* is pronounced as a syllable.
   Sis's lunch, Russ's car, Buzz's average

3. Add ' only if the ending *s* or *z* is awkward to pronounce.
   series' outcome, ladies' shoes, Delibes' music, Cortez' quest

4. Add 's to a plural noun that does not end in *s*.
   men's notions, children's toys, mice's tracks

5. Add only ' after a plural noun ending in *s*.
   horses' hooves, lamps' shades

6. Add 's after the last noun in a series to show joint possession of two or more people.
   Jack and Judy's house; Peter, Paul, and Mary's song

7. Add 's to each noun to show individual possession of two or more persons.
   Li's and Ted's tools, Jill's and Ed's races.

Drill 4

Key the sentences, correcting all errors in apostrophes. DS between items. Save as apostrophes-drill4.

1. Mary Thomas, my neighbors sister, will take care of my son.
2. The assistant gave him the instructors telephone number.
3. The announcers microphone is never shut off.
4. His father-in-laws home will be open for touring next week.
5. Two hours time is not sufficient to set up the exhibit.
6. Someones car lights have been left on.

Drill 2

Open the following Web sites. Identify the high-level domain for each site.

1. http://www.weather.com _____

2. http://fbla-pbl.org _____

3. http://www.army.mil _____

4. http://www.senate.gov _____

Drill 3

Open the following Web sites and identify the filenames.

1. http://www.cnn.com/TRAVEL/ _____

2. http://espn.go.com/ncaa/ _____

3. http://www.usps.gov/ctc/welcome.htm _____

Explore the Browser's Toolbar

The browser's toolbar is very valuable when surfing the Internet. Become familiar with your browser's toolbar by studying the screen. Browsers may vary slightly.

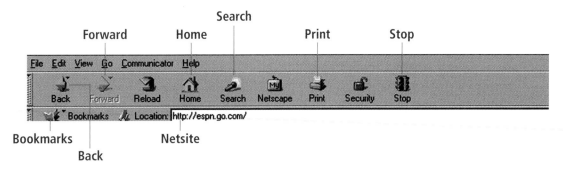

Netsite entry box	Displays the active URL or Web site address.
Back	Moves to Web sites or pages visited since opening the browser.
Forward	Moves forward to sites visited prior to using the Back button. (The Forward button is ghosted if the Back button has not been used.)
Print	Prints a Web page.
Home	Returns to the Web page designated as the Home or Start Page.
Stop	Stops computer's search for a Web site.
Search	Opens one of the Internet search engines.
Bookmarks	Moves to the list of Web sites marked for easy access.

Drill 4

1. Open the following Web sites:
   a. http://nike.com
   b. http://realage.com
   c. http://mapquest.com
   d. A site of your choice

2. Click the **Back** button twice. The_____Web site displays.

3. Click the **Forward** button once. The_____Web site displays.

4. Print the active Web page.

COMMUNICATION SKILLS 3

Pronoun Guides

Pronoun Case

Use the **nominative case** (*I, you, we, she, he, they, it, who*):

1. When the pronoun acts as the **subject of a verb**.

> Jim and *I* went to the movies.
> Mike and *she* were best friends.

2. When the pronoun is used as a **predicate pronoun**. (The verb *be* is a linking verb; it links the noun/pronoun to the predicate.)

> It was *she* who answered the phone.
> The person who objected was *I*.

Use the **objective case** (*me, you, us, her, him, them, it, whom*):

3. When the pronoun is used as a **direct** or **indirect object**.

> Jill invited *us* to the meeting.
> The printer gave Bill and *me* tickets to the game.

4. When the pronoun is an **object of the preposition**.

> I am going with **you** and **him**.
> This issue is between **you** and **me**.

Pronoun-Antecedent Agreement

1. The **antecedent** is the word in the sentence that the pronoun refers to. In the examples, the antecedent is bold and the pronoun is in italics.

> **Players** must show *their* birth certificates.
> The *boy* lost **his** wallet.

2. The antecedent must agree with the pronoun in **person** (first, second, third).

> **I** am pleased that *my* project placed first. (Both are first person.)
> **You** must stand by *your* display at the science fair. (Both are second person.)
> The ash **tree** has lost *its* leaves. (Both are third person.)

3. The antecedent must agree with the pronoun in **gender** (neuter when gender of antecedent is unknown).

> **Gail** said that *she* preferred the duplex apartment.
> The adjustable **chair** sits firmly on *its* five-leg base.
> The **dog** looked for *its* master for days.

4. The antecedent must agree with the pronoun in **number**. If the antecedent of a pronoun is singular, use a singular pronoun. If the antecedent is plural, use a plural pronoun.

> All **members** of the class paid *their* dues.
> **Each** of the Girl Scouts brought **her** sleeping bag.

D r i l l   1

PRONOUN CHOICE

1. Open **pronoun** from the data files. Save it as **pronoun-drill1**.
2. Follow the specific directions provided in the data file. Save again and print.

Bookmark a Favorite Web Site

When readers put a book aside, they insert a bookmark to mark the place. Internet users also add bookmarks to mark their favorite Web sites or sites of interest for browsing later.

To add a bookmark:

1. Open the desired Web site.

2. Click **Bookmarks** and then **Add Bookmark**. (Browsers may vary on location and name of Bookmark button.)

To use a bookmark:

1. Click **Bookmarks** (or **Communicator**, **Favorites**, or **Window Bookmarks**).

2. Select the desired bookmark. Click or double-click, depending on your browser. The desired Web site displays.

Drill 5

1. Open these favorite Web sites and bookmark them on your browser.

   a. http://www.weather.com

   b. http://www.cnn.com

   c. http://ask.com

   d. Key the Web address of a city you would like to visit (destin.com)

2. Use the bookmarks to go to the following Web sites to find answers to the questions shown.

   a. The Weather Channel—What is today's temperature in your city? _____

   b. CNN—What is today's top news story? _____

   c. Ask Jeeves. Ask a question; then find the answer. _____

   d. City Web site you bookmarked—Find one attraction in the city to visit. _____

Activity 2

Set up e-mail addresses

Electronic mail

Electronic mail or **e-mail** refers to electronic messages sent by one computer user to another computer user. To be able to send or receive e-mail, you must have an e-mail address, an e-mail program, and access to the Internet or an intranet (in-house network).

Many search engines such as Excite, Google, Lycos, Hotbot and others provide free e-mail via their Web sites. These e-mail programs allow users to set up an e-mail address and then send and retrieve e-mail messages. To set up an account and obtain an e-mail address, the user must (1) agree to the terms of agreements, (2) complete an online registration form, and (3) compose an e-mail name and password.

Drill 1

1. Click the Search button on the browser's toolbar. Click a search engine that offers free e-mail.

2. Click **Free E-mail** or **Mail**. (Terms will vary.)

3. Read the Terms of Agreement and accept.

4. Enter an e-mail name. This name will be the login-name portion of your e-mail address.

5. Enter a password for your e-mail account. For security reasons, do not share your password, do not leave it where others can use it, and avoid choosing pet names or birth dates.

6. Review the entire registration form and submit it. You will be notified immediately that your e-mail account has been established. (If your e-mail name is already in use by someone else, you may be instructed to choose a different name before your account can be established.)

MODULE 6 Checkpoint

Objective Assessment

Answer the questions below to see if you have mastered the content of Module 6.

1. A vertical list of information within a table is referred to as a(n) _____.
2. To move to the next cell in a table, press the _____ key.
3. A quick way to select an entire table is by clicking on the _____ _____ _____ .
4. To center a table horizontally on the page, use the _____ _____ option.
5. Preformatted styles can be applied to tables by using the _____ feature.
6. A row can be added at the end of the table by clicking the insertion point in the last cell and pressing _____.
7. The Table feature that allows you to join cells is referred to as _____ Cells.
8. Text can be rotated within the cell by clicking on the _____ _____ _____ button.
9. The _____ toolbar provides easy access to features that change the appearance of a table.
10. Whole numbers are generally aligned at the _____; whereas text is generally aligned at the _____.

Performance Assessment

Document 1
Create Table

1. Format the main and secondary headings in 14-point bold. Increase row 1 height to approximately 1", and apply 15% shading.
2. Increase row 2 height to .45". Center the headings vertically within the cells.
3. Right-align column B. Set a decimal tab in column C to align numbers and center under column head.
4. Change line spacing of rows 3–9 to 1.5. Adjust column widths, and center the table horizontally and vertically.
5. Save as **checkpoint6-d1**. Print but do not close.

UNIVERSITY OF NEVADA		
College of Business		
Department	**Majors**	**Growth Rate**
Accounting	945	3.65%
Banking, Finance, and Insurance	1,021	2.17%
Communications	326	-2.5%
Economics	453	1.4%
International Business	620	14.74%
Management Science	1,235	11.8%
Marketing	1,357	10.38%

Document 2
Edit table

1. Save the table as **checkpoint6-d2**.
2. Add a row in alphabetical order for **Computer Information Systems** that has **8,756** majors and a **14.5%** growth rate. Save and print.

Send E-mail Message

To send an e-mail message, you must have the address of the computer user you want to write. Business cards, letterheads, directories, etc., now include e-mail addresses. Often a telephone call is helpful in obtaining e-mail addresses. An e-mail address includes the user's login name followed by @ and the domain (sthomas@yahoo.com)

Creating an e-mail message is quite similar to preparing a memo. The e-mail header includes TO, FROM, and SUBJECT. Key the e-mail address of the recipient on the TO line, and compose a subject line that concisely describes the theme of your message. Your e-mail address will automatically display on the FROM line.

Drill 2

1. Open the search engine used to set up your e-mail account. Click **E-mail** or **Mail**. (Terms will vary.)

2. Enter your e-mail name and password when prompted.

E-mail Message 1

3. Enter the e-mail address of your instructor or another student. Compose a brief message describing the city you would like to visit. Mention one of the city's attractions (from Activity 1, Drill 5). Include a descriptive subject line. Send the message.

E-mail Message 2

4. Enter your e-mail address. The subject is **Journal Entry for March 29, 200-**. Compose a message to show your reflections on how keyboarding is useful to you. Share your progress in the course and your plan for improving this week. Send the message.

Respond to Messages

Replying to e-mail messages

Reading one's e-mail messages and responding promptly are important rules of netiquette (etiquette for the Internet). However, avoid responding too quickly to sensitive situations.

Forwarding e-mail messages

Received e-mail messages are often shared or forwarded to other e-mail users. Be sure to seek permission from the sender of the message before forwarding it to others.

Drill 3

1. Open your e-mail account if it is not open.

2. Read your e-mail messages and respond immediately and appropriately to any e-mail messages received from your instructor or fellow students. Click **Reply** to answer the message.

3. Forward the e-mail message titled *Journal Entry for March 29, 200-* to your instructor.

4. Delete all read messages.

Attach a Document to an E-mail Message

Electronic files can be attached to an e-mail message and sent to another computer electronically. Recipients of attached documents can transfer these documents to their computers and then open them for use.

Drill 4

1. Open your e-mail account if it is not open.

2. Create an e-mail message to your instructor that states your homework is attached. The subject line should include the specific homework assignment (**xx-profile**, for example).

3. Attach the file by clicking **Attach**. Use the browser to locate the homework assignment. (E-mail programs may vary.)

4. Send the e-mail message with the attached file.

45d-d3
Table in Landscape Orientation

1. Open **45d-d2** and save it as **45d-d3**.
2. Change the orientation to landscape.
3. Insert a new column between columns A and B. Remerge the cells in row 1, and adjust the width of row 1 to the size of the table.
4. Key the data below in the new column; then adjust the column widths.

   Publisher
   Bodwin
   American
   TWSS
   Bodwin
   TWSS

5. Insert a new row above *Pommery Mountain*, add the information below, center the table again, and save the file.

   The Lion and the Mouse   **American**   **2002 63,500.00**   **22.75**

45d-d4
Table with Merged Cells and Rotated Text

1. Create a nine-row, seven-column table. Then merge the cells in row 1, and key the main heading. Adjust row 1 height to approximately .5".
2. Merge the appropriate cells in row 2, and key the heading **Reporting Method**.
3. Merge cells A2 and A3, and key the heading **Type of Request**. Key the other headings in row 3, and rotate the text to read from bottom to top.
4. Adjust the column widths, and align the rotated headings at the bottom and horizontal center. Align all other headings vertically and horizontally at center.
5. Center the *X*s in the columns, apply 1.5 spacing to these columns, and change the outer border to a double line.
6. Center the table vertically and horizontally on the page. Save as **45d-d4**.

LOAN CHANGE REQUEST GUIDELINES						
	Reporting Method					
Type of Request	Electronic Branch	On-line FAPS	E-Mail	Phone	Fax	Paper Form
Address Change/Correction	X	X	X	X	X	
Disbursement Increase	X	X	X	X	X	FFELP 18
Enrollment Status Change	X	X	X	X	X	SSCR 21
Late Guarantee	X	X			X	FFELP 1, 3
Name Change/Correction	X	X	X	X	X	
SSN Change			X	X	X	

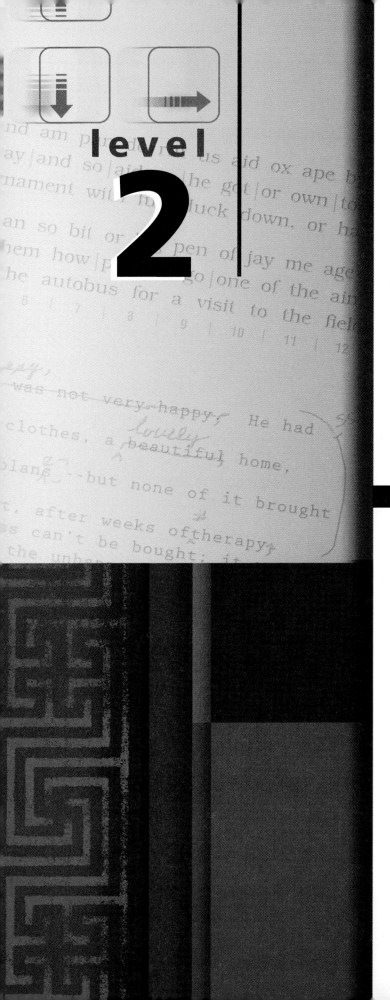

level 2

Formatting Business Documents

KEYBOARDING

To key about 40 *wam* with good accuracy.

DOCUMENT DESIGN SKILLS

To format accurately business letters, memos, reports, and tables.

To apply basic design skills to newsletters and announcements.

WORD PROCESSING SKILLS

To learn the basic word processing competencies (Core).

To create, edit, and format documents efficiently.

COMMUNICATION SKILLS

To apply proofreaders' marks and revise text.

To compose simple e-mails and other documents.

Applications

45d-d1
Table without Borders

1. Set 1" side margins, and leave an approximate 2" top margin. Prepare the following document as a table; however, do not print any borders.
2. Number the bold items in column A. Use **Decrease Indent** to move the numbers to the left margin. Change the width of column A to approximately 2.25". Add a blank line below each row except the last. Save the file as **45d-d1**.

NOTEBOOK SECURITY GUIDELINES

Choose an easy-to-use security system.	Select a security system that is easy to use. If the security system is difficult to use and requires complicated steps, users will either not use it or look for ways to defeat it.
Assign someone to be in charge of notebook security.	One or more persons in the company should be responsible for monitoring the hardware and software on notebook computers. This person needs to be in charge of disseminating security rules and making sure that the rules are followed.
Apply several levels of security.	Different levels of security should be applied to different levels of employees. A CEO or an engineer working in the company's R & D department may be working with data that will require a higher level of security than someone in the art department. Don't bog down the artist with the high level of security needed for the CEO.
Most laptop/notebook thefts are opportunistic.	Train users to be alert and to keep an eye on their computers at all times. Remind them to use extra caution when passing through airports and staying in hotels.
Hold users responsible for their computers.	Encourage users to take precautions, and punish those who are careless by taking away laptop privileges.

45d-d2
Table with AutoFormat

1. Key the table. Center column B; set decimal tabs for columns C and D, resulting in the numbers appearing centered within the columns.
2. Adjust the column widths, change the line spacing to 1.5 for rows 2–7, and apply Table List 4 style.
3. Increase row 1 height to approximately .45", center the table vertically and horizontally, and save the file as **45d-d2**.

LARSON LEARNING			
Book Title	**Publication**	**Sales**	**Unit Price**
Adventures of Sally Boyer	2002	478,769.00	22.85
Tale of Five Cities	2001	91,278.00	32.50
Horrel Hill Adventures	2002	89,412.00	29.00
Pommery Mountain	2002	194,511.00	33.75
Tom Creek's Adventures	2001	105,750.00	27.50

module 3

Word Processing Basics

OBJECTIVES

* Create and format memos.
* Save, preview, and print documents; use Help.
* Create and modify character and paragraph formats.
* Apply communication skills.

LESSON 26 | Get Started

New Functions
26a

Start Word

You are about to learn one of the leading word processing packages available today. At the same time, you will continue to develop your keyboarding skill. You will use *Microsoft Word*® to create and format professional-looking documents. *Word* will make keying documents such as letters, tables, and reports easy and fun.

When you first start *Word*, the screen appears with two windows. The left area is a blank document screen where you can enter text. The right area is called the **Task Pane**. The available options on the Task Pane are:

Open a Document: Lists files that you can click to open.

New: Lists types of new documents that can be created.

New from Existing Document: Enables you to create a new file from an existing file.

New from Template: Enables you to create a new file from a template.

Follow the steps in Drill 1 to start *Microsoft Word*; then study the illustration of the opening *Word* screen to learn the various parts of the screen.

LESSON 45 | Table Assessment

Skillbuilding

45a
Warmup
Key each line three times SS; DS between 3-line groups.

alphabet	1	Jacob Kazlowski and five experienced rugby players quit the team.
figures	2	E-mail account #82-4 is the account for telephone (714) 555-0108.
double letters	3	Anne will meet with the committee at noon to discuss a new issue.
easy	4	The men may pay my neighbor for the work he did in the cornfield.

| 1 | 2 | 3 | 4 | 5 | 6 | 7 | 8 | 9 | 10 | 11 | 12 | 13 |

45b
Timed Writing
Assess Straight-Copy Skill

Take two 3' timings. Strive to key with control and fluency.

  all letters

	gwam	3'	5'

Whether any company can succeed depends on how well it fits into the economic system. Success rests on certain key factors that are put in line by a management team that has set goals for the company and has enough good judgment to recognize how best to reach these goals. Because of competition, only the best-organized companies get to the top.

A commercial enterprise is formed for a specific purpose: that purpose is usually to equip others, or consumers, with whatever they cannot equip themselves. Unless there is only one provider, a consumer will search for a company that returns the most value in terms of price; and a relationship with such a company, once set up, can endure for many years.

Thus our system assures that the businesses that manage to survive are those that have been able to combine successfully an excellent product with a low price and the best service—all in a place that is convenient for the buyers. With no intrusion from outside forces, the buyer and the seller benefit both themselves and each other.

gwam 3'/5':
4 2
8 5
13 8
17 10
21 13
23 14
27 16
31 19
36 21
40 24
43 27
47 28
51 31
56 33
60 36
64 39
69 41
70 42

3' | 1 | 2 | 3 | 4 |
5' | 1 | 2 | 3 |

Assessment: Tables

45c
Timed production: 25'

 Continue

 Check

With CheckPro 2002: When you complete a document, proofread it, check the spelling, and preview for placement. When you are completely satisfied with the document, click the **Continue** button to move to the next document. You will not be able to return and edit a document once you continue to the next document. Click the **Check** button when you are ready to error-check the test. Review and/or print the document analysis results.

Without CheckPro 2002: On the signal to begin, key the documents in sequence. When time has been called, proofread all documents again; identify errors, and determine *g-pwam*.

$$g\text{-}pwam = \frac{\text{total words keyed}}{25}$$

D r i l l   1 | START WORD

1. Turn on the computer and the monitor. When the *Windows* Log On screen displays, key your password and click **OK** to display the *Windows* desktop.

2. Click the **Start** button at the bottom of the screen. Point to **Programs** to display the Programs menu; then click **Microsoft Word 2002** to display the *Microsoft Word* document screen.

3. If the program does not fill the entire screen, you will need to maximize the window. You will learn about the Maximize button in the next section.

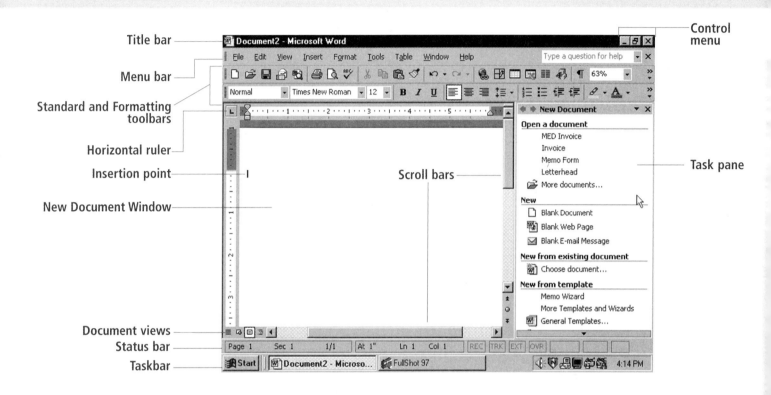

Title bar	Displays the name of the application and document that are currently open.
Control menu	Buttons that size (enlarge or shrink) and close a window. Buttons include Minimize, Restore, and Close.
Menu bar	Displays drop-down menus from which commands can be selected.
Standard toolbar and Formatting toolbar	Display buttons that provide access to common commands. The name of each button displays when you point to it.
Horizontal ruler	Displays the margins, tabs, and indents. To change the display of the Ruler, choose **Ruler** from the View menu. A vertical ruler displays in Print Layout View.
New Document window	A blank area on the screen where you can enter text.
Task Pane	Displays options for opening files and creating new documents.
Insertion point	Blinking vertical line that shows where the text you key will appear. Moving the pointer with the mouse does not move the insertion point until you click the mouse.
Document views	Display documents in four views: Normal, Print Layout, Outline, and Web Layout. You will use Normal most of the time, which enables you to see more of the document.
Scroll bars	Enable you to move rapidly through documents.
Status bar	Displays information about the document such as page number and position of the insertion point.
Taskbar	Displays the Start button and whatever programs are currently running.

44c-d4
Table in Landscape Orientation

1. Key the table. Then apply the bullets. Align the bullets at the left edge of the cell.
2. Bold column A. Align the text at the left, and center it vertically within the cells.
3. Change the table border using the Grid setting on the Tables and Borders toolbar; change the line width to 2¼.
4. Change the table to landscape orientation, and widen column B so that all but the two longest entries fit on one line. Preview the document and, if necessary, adjust the column widths again to improve the appearance.
5. Center the page vertically.
6. Use Table AutoFormat to apply the Table Professional style. Center-align the main heading vertically and horizontally. Align the text in column A at the left, and center it vertically again. Save the table as **44c-d4**.

BENEFITS OF DSL SERVICE	
Improves productivity and eliminates frustration	▪ Never a busy tone; always on, ends busy signals and dropped calls. ▪ High-speed Internet access; greatly reduces wait time when uploading or downloading files.
Saves money	▪ Unlimited Internet access for one affordable flat rate. ▪ One dedicated connection; no extra costs for network of multiple users. ▪ No additional telephone company fees or usage charges.
Maximizes growth potential	▪ Increased bandwidth enables you to fully take advantage of the Internet. ▪ Scalable enhanced services and applications that can accommodate change and growth with your business needs.

COURTESY OF © PHOTODISC, INC.

N E W S | on casual dress

Many companies have now established casual dress codes. Casual dressing implies that the clothing is appropriate for business yet still commands respect. Examples of casual attire are slacks, khakis, polo shirts, blouses, and other comfortable apparel. Casual dress code does not mean that employees may look sloppy. Tee-shirts, old sneakers, or improperly fitting clothing are not appropriate.

Appropriate dress plays an important role in the impression an employee creates with clients, customers, and even other employees. If you are hoping to climb the corporate ladder, you need to plan your dress carefully and always look professional.

Enter Text

When you key text, it is entered at the insertion point (the blinking vertical bar). When a line is full, the text automatically moves to the next line. This feature is called **wordwrap.** To begin a new paragraph, press ENTER. To indent the first line of a paragraph to the first default tab, press the TAB key.

To change or edit text, you must move the insertion point around within the document. You can move to different parts of the document by using the mouse or the keyboard. To use the mouse, move the I-beam pointer to the desired position and click the left mouse button. You can also use the arrow keys on the keyboard to move the insertion point to a different position.

D r i l l   2 | ENTER TEXT

1. If the opening *Word* screen does not fill your entire screen, click the **Maximize** button.

2. Key the text that follows using wordwrap. Press ENTER twice only at the ends of paragraphs to DS between paragraphs. Ignore any red and green wavy lines that may appear under text as you key.

3. Using the mouse, move the insertion point immediately before the *S* at the beginning of the document.

4. Key your name. Press ENTER four times. Notice that paragraph 1 moves down four lines.

5. Use the Right arrow key to move the insertion point to the left of the *h* in *homework*. Key the word **new** followed by a space. Notice that text moves to the right.

6. Keep the document on the screen for the next drill.

Serendipity, a new homework research tool from Information Technology Company, is available to subscribers of the major online services via the World Wide Web. **(Press ENTER two times.)**

Offered as a subscription service aimed at college students, Serendipity is a collection of tens of thousands of articles from major encyclopedias, reference books, magazines, pamphlets, and Internet sources combined into a single searchable database.

Serendipity puts an electronic library right at students' fingertips. The program offers two browse-and-search capabilities. Users can find articles by entering questions in simple question format or browse the database by pointing and clicking on key words that identify related articles. For more information, call 800-555-0174 or address e-mail to lab@serendipity.com.

Menu Bar Commands

The commands available in *Word* are listed in menus located on the menu bar at the top of your screen. The names of the menus indicate the type of commands they contain. You can execute all commands using the proper menu. When you click an item on the menu bar, a menu cascades or pulls down and displays the available commands. Note that common shortcuts including toolbar buttons and keyboard commands are provided when appropriate. The File menu that follows illustrates the main characteristics of pull-down menus.

Applications

Center all tables
vertically on the page.

44c-d1
Table with
Rotated Cells

To size columns to the same
width quickly, select the
columns, on the Table menu
click **AutoFit**, and then click
**Distribute Columns
Evenly**.

✳ 1. Key the table. Then increase the width of column A to fit the longest line on one line. Rotate the headings for columns B–G. Adjust columns B–G so they are approximately the same width. Increase the height of row 2 so the rotated headings display attractively.

2. Align the column headings at center.

3. Change line spacing to 1.5 for rows 3–7. Increase the height of row 1 to .75", and align the text in the center. Save the file as **44c-d1**.

COMPARISON OF TOP-RATED LAPTOP COMPUTERS						
Manufacturer/Model	17" XGA display	Integrated modem	DVD drive	CD drive	Extra power supply	Carrying case
Americorp Ultra 450	X	X		X		X
BroadConnection L-2001		X	X		X	X
Davis-Packard V190	X	X	X		X	X
Standford Super Laptop	X	X	X		X	X
VMP L-7611		X		X	X	X

44c-d2
Create and Edit a Table

1. Increase the height of row 1 to 1". Center the text vertically within the cell, and add 15% shading.

2. Adjust the column widths attractively, and center the table horizontally and vertically.

3. Add two items to the agenda in correct sequence: **9:00-9:50 Mark Baker, Project Manager; 3:45-4:30 Jan Mason, Human Resources Manager**. Center-align the text in column A. Save it as **44c-d2**.

INTERVIEW SCHEDULE	
Conference Room 1	
10:00-10:50 a.m.	Alice Salva, Marketing Manager
11:00-11:50 a.m.	Roger Eason, Advertising Director
12:15-1:45 p.m.	Catered Lunch with Sales Team
2:00-3:30 p.m.	Ginger Folger, Vice President of Marketing

44c-d3
Revise Table with
Rotated Text

1. Open document **44c-d1**, and add the following manufacturers in alphabetical order.
   Royal Computers L210 offers an integrated modem, DVD drive, extra power supply, and carrying case.
   CNS Computers U550 offers the 17" XGA display, an integrated modem, CD drive, and carrying case.

2. Use Table AutoFormat to apply the Table Professional style.

3. Center the text vertically in row 1. Save the document as **44c-d3**.

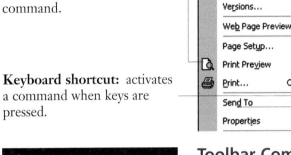

Toolbar button: indicates button to click to activate a command.

Keyboard shortcut: activates a command when keys are pressed.

Ellipsis (...): indicates dialog box will display.

Arrow: indicates additional commands are available.

Bold: indicates the command can be used.

Dimmed command: indicates the command cannot be used.

Underlined letter: activates a command when keyed.

Bottom arrow: indicates additional commands are available.

✳ Discover

If the Standard and Formatting toolbars do not display on separate lines:

■ Click the chevrons (>>) at the right of the toolbar.

■ Click the option **Show Buttons on Two Rows**.

Option: Click **Customize** on the toolbar menu. On the **Options** tab, a checkmark should display beside **Show the Toolbars on Two Rows**.

Toolbar Commands

Frequently-used commands also can be accessed using the buttons on the Standard and Formatting toolbars. Whenever you use *Word*, make sure that both toolbars are displayed, with the Standard toolbar on top of the Formatting toolbar. If either toolbar is missing or other toolbars display, change the display following these steps. ✳ See Discover box at left.

Chevrons

To display or hide a toolbar:

1. Position the mouse pointer over any toolbar and click the right mouse button; a shortcut menu appears listing all of the toolbars that are available. (*Option:* Click **View** on the menu bar; then click **Toolbars**.)

2. Click to the left of **Standard** or **Formatting**, placing a checkmark next to its name. The toolbar displays. If toolbars other than the Standard or Formatting toolbars are displayed, click the toolbar name to remove the checkmark and hide the toolbar.

3. If Task Pane is checked, click to the left of it to close the window. You can also close the Task Pane by clicking the Close button at the upper right of the Task Pane.

Drill 3 | COMMANDS

1. Check that the Standard and Formatting toolbars are the only ones that are displayed and that they each display on a separate row.

2. Point to several buttons on the Standard and Formatting toolbars. Notice the name of each button as it displays.

3. Click **File** on the menu bar. Point to the arrow at the bottom of the File menu, and click the left mouse button to display additional commands. If there is no arrow at the bottom of the File menu, then your entire menu is already displayed.

4. Click **Edit** on the menu bar. Note that *Cut* is dimmed. A dimmed command is not available; making it available requires another action.

5. Click **File** on the menu bar again. Note that the Save As command is followed by an ellipsis (...). Click **Save As** to display the Save As dialog box. Click **Cancel** to close the Save As dialog box.

6. Click each of the different View buttons on the status bar. Notice that a button is highlighted when that view is active. Return to Normal view.

Change Table Borders and Lines

You can change the appearance of a table by changing the style, width (thickness), and color of the lines. You also can apply different borders to different parts of the table.

When working with borders, keep in mind the difference between gridlines and borders. **Gridlines** are light gray lines that show the structure of a table; **borders** are solid lines over the gridlines. Gridlines do not print, but borders do.

To change table borders:

1. Click in the table, and choose **Borders and Shading** from the Format menu.

2. If necessary, click the **Borders** tab, and choose an appropriate setting.

   a. **None**: No borders on cells; gridlines display but do not print.

   b. **Box**: Borders only on the outside of the table; gridlines display but do not print.

   c. **All**: Borders on all cells.

3. To change the border style, scroll through the Style list and choose a border.

4. To change the color, click the **Color** down arrow and select a border color.

5. To change the border width (thickness), click the **Width** down arrow and select a width.

6. To apply changes to the entire table, be sure that *Table* is displayed in the Apply to list box. To change a cell, click the down arrow in the Apply to list box and select **Cell**.

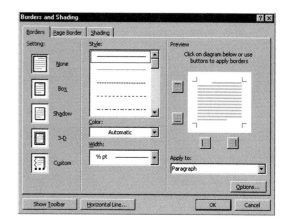

D r i l l   2   TABLE BORDERS

1. Open **44b-drill1**. Click anywhere in the table. In the Borders and Shading dialog box, experiment by changing the border settings to **None**, then **Box**, and then **All**. With each choice, notice what happens to the borders of the table in the Preview area of the screen.

2. Change the border settings of the table to **Box**. Notice that the Box setting applies a black border over the outside border; gridlines within the table do not print. Change the border style to a double line. Save as **44b-drill2**.

D r i l l   3   CELL BORDERS

1. Open **44b-drill 1**. Save it as **44b-drill3**.

2. Change the borders only in row 1. Select row 1. Display the Tables and Borders dialog box; notice that the Apply to box displays *Cell*. Change the border color to red and the width to 2¼ pt. Save the file again.

3. Open **44b-drill2**. Select row 1. Change the setting of row 1 to Grid, the width of the border to 1½ pt, and the color to blue. Save the file as **44b-drill4**. Notice that the gridlines and other changes appear only in row 1.

Save/Save As

Saving a document preserves it so that it can be used again. If a document is not saved, it will be lost once the computer is shut down. It is a good idea to save a document before printing. The first time you save a document, you must give it a filename. Filenames should accurately describe the document. In this course, use the exercise number as the filename (for example, **26b-drill4**).

The Save As command on the File menu is used to save a new document or to rename an existing document. The Save As dialog box contains a Save In list box, a File Name list box, and a Files of Type list box. The Save As dialog box may either be blank or display a list of files that have already been saved.

Word makes it easy to create a new folder when a file is saved. A folder would be created for storing related files. The Create New Folder button is located near the top of the Save As dialog box.

To save a new document:

1. Click the **Save** button on the Standard toolbar. (*Option:* Click **File** on the menu; then click **Save As**.) The Save As dialog box displays.

2. If necessary, change the folder or drive in the Save In box. Use the down arrow to locate the desired drive.

3. To save the document in a new folder, click the **Create New Folder** button at the top of the dialog box. Key the folder name (for example, **Module 3**).

4. Key the filename in the File Name text box.

5. Click the **Save** button or press ENTER. *Word* automatically adds the file extension **.doc** to the filename. This extension identifies the document as a *Word* document.

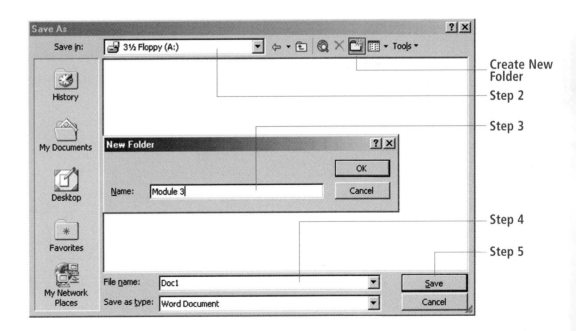

LESSON 44 | Change Appearance of Tables

Skillbuilding

44a
Warmup
Key each pair of
lines twice at
a controlled rate.

1st and 2d 1 Mickey teaches golf three times this month to young children.
fingers 2 Jenny might meet her husband at the new stadium before the match.

3d and 4th 3 Wallace was so puzzled over the sizable proposal due in six days.
fingers 4 Paula will wash, wax, and polish Polly's old, aqua car quite soon.

direct 5 Kilgore, located in a low-lying area, was destroyed by the flood.
reach 6 Dennie framed the ball to help the Jupiter pitcher earn a strike.

| 1 | 2 | 3 | 4 | 5 | 6 | 7 | 8 | 9 | 10 | 11 | 12 | 13 |

New Functions

44b

help keywords
rotate

Rotate Text in a Cell

Sometimes a table is more functional or readable when text or graphics are rotated or turned within the cells. Text can be rotated using the Change Text Direction button on the Tables and Borders toolbar or Text Direction on the Format menu.

To change text direction:

1. Select the row or cells in which you want to change the text direction.

2. Click the **Change Text Direction** button on the Tables and Borders toolbar until the text displays in the desired direction. There are three possible positions: left to right, top to bottom, and bottom to top.

Drill 1 | ROTATE CELLS

1. Create and key the five-column, four-row table shown below.

2. Adjust column widths so that column A is about 3" and the others are about .6". Save the table as **44b-drill1**.

3. Display the Tables and Borders toolbar. Select columns B–E in row 1, and click the **Change Direction** button until the text is rotated in the cells as shown.

4. Click the **Align** button on the Tables and Borders toolbar, and align the headings in row 1 vertically and horizontally within the cells. Save again and print.

Name of Client	Week 1	Week 2	Week 3	Week 4

Name of Client	Week 1	Week 2	Week 3	Week 4

D r i l l 4 | SAVE A FILE

1. The document you keyed in Drill 2 should be displayed. If you are saving your files to a floppy disk, insert a disk into Drive A.

2. Click the **Save** button. The Save As dialog box displays.

3. Click the arrow in the Save In list box to locate the drive you will use. Point to Drive A to highlight it; then click the left mouse button to select it.

4. Click the **Create New Folder** button. The New Folder dialog box displays. Key the name **Module 3 Keys** in the text box; then click **OK**.

5. With the insertion point in the File Name text box, key **26a-drill4** as the filename.

6. Check to see that the default (*Word Document*) is displayed in the Files of Type list box. If not, click the down arrow and select **Word Document**.

7. Click the **Save** button or press ENTER to close the dialog box and return to the document window.

8. Keep the document on the screen for the next drill.

Print Preview

Print Preview enables you to see how a document will look when it is printed. Use Print Preview to check the layout of your document, such as margins, line spacing, and tabs, before printing.

To preview a document:

1. Click **Print Preview** on the Standard toolbar. A full-page version of the document displays. Print Preview displays the page where the insertion point is located.

2. Click **Close** to return to the document screen.

In Print Preview, a special toolbar displays with additional options for viewing the document. For example, when you click on the Magnifier button the mouse pointer changes to a magnifying glass. When you click the magnifying glass on the page, you can see a portion of the document at 100%.

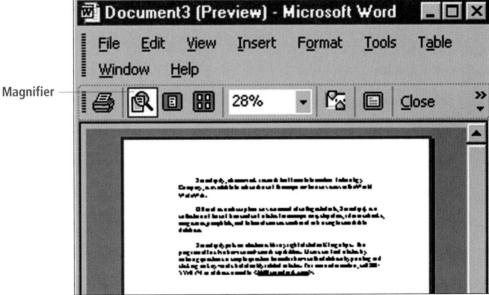

43c-d3
Table with Merged and Split Cells

1. Create a three-column, nine-row table, and change the line spacing of rows 2–9 to 1.5.
2. Merge the cells in row 1, key the title, add 15% shading, and change the row height to 0.5".
3. Key the braced headings (headings that apply to more than one column) in row 2.
4. Split cells B3–B9 into two columns and seven rows. Repeat with cells C3–C9, and key the rest of the table.
5. Center-align the text in row 3. Right-align the numbers in columns B and D. Set a decimal tab to make the numbers in columns C and E appear centered.
6. Adjust column widths; center the table vertically and horizontally, and save it as **43c-d3**.

INTERNATIONAL EXPORTS				
Exports	2001		2002	
Goods and Services	$ Millions	% of Total	$ Millions	% of Total
Agriculture	3,798	8.8	4,783	9.5
Mining	23,587	54.6	25,261	50.4
Manufacturing	11,582	26.8	15,438	30.8
Other Goods	410	1.0	518	1.0
Services	3,791	8.8	4,155	8.3
Total	43,168	100.0	50,155	100.0

43c-d4
Table with Split Columns

1. Create a three-column, ten-row table. Split the column in rows 3–10.
2. Adjust the height of row 1 to .45"; center the text vertically, and add 15% shading.
3. Adjust column widths, center the table vertically and horizontally, and save it as **43c-d4**.

CANADA GEOGRAPHICAL INFORMATION					
Key Islands		Key Mountains		Key Lakes	
Island	Sq. Miles	Mountain	Height	Lake	Sq. Miles
Baffin	195,928	Logan	19,524	Superior	31,700
Victoria	83,897	St. Elias	18,008	Huron	23,000
Ellesmere	75,767	Lucania	17,147	Great Bear	12,095
Newfoundland	42,031	Fairweather	15,300	Great Slave	11,030
Banks	27,038	Waddington	13,104	Erie	9,910
Devon	21,331	Robson	12,972	Winnipeg	9,416
Melville	16,274	Columbia	12,294	Ontario	7,540

Print

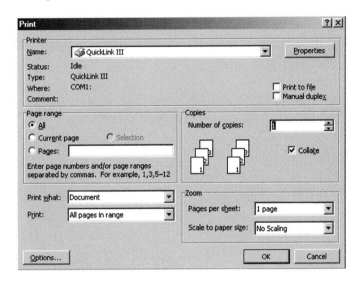 You can print a document by clicking Print on the File menu or by clicking the Print button on the Standard toolbar. Clicking the Print button immediately prints the document using all of the default settings. To view or change the default settings, click **Print** on the File menu or use the keyboard shortcut Ctrl+P to display the Print dialog box.

D r i l l   5 | PREVIEW AND PRINT

1. The document **26a-drill4** should be displayed on your screen.

2. Click the **Print Preview** button to view your document.

3. Change the magnification to **75%**; then change it to **Whole Page**.

4. Click the **Close** button to return to Normal view.

5. Check to be sure that your printer is turned on and has paper.

6. Click **File** on the menu bar, and then click **Print**. Compare your dialog box with the one above. Your printer name may differ, but other choices should be the same. Verify that you will print one copy, and then click **OK**.

Help

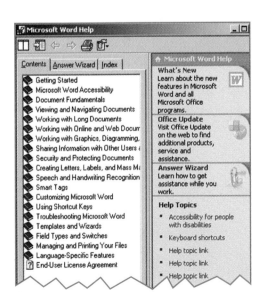

Help provides you with quick access to information about commands, features, and screen elements. To access it, click **Help** on the menu bar, and then click **Microsoft Word Help**. This option includes Contents, Answer Wizard, and Index.

Contents displays a list of topics you can click on to display helpful information.

Answer Wizard enables you to ask a question. When you click **Search,** the Wizard displays a list of topics pertaining to your answer. Click on a topic to display additional information.

Index enables you to key a word or select a keyword to display a list of topics pertaining to the keyword. Click **Search** and then click on the topic to display the information in the right window.

Click outside the Help window to remove the window from the screen.

To align text vertically within a cell:

1. Position the insertion point in the row or cell (or select the rows and columns) in which you want to align the text.

TOP·SALES·REPRESENTATIVES¤		
Sales·Representative¤	Region¤	Sales¤
Avery,·Thomas¤	Northeast¤	100,500¤
Brewer,·Lorraine¤	Plains¤	100,250¤

2. Right-click the mouse.

3. Choose **Cell Alignment** from the shortcut menu; then click the vertical and horizontal center button.

Option: Display the Tables and Borders toolbar, and click the **Cell Alignment** button.

D r i l l 4 ADJUST ROW HEIGHT

1. Open **43b-drill1**. Switch to Print Layout view.

2. Position the mouse pointer on the bottom gridline in row 1 so that the pointer changes to a double vertical arrow. Hold down the ALT key and click the left mouse button. The vertical ruler shows that row 1 measures approximately .29".

3. Drag the bottom gridline until the cell height is approximately 0.5".

4. With the insertion point in row 1, align the text within the cell both vertically and horizontally.

5. Save the document as **43b-drill4**.

Applications

43c-d1
Table with Shading and Adjusted Row Height

1. Key the table following the Table Format Guides on page 146. Leave a 2" top margin.

2. Adjust the height of row 1 to approximately 0.5". Center the text vertically and horizontally, and add 15% shading.

3. Adjust column widths, center the table horizontally, and save it as **43c-d1**.

SAFETY AWARDS		
Award Winner	**Department**	**Amount**
Lorianna Mendez	Accounting	2,000
William Mohammed	Marketing	2,000
Marjorie Adams	Engineering	1,500
Charles Drake	Purchasing	1,000

43c-d2
Table with Rows Inserted and Deleted

1. Open **43c-d1** and make the following changes:

   a. Insert a row after Lorianna Mendez, and add the following information: **Robert L. Ruiz, Research, 2,250**

   b. Insert a row at the end of the table, and add the following information: **Franklin T. Cousins, Security, 500**

   c. Delete the row for William Mohammed, and save the table as **43c-d2**.

Close

Close clears the screen of the document and removes it from memory. You will be prompted to save the document before closing if you have not saved it or to save your changes if you have made any to the document since the previous save. It is necessary to close each document that is open.

To close a document, do one of the following:

- Click **File** on the menu bar; then click **Close**.
- Click the **Close** button at the top right side of the document title bar.

File	Edit
New...	
Open...	
Close	

New

When all documents have been closed, *Word* displays a blank screen. To create a new document, click the **New Blank Document** button on the Standard toolbar.

Open

Any documents that have been saved can be opened and used again. When you open a file, a dialog box displays the names of folders or files within a folder. You can also select files saved on a floppy disk.

To open a document:

1. Click **Open** on the File menu. (*Option:* Click the **Open** button on the Standard toolbar.) The Open dialog box displays.
2. In the Look In box, click the down arrow; then click the drive where your files are stored (Drive A).
3. If necessary, double-click the folder name to display the filenames. Click the desired filename; then click **Open**.

D r i l l 6 | **CLOSE AND OPEN A DOCUMENT**

1. Close the file **26a-drill4** that you saved in Drill 4.
2. Click **New Blank Document** on the Standard toolbar.
3. Close the blank document.
4. Click **Open** on the Standard toolbar, and open the file **26a-drill4**.
5. Click **Save As** on the File menu. In the Save As dialog box, save the file again as **26a-drill4a**. Leave the document on the screen for the next drill.

Exit

Exit saves all documents that are on the screen and then quits the software. When you exit *Word*, you close both the document and the program window. You will be prompted to save before exiting if you have not already saved the document or if you have made changes to it since last saving. Click the **Close** button in the title bar (top bar) to exit *Word*.

Insert and Delete Columns and Rows

Columns can be added to the left or right of existing columns. Rows can be added above or below existing rows. A row also can be added at the end of the table by clicking the insertion point in the last cell and pressing TAB.

To insert rows or columns in a table:

1. Click the insertion point where the new row or column is to be inserted. If several rows or columns are to be inserted, select the number you want to insert.
2. Choose **Insert** from the Table menu.
3. Choose **Rows Above** or **Rows Below** to insert rows. Choose **Columns to the Left** or **Columns to the Right** to insert columns.

To delete rows or columns in a table:

1. Click the insertion point in the row or column to be deleted. If you want to delete more than one row or column, you must first select them.
2. Choose **Delete** from the Table menu, and then choose **Rows or Columns**.

Drill 2 | INSERT ROWS

1. Open **43b-drill1** and insert the following information so that the representatives' names are in alphabetical order.
2. Delete the row containing Heil, Clinton.
3. Save the document as **43b-drill2**, and leave it open.

Connors, Margaret	**South**	**87,560**
Roberts, George	**East**	**97,850**
Zales, Laura	**West**	**93,500**

Drill 3 | INSERT COLUMNS

1. Open **42b-drill1**. Click the insertion point in cell B1, and insert a column to the right.
2. Key the data at the right. Left-align the column data. Adjust the column widths so that all copy fits on one line.
3. Save the document as **43b-drill3**.

Office
Wilshire
Toledo
Lake Forest
Tampa

Adjust Row Height and Align Text Vertically

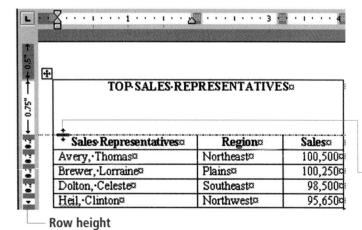

Row height

Row heights can be adjusted to make the table more attractive. They can be adjusted by dragging the row border or by using the Table Properties dialog box. Once cell height is adjusted, the text within the cell will need to be centered vertically.

To adjust row height with the mouse:

1. Switch to Print Layout view to display the Vertical Ruler.
2. Click the insertion point on the gridline of the row to be adjusted. The pointer changes to a double vertical arrow.
3. Drag the gridline up or down until the cell is the height that you want. Hold down the ALT key while dragging the gridline to display the row height.

1. Document **26a-drill4a** should be displayed on your screen. Click **Help** on the menu bar, click **Microsoft Word Help**, and then click the **Index** tab.

2. Key **Thesaurus** as the keyword; then click **Search.**

3. Click **Look up words in the Thesaurus** to view the information in the right window.

4. Key **save** in the keyword box; then click **Search.** Click **Save a document** to view the information.

5. Close document **26b-drill4a**, and exit *Microsoft Word.*

Applications

26b-d1
Create a New Document

1. Start *Microsoft Word.*

2. Create a document by keying the text below. Double-space (DS) between paragraphs.

3. Save the document as **26b-d1.** Print, then close the document.

In Lesson 26, I have learned the basic operations of my word processing software. Today I opened the word processor, created a new document, saved the document, printed the document, closed the document, and exited the software. This new document that I am creating will be named 26b-d1. I will save it so that I can use it in the next lesson to open an existing document.

(Press ENTER two times)

Help is available online for me at all times. If I get stuck on a test, and I cannot use my textbook or solicit the help of my teacher or classmates, I can still rely on using the Microsoft Word Help.

26b-d2
Create a New Document

1. Open a new blank document and key the text below. Press TAB to indent the first line of each paragraph. Double-space (DS) between paragraphs.

2. Save the document as **26b-d2** and print. Close the document. Then exit *Word.*

As the man says, "I have some good news and some bad news." Let me give you the bad news first.

Due to a badly pulled muscle, I have had to withdraw from the Eastern Racquetball Tournament. As you know, I have been looking forward to the tournament for a long time, and I had begun to hope that I might even win it. I've been working hard.

That's the bad news. The good news is that I have been chosen to help officiate, so I'll be coming to Newport News anyway. In fact, I'll arrive there a day earlier than I had originally planned.

So, put the racquet away, but get out the backgammon board. I'm determined to win something on this trip!

Lesson 43 | Revise Tables

Skillbuilding

43a

Key each pair of lines three times at a controlled rate. DS between 6-line groups.

direct 1 June and my brother, Bradly, received advice from junior umpires.

reaches 2 My bright brother received minimum reward for serving many years.

adjacent 3 Clio and Trey were sad that very few voters were there last week.

reaches 4 Western attire was very popular at the massive auction last week.

double 5 Tommie Bennett will go to a meeting in Dallas tomorrow afternoon.

letters 6 Lee will meet Joanne at the swimming pool after accounting class.

New Functions

43b

help keywords
cell

Tables can be revised in a variety of ways including splitting and merging (joining) cells, inserting and deleting columns and rows, adjusting the height of rows and the width of columns, changing the page orientation, or even rotating text.

Merge/Split Cells

Cells can be joined or divided horizontally or vertically by selecting the cells and then choosing the Merge Cells or the Split Cells command on the Table menu or the Tables and Borders toolbar. Frequently, main and secondary headings are included in the table by merging the cells in row 1 and centering the headings in the row.

To merge cells:

Select the cells to be merged. Choose **Merge Cells** from the Table menu, or click the **Merge Cells** button on the Tables and Borders toolbar.

To split cells:

1. Select the cells to be split. Choose **Split Cells** from the Table menu, or click the **Split Cells** button on the Tables and Borders toolbar.
2. In the Split Cells dialog box, indicate the number of columns and rows; click **OK**.

D r i l l   1 | MERGE

1. Create a three-column, eight-row table.
2. Select row 1 and merge the cells. Bold and center the main heading in row 1.

3. Adjust the column widths; right-align column C; center-align the column headings.
4. Center the table horizontally, and center the page vertically. Save it as **43b-drill1**.

TOP SALES REPRESENTATIVES		
Sales Representative	**Region**	**Sales ($)**
Avery, Thomas	Northeast	100,500
Brewer, Lorraine	Plains	100,250
Dolton, Celeste	Southeast	98,500
Heil, Clinton	Northwest	95,650
Packard, Hillary	Southwest	94,800
Stevens, Richard	Central	92,000

LESSON 27 | Edit and Format Text

New Functions

27a

Navigate in a Document

The document window displays only a portion of a page at one time. There are several ways to move quickly through a document to view it.

Keyboard

To move through a document using the keyboard, study the following shortcuts.

To move	Press
Next word	CTRL + ← or → arrow key
One paragraph up or down	CTRL + ↑ or ↓ arrow key
To beginning of line	HOME
To end of line	END
Up one screen	PgUp
Up one page	ALT + CTRL + PgUp
To beginning of document	CTRL + HOME
To end of document	CTRL + END

Scroll Bars

To move through the document using the mouse, use the scroll bars. The vertical scroll bar enables you to move up and down through a document. The horizontal scroll bar enables you to move left and right across a line. Scrolling does not change the position of the insertion point, only your view of the document.

To scroll	Click
Up or down	Scroll bar and drag or click Up and Down arrows
Up one screen	Above the scroll box
Down one screen	Below the scroll box
To a specific page	Drag the vertical scroll box and watch for page number
Left or right	Scroll bar and drag or click arrows

Select Text

To make any formatting changes to existing text, you must first select the text you want to change. Selected text is highlighted in black. You can select text using either the mouse or the keyboard. To deselect text, click anywhere outside of the selected text.

To select text with the mouse:

To select	Do this
Any amount of text	Click at the beginning of the text and drag the mouse over the text.
A word	Double-click the word.
A line	Click in the area left of the line.
Multiple lines	Drag in the area left of the lines (selection bar).
A paragraph	Double-click in the selection bar next to the paragraph, or triple-click anywhere in the paragraph.

42c-d3

Table with AutoFormat

1. Key the table; then apply List 8 style.

2. Center column B, and align column C in the approximate center with a decimal tab.

✳ 3. Total the figures in column C using AutoSum from the Tables and Borders toolbar. Center the table vertically and horizontally.

4. Save the document as **42c-d3** and print.

✳ 5. Change the price of dinner rolls to $20. Recalculate the total. Save as **42c-d3a** and print again.

QUEEN'S BAKERY AND PASTRIES
Catering Invoice

Item	Quantity	Total Price ($)
Cherry nut muffins	3 dozen	25.75
Dinner rolls	4 dozen	18.50
Whole wheat breadsticks	2 dozen	10.00
Brownies	2 dozen	16.00
Assorted pastries	3 dozen	24.00
Total		

42c-d4

Table in Landscape Orientation

✳ 1. Change the page to landscape orientation to position the document horizontally on the page (11" × 8.5"). Landscape orientation is appropriate for tables with many columns or with wide columns. Create and key the table.

2. Adjust the column widths so that all column headings fit on a single line.

3. Select the numbers in column D, and set a decimal tab that aligns the numbers so they appear centered in the column. Center-align columns A, E, F, and G.

4. Change the line spacing to 1.5. Center the table vertically and horizontally on the page, save it as **42d-d4**, and then print.

INTERNATIONAL FINANCIAL SYSTEMS
Collection Status Report

Client Number	Last Name	First Name	Current Balance	Age	Service Started	Last Activity
1002	Castillo	Robert	2,861.63	6-4-99	9-5-00	11-8-00
1003	Aguirre	Janna	115.02	11-30-99	9-6-00	11-30-00
1007	Perez	Linda	1,194.30	3-13-00	9-11-00	12-05-00
1008	Nieto	Victor	1,746.80	12-14-98	9-11-00	12-05-00
1009	Plate	Sharon	1,352.00	8-18-00	9-11-00	12-05-00
1011	Mau	Marianne	942.25	6-10-00	9-11-00	1-15-01

To select text with the keyboard:

To select	Do this
One character to left or right	SHIFT + LEFT or Right arrow
Beginning or end of word	CTRL + SHIFT + Right or Left arrow
End of line	SHIFT + END
Beginning of line	SHIFT + HOME

Drill 1 | NAVIGATE AND SELECT TEXT

1. Open the file you created in Lesson 26, **26b-d1.**

2. Move to the end of the document (CTRL + END).

3. Move to the top of the document (CTRL + HOME).

4. Select the first sentence; then deselect the sentence.

5. Move to the last sentence and select the word **Microsoft**.

6. Move to the beginning of the line (HOME), and select the first sentence.

7. Move to the top of the document (CTRL + HOME), and key your name followed by a DS.

8. Save the document as **27a-drill1**; then close the document.

Character Formats

Character formats apply to letters, numbers, and punctuation marks and include such things as bold, underline, italic, fonts, and font sizes. The Formatting toolbar provides an efficient way to apply character formats. Formatting toolbar buttons also make it easy to align text.

Font style   Font size

To apply character formats as you key:

1. Click the appropriate format button, and key the text to be formatted.

2. When you finish keying the formatted text, click the same button again to turn off the format. Notice that a format button is highlighted when the feature is on.

To apply character formats to existing text:

1. Select the text.

2. Click the appropriate format button.

Font Size and Styles

Word's default font is 12-point Times New Roman. Font size is measured in points. One vertical inch equals 72 points. Most text is keyed in a 10-, 11-, or 12-point font, although a larger font may be used to emphasize headings. *Word* has a variety of font styles available.

To change font size:

1. Select the text to be changed.

2. Click the **Font Size** down arrow.

3. Scroll through the list of available sizes, and click the desired font size.

1. The table **42b-drill2** should be displayed. Click the insertion point in the table.
2. Apply a style of your choice.
3. Save the document as **42b-drill3**.

Applications

42c-d1
Memo with Table with Decimal Tabs

1. Key the following memo to **Robert May**, from **Marcia Lewis**. The subject is **Purchase Order 5122**.
2. Center the data in column A, set a decimal tab to align column C in the approximate center of the column, apply 15% shading to Row 1, adjust the columns widths, and center the table horizontally.
3. DS after the table, and add your reference initials. Save it as **42c-d1**.

The items that you requested on Purchase Order 5122 are in stock and will be shipped from our warehouse today. The shipment will be transported via Romulus Delivery System and is expected to arrive at your location in five days.   ↓2

Item Number	Description	Unit Price
329	Lordusky locking cabinet	212.00
331	Anchorage heavy duty locking cabinet	265.00
387	Lordusky locking cabinet (unassembled)	175.00

↓2

42c-d2
Table with Shading

1. Key the table. Then set a decimal tab to align columns B and C in the approximate center of the column, and add 15% shading to row 1.
2. Adjust the column widths, center the table horizontally, and center the page vertically. Save the table as **42c-d2**.

LOS ALTOS DRY CLEANING SPECIALS

Garment	Regular Price	Special Price
Wool sweater	6.50	5.00
Men's two-piece suit	8.00	6.75
Women's two-piece suit	8.00	6.75
Leather jacket	20.00	18.00
Leather pants	16.00	14.50
Slacks	4.50	3.75
Skirt	4.00	3.00
Blazer	5.00	3.75
Silk shirt/blouse	5.00	4.25

To change font style:

1. Select the text to be changed.
2. Click the **Font** down arrow.
3. Scroll through the list of available styles, and click the desired style.

D r i l l   2   CHARACTER STYLES

1. Open a new blank document.
2. Key your name, and press ENTER.
3. Key the document name **27a-drill2**, and press ENTER four times.
4. Key the sentences that follow, applying the formats as you key.
5. Save the document as **27a-drill2**.

This sentence is keyed in bold.

This sentence is keyed in italic.

This sentence is underlined.

This sentence is keyed in bold and italic and underlined.

This sentence is keyed in 14-point Times New Roman.

This sentence is keyed in 12-point Arial.

Paragraph Formats

Paragraph formats apply to an entire paragraph and can be applied before or after a paragraph has been keyed. Each time you press ENTER, *Word* inserts a paragraph mark and starts a new paragraph. Thus, a paragraph may consist of a single line followed by a hard return (¶ mark) or several lines that wrap and are followed by a hard return. In order to apply paragraph formats such as line spacing or alignment, you must be able to see where paragraphs begin and end. Show/Hide displays hard returns as a paragraph mark (¶).

Show/Hide

¶ Click the **Show/Hide** button on the Standard toolbar to display all nonprinting characters such as paragraph markers (¶) and spaces (··). The Show/Hide button appears highlighted or depressed when it is active. To turn nonprinting characters off, click the **Show/Hide** button again.

Alignment

Alignment refers to the way in which the text lines up. Text can be aligned at the left, center, right, or justified (lined up with both margins). Use the Alignment buttons on the Formatting toolbar to quickly align paragraphs.

To align existing text:

1. Place the insertion point in the paragraph to be changed. If more than one paragraph is affected, select the paragraphs to be aligned.
2. Click the appropriate **Align** button.

To align text as you key:

1. Click the appropriate **Align** button.
2. Key the text. This alignment will remain in effect until you click the button again.

Tables and Borders Toolbar

You can change the appearance of tables by adding shading, borders, patterns, and color. You can use Table AutoFormat to apply a preformatted design to the table, or display the Tables and Borders toolbar, which provides you with many formatting options. To display this toolbar, click **View** on the menu; then click **Toolbars, Tables and Borders**.

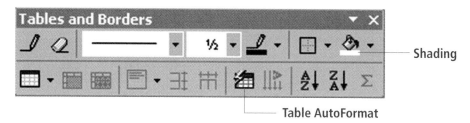

Shading

Table AutoFormat

Shading Cells

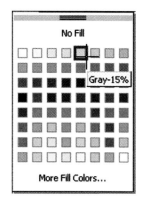

Shading can be applied to cells for emphasis. Normally, shading is applied to emphasize headings, totals, or divisions and sections of a table.

To add shading to cells:

1. Select the cells to be shaded, and click the **Shading** button on the Tables and Borders toolbar.

2. Click the down arrow, and choose a color or shade of gray. For class assignments, choose 15% gray (row 1, item 5).

Option: Choose **Borders and Shading** on the Format menu. Click on the **Shading** tab. Under Style, click the down arrow to change *Clear* to 15%; then click **OK**.

D r i l l   2 | SHADING

1. Drill **42b-drill1** should be displayed.

2. Display the Table and Borders toolbar (**View menu, Toolbars**).

3. Select row 1 and apply 15% shading.

4. Save as **42b-drill2**. Print. Leave the document displayed for the next drill.

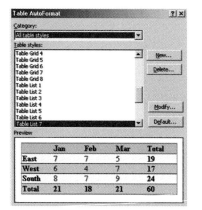

Table AutoFormat

AutoFormat enables you to apply one of *Word*'s many preformatted styles to tables. You can view those styles in the Preview box. Choose a style based on the information in the table. For example, a style with shading in the last row is well suited to a table with totals.

To use AutoFormat:

1. Create the table and key the table data without formats.

2. Click the insertion point in the table, and then click the **AutoFormat** button on the Tables and Borders toolbar.

3. In the Table AutoFormat dialog box, check to see that All table styles is displayed in the Category list box; then choose a style from the Table styles list box.

4. Click **Apply** to apply the style, and return to the table.

Option: Choose Table AutoFormat from the Table menu. Continue with Step 3 above.

D r i l l 3 | ALIGNMENT

1. Open a new blank document, and center **USING ALIGNMENTS** in 14 point and bold. Strike ENTER twice to create a DS.

2. Change to left alignment and 12 point to key the first paragraph.

3. Apply the formatting and alignment as shown in the following document.

4. Save the document as **27a-drill3,** and print a copy. Leave the document on the screen for the next drill.

USING ALIGNMENTS

Left alignment is used for this first paragraph. When left alignment is used, each line in the paragraph begins at the same position on the left side. The right margin will be uneven.

Center alignment

Center titles and short lines.

Use for invitations, announcements, and other documents.

Right alignment is used for this third paragraph. When right alignment is used, each line in the paragraph ends at the same position on the right side. The left side will be uneven.

Justify is used for this fourth paragraph. When justification is used, all lines (except the last line of a paragraph) begin and end at the same position at the left and right margins. Extra spaces are automatically inserted to achieve this look.

Line Spacing

Word's default line spacing is single. When paragraphs are single spaced, the first line of the paragraph normally is not indented. However, a blank line is inserted between paragraphs to distinguish them and to improve readability. Double spacing leaves a blank line between every keyed line. Therefore, it is necessary to indent the first line of each double-spaced paragraph to indicate the beginning of the paragraph. To indent the first line of a paragraph, press the TAB key. The default indention is 0.5".

To change line spacing:

1. Position the insertion point in the paragraph in which you want to change the line spacing. If more than one paragraph is to be changed, select all the paragraphs.

2. Click **Format** on the menu bar; then click **Paragraph**.

3. Select the **Indents and Spacing** tab.

4. Click the arrow in the Line Spacing box; then click **Double**. Click **OK**.

Line spacing can also be changed using the Formatting toolbar. Place the cursor in the paragraph in which the spacing will be changed. Click the **Line Spacing** button; click the Down arrow; then click the desired line spacing. If the Line Spacing button is not displayed, click the chevrons at the right of the toolbar (>>) to display additional formatting options.

LESSON 42 | Format Tables

Skillbuilding

42a
Warmup
Key the entire drill working at a controlled rate. Repeat.

adjacent 1 her err ire are cash free said riot lion soil join went wean news

key 2 sat coil riot were renew forth weed trade power grope owner score

one hand 3 him bear joy age kiln loup casts noun loop facet moon deter edges

4 get hilly are fear imply save phony taste union versa yummy wedge

balanced 5 oak pay hen quay rush such burp urus vial works yamen amble blame

hand 6 cot duty goal envy make focus handy ivory lapel oriel prowl queue

| 1 | 2 | 3 | 4 | 5 | 6 | 7 | 8 | 9 | 10 | 11 | 12 | 13 |

New Functions

42b

Decimal Tabs

 Decimal tabs are used to align numbers at their decimal points when numbers have varying lengths of decimal places. Dollar amounts and other numbers should be aligned at the right.

— Tab marker

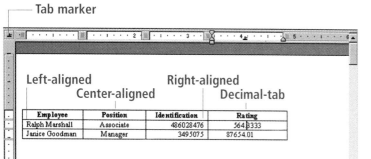

To set a decimal tab:

1. Display the Horizontal Ruler (**View menu, Ruler**).

2. Select the column or cells to be aligned (do not include the column heading).

3. Click the **tab marker** at the far left of the Horizontal Ruler, and change the tab type to a decimal tab.

4. Click the Horizontal Ruler to set a decimal tab.

Drill 1 | DECIMAL TABS

1. Create and key the table. Change the line spacing to 1.5.

2. Center the column headings.

3. Select column B, and center-align the column. Right-align column C.

4. Select cells D2–D5 and set a decimal tab at about 5.4" to align the numbers near the center of the column.

5. Save the document as **42b-drill1**. Keep the document displayed on your screen.

Employee	Position	Identification	Rating
Ralph Marshall	Associate	486028776	564.333
Janice Goodman	Manager	3495075	87654.01
Frank Wiley	Associate	9376	157.198
Dinh Lee	Manager	732	96.52

D r i l l 4 | LINE SPACING

1. Document **27a-drill3** should be on your screen.
2. Click in the first paragraph and change the line spacing to double.
3. Click on **Center Alignment** in the second paragraph. Change the line spacing to 1.5. Note that the spacing change affects only paragraph 2—the paragraph where the insertion point is located.

4. Click in the third paragraph and change the line spacing to Multiple. Leave the document on the screen for the next drill.

Undo/Redo

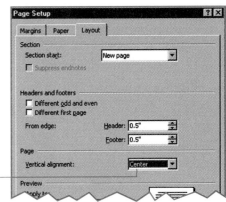 To reverse the most recent action you have taken (such as inserting or deleting text, formatting in bold or underline, changing line spacing, etc.), click the **Undo** button. To reverse several actions, click the Down arrow beside Undo to display a list of recent actions. Then click the action you wish to reverse. Note, however, that all actions you performed prior to the action you select also will be reversed. Commands such as Save and Print cannot be undone this way.

Redo reverses the last Undo and can be applied several times to redo the past several actions. Click on the Down arrow beside Redo to view all actions that can be redone.

D r i l l 5 | UNDO/REDO

1. Document **27a-drill3** should be on your screen.
2. Undo the line spacing change to paragraph 3.
3. Redo the line spacing change.

4. Select the first sentence in paragraph 4, and delete the underline.
5. Redo the underline.
6. Leave the document on the screen for the next drill.

Center Page

The **Center Page** command centers a document vertically on the page. Should extra hard returns (¶) appear at the beginning or end of a document, these are also considered to be part of the document. Be careful to delete extra hard returns before centering a page.

To center a page vertically:

1. Position the insertion point on the page to be centered.
2. From the File menu, select **Page Setup**. The Page Setup dialog box displays.
3. Click the **Layout** tab.
4. Click the **Vertical alignment** down arrow. Select **Center**; then click **OK**.

D r i l l 6 | CENTER PAGE

1. Document **27a-drill3** should be open on your screen.
2. On the File menu, click **Page Setup**; then center the page vertically.

3. Click **Print Preview** to view the entire document, and notice that there is equal space at the top and bottom of the page.
4. Return to Normal view, and save the document as **27a-drill6**.

Applications

41d-d1

Table

1. Leave an approximate 2" top margin. SS the 2-line main heading. Center-align and bold the heading; press ENTER twice. Change the alignment to left, and turn bold off.
2. Create the table using the Table button and key the information in the cells.
3. Select row 1. Bold and center-align the column headings.
4. Adjust the column widths, and center the table horizontally. Select the table, and change the line spacing to 1.5. Save the document as **41d-d1**.

COMPARISON OF CIVILIAN AND MILITARY TIMES

Civilian Time	Military Time
1:00 a.m.	0100
2:00 a.m.	0200
4:15 a.m.	0415
Noon	1200
2:20 p.m.	1420
6:00 p.m.	1800
Midnight	2400

41d-d2

Table

1. Key and format the main heading. Create and key the table.
2. Format the table: center and bold the column headings; change the line spacing to 1.5; adjust the column widths; then center the table horizontally. Save as **41d-d2**.

STAGES OF LIFE SPAN DEVELOPMENT

Stage	Approximate Age
Infancy	Birth to 1 year
Toddler	1 to 3 years
Preschool	3 to 5 years
School age	6 to 12 years
Adolescence	13 to 19 years
Early adulthood	20 to 39 years
Middle adulthood	40 to 65 years
Late adulthood	65 years and over

Edit Text

Once text is keyed, it often needs to be corrected or changed. *Word* automatically corrects some text as you key it and provides various other methods for editing text. These methods are described below.

Insert: Insert mode is the *Word* default. To insert text, click or move the insertion point where the new text is to appear and key the text. Existing text moves to the right.

Delete: Delete is used to remove text that is no longer wanted. To delete a single character, click the insertion point to the left of the character and press DELETE. To delete a word, double-click the word and press DELETE.

Overtype: Overtype replaces existing text with new text that is being keyed. To turn on Overtype, double-click **OVR** on the status bar. To return to Insert mode, double-click **OVR** again.

Drill 7 | EDIT TEXT

1. Open document **26a-drill4.**

2. Edit the document as indicated by the proofreaders' marks below. Use the most efficient method to move within the document to make the changes.

3. Change the line spacing to double. If necessary, delete any extra hard returns between paragraphs.

4. Tab to indent the first line of each paragraph.

5. Print the document, and then save it as **27a-drill7**.

Serendipity, a ~~new homework~~ research tool from Information Technology Company, is available to subscribers of ~~the major~~ online services via the World Wide Web.

Offered as a subscription service aimed at ~~college~~ students, Serendipity is a collection of tens of thousands of articles from ~~major~~ encyclopedias, reference books, magazines, pamphlets, and Internet sources combined into a single searchable database. *with just a computer and a modem*

Serendipity puts an electronic library right at students' fingertips. The program offers two browse-and-search capabilities. Users can find articles by entering questions in simple question format or browse the database by pointing and clicking on key words that identify related articles. For more information, call 800-555-0174 or address e-mail to lab@serendipity.com. *on just about any subject*

Adjust Column Widths

Tables extend from margin to margin when they are created, regardless of the width of the data in the columns. Some tables, however, would be more attractive and easier to read if the columns were narrower. Column widths can be changed manually using the mouse or automatically using AutoFit. Using the mouse enables you to adjust the widths as you like. Once you change the width of a table, you will need to center it horizontally.

Column marker

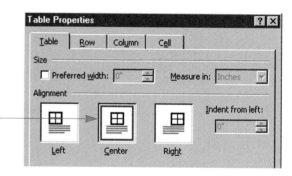

To adjust column widths using the mouse:

1. Point to the column border between the first and second columns in the table.

2. When the pointer changes to ✛, drag the border to the left to make the column narrower or to the right to make the column wider.

3. Adjust the column widths attractively. Leave approximately 0.5" to .75" between the longest line and the border. Use the Horizontal Ruler as a guide.

4. You can display the width of the columns by pointing to a column marker on the ruler, holding down the ALT key, and clicking the left mouse button.

To center a table horizontally:

1. With the insertion point in the table, choose **Table Properties** from the Table menu.

2. Click the **Table tab**, if necessary.

3. Choose the **Center** option in the Alignment box, and click **OK**.

Drill 3 | ADJUST COLUMN WIDTH

1. The document **41b-drill2** should still be displayed on the screen.

2. Use the mouse to adjust the width of the columns so they look attractive.

3. Center the table horizontally.

4. Save the table as **41b-drill3;** then print a copy.

Document Design

41c

Table Format Guides

1. Leave an approximate 2" top margin, or center the table vertically on the page.

2. **Headings:** Center, bold, and key the main heading in all caps. Key the secondary heading a DS below the main heading in bold and centered; capitalize main words. Center and bold all column headings.

3. Adjust column widths attractively, and center the table horizontally.

4. Change the line spacing of the table to 1.5.

5. Align text within cells at the left. Align numbers at the right. Align decimal numbers of varying lengths at the decimal point.

6. When a table appears within a document, DS before and after the table.

Applications

27b-d1
Rough Draft

1. Key the following paragraphs DS, and make the revisions shown.
2. Save the document as **27b-d1**. Print the document.

The World Wide Web (www) and Internet Usenet News groups are electronic fan clubs that offers users a ways to exchange views and information on just about any topic imaginable with people all around the world.
World Wide Web screens contain text, graphics, and pictures *and often audio and video*. Simple pointing and clicking on the pictures and links (underlined words) bring users to new pages or sites of information.

27b-d2
Revising a Document

To save a file in a different file format, click the **Save as type** down arrow and select the desired type.

1. Open the document **27a-drill7**. Select the entire document using the mouse, and change the font to Arial 12 point.
2. Center-align and bold your name.
3. Change the line spacing to 1.5.
4. Italicize Information Technology Company.
5. Center the document on the page.
6. Preview the document, print a copy, and then save it as **27b-d2**.
7. Sometimes it is necessary to save a file in a different file format such as an earlier version of *Word*, in a different application such as *WordPerfect*, or without any formatting (Rich Text Format).
   a. Save **27b-d2** as a *WordPerfecct 5.0* file using the same file name.
   b. Save **27b-d2** in Rich Text Format.
8. Open **27b-d2.rtf**. Display **All Files** in the Files of type entry box. Close without saving or printing.

Skillbuilding

27c
Skill Builder, Lesson A

Use the remaining class time to build your skills using the Skill Builder module within *Keyboarding Pro Multimedia*. Complete these lessons as time permits.

1. Open *Keyboarding Pro Multimedia*. Log on in the usual manner.
2. Click **Edit** on the menu bar and then **Preferences**. On the Preferences dialog box under Skill Builder, click the radio button for **Speed** and then **OK**. (You must choose your preference before entering Skill Builder.)
3. Open the Skill Builder module, and select Lesson A.
4. Beginning with Keyboard Mastery, complete as much of the lesson as time permits.
5. Exit the software. Remove your storage disk. Store your materials as directed.

Format Table, Rows, Columns, or Cells

If you wish to apply a format such as bold, alignment, or line spacing to the table, you must first select the table. Likewise, to format a specific row, column, or cell, you must select the table parts and then apply the format. Editing features such as delete and undo work in the usual manner. Follow these steps to select various parts of the table:

To select	Move the insertion point:
Entire table	Over the table and click the table move handle in the upper left of the table. (Option: **Table menu, Select, Table**). To move the table, drag the table move handle to a new location.
Column	To the top of the column until a solid down arrow appears; click the left mouse button.
Row	To the left area just outside the table until the pointer turns to an open arrow (↗), then click the left mouse button.

Note: You can also select rows and columns by selecting a cell, column, or row, and dragging across or down.

Drill 2 | **CREATE TABLES**

1. Center-align and key the main heading in bold; press ENTER twice.

2. Change the alignment to left and turn bold off.

3. Create a three-column, four-row table.

4. Key the table shown below; press TAB to move from cell to cell.

5. Select row 1; then bold and center-align the column headings. Row 1 is called the **header row** because it identifies the content in each column.

6. In Print Layout View, click the table move handle to select the entire table. Change the line spacing to 1.5.

7. Create the folder **Module 6 keys** and save the table as **41b-drill2** in this folder. Leave the table on the screen for the next drill.

COLLEGE SPORTS PROGRAM

Fall Events	Winter Events	Spring Events
Football	Basketball	Golf
Soccer	Gymnastics	Baseball
Volleyball	Swimming	Softball

LESSON 28 | Create an Interoffice Memo

New Functions

28a

Spelling and Grammar

When you key, *Word* places a red wavy line under misspelled words and a green wavy line under potential grammar errors. Clicking the right mouse button in a marked word displays a shortcut menu with suggested replacement words that you can use to correct the error.

The Spelling and Grammar Status button on the status bar also informs you if there is an error in the document.

 no error

error

To manually check a document, click the Spelling and Grammar button on the Standard toolbar to start the checking process.

When *Word* locates a possible error, the Spelling and Grammar dialog box displays. You can change words marked as errors or ignore them. You can click the **Add** button to add correct words not recognized by *Word* to the dictionary. If you choose Ignore All and Change All, the marked words will either be ignored or changed throughout the entire document

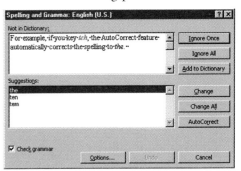

AutoCorrect

As you key, common errors are automatically corrected. For example, if you key *teh*, the AutoCorrect feature automatically corrects the spelling to *the*. When this feature is enabled, *Word* automatically replaces errors using the spell checker's main dictionary. You can customize or add words to the software's dictionary by accessing AutoCorrect Options on the Tools menu. Additional AutoCorrect options enable you to format text and automatically insert repetitive text as you key.

Drill 1 | SPELLING AND GRAMMAR AND AUTOCORRECT

1. On the Tools menu, select **AutoCorrect Options**. Note the available options, and then scroll through the list of replacement words (you can add additional words).

2. Key the following sentences exactly as they are shown; include the misspellings and abbreviations. Note that many errors are automatically corrected as you key.

3. In the last sentence, press ENTER to accept the AutoText entry at the beginning of the sentence.

4. Right-click on the words marked with a wavy red line, and correct the errors.

5. Proofread the lines to find two unmarked errors.

6. Save the document as **28a-drill1**. Print and close the document.

i beleive a lot of dissatisfied customers will not return.

a seperate committee was formed to deal with the new issues.

please includ a self-addressed stampted envelope with you letter.

To Whom It May Concern: If you don't receive a repsonse to you e-mail messige, call Robbins and Assocaites at 555-0106.

You can create tables using the Table menu or the Table button on the Standard toolbar. Either method produces the same results. Position the insertion point where you want the table to appear in the document before you begin.

To create a table using the Table menu:

1. From the Table menu, choose **Insert**; then **Table**. The Insert Table dialog box displays. The default setting of AutoFit is set to create a table with a fixed width. The columns will be of equal width and spread across the writing line.

2. Click the up or down arrows to specify the number of rows and columns. Click **OK**. The table displays.

Notice that column widths are indicated by column markers on the Ruler.

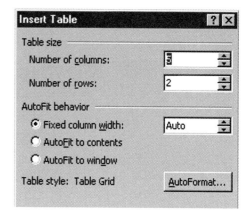

To create a table using the Insert Table button:

1. Click the **Insert Table** button on the Standard toolbar. A drop-down grid displays.

2. Click the left mouse button, and drag the pointer across to highlight the number of columns in the table and down to highlight the number of rows in the table. The table displays when you release the left mouse button.

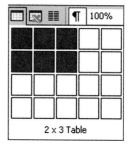

2 x 3 Table

Move Within a Table

When a table is created, the insertion point is in cell A1. To move within a table, use the TAB key or simply click within a cell using the mouse. Refer to this table as you learn to enter text in a table:

Press	Movement
TAB	To move to the next cell. If the insertion point is in the last cell, pressing TAB will add a new row.
SHIFT + TAB	To move to the previous cell.
ENTER	To increase the height of the row. If you press ENTER by mistake, press BACKSPACE to delete the line.

D r i l l   1   CREATE TABLES

1. Create a two-column, five-row table using the Table menu.

2. Turn on **Show/Hide** and notice the marker at the end of each cell and each row. Hold down the ALT key, and click on one of the column markers on the ruler. Notice that the width of the column is displayed in inches (2.93").

3. Close the table without saving it.

4. Create a four-column, four-row table using the Table button on the Standard toolbar.

5. Move to cell B3. Move to cell B2.

6. Move to cell A1 and press ENTER.

7. Move to cell D4 and press TAB.

8. Close the table without saving it.

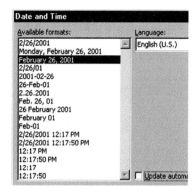

Date and Time

The current date and time can be inserted into documents using the **Date and Time** command from the Insert menu.

1. Choose **Date and Time** from the Insert menu.

2. Choose a format from the Available Formats box. Standard business format is the month-day-year format.

Note: The date is inserted as text and will not change. To update the date each time the document is opened, click the **Update Automatically** check box.

D r i l l   2 | **INSERT DATE**

1. Open **27b-d2**. Press CTRL + END to go to the end of the document. Press ENTER and key your name.

2. Press ENTER and insert the date below your name. Use the format day/month/year.

3. Spell-check the document and, if necessary, make any corrections.

4. Save the document as **28a-drill2**.

Document Design

28b

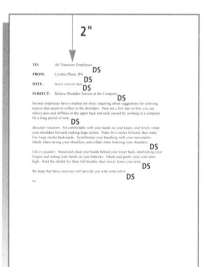

Interoffice Memorandums

Messages sent to persons within an organization are called **memorandums** (memos for short). A popular memo form is an e-mail, which is mailed electronically. Memos are printed on plain paper and sent in plain or interoffice envelopes. Memos consist of the heading, a body, and one or more notations.

To format a memo:

1. At the top of a document, change the line spacing to double (DS). Strike ENTER three times to leave an approximate 2" top margin.

2. Format the memo headings in bold and all caps. Turn off bold and all caps, and strike TAB once or twice after each heading to align the information. Generally, courtesy titles (Mr., Ms., etc.) are not used; however, if the memo is formal, the receiver's name may include a title.

3. Single-space the body of the memo. Set the line spacing to single at the beginning of the first paragraph. DS between paragraphs.

4. Add reference initials a DS below the body if the memo is keyed by someone other than the sender. Do not include initials when keying your own memo.

5. Items clipped or stapled to the memo are noted as attachments; items included in an envelope are enclosures. Key these notations a DS below the reference initials.

Proofread and Finalize a Document

Before documents are complete, they must be proofread carefully for accuracy. Error-free documents send the message that you are detail oriented and capable. Apply these procedures when processing all documents:

1. Use Spelling and Grammar to check spelling when you have completed the document.

2. Proofread the document on screen to be sure that it makes sense.

3. Preview the document, and check the overall appearance.

4. Save the document, and then print it.

5. Compare the document to the source copy (textbook), and check that text has not been omitted or added. Revise, save, and print if necessary.

Table Basics

OBJECTIVES

* Create tables.
* Format tables using the Tables toolbar and AutoFormat.
* Edit table and cell structure.
* Build keying speed and accuracy.

LESSON 41 | Create Tables

Skillbuilding

41a
Warmup

Key each line twice; DS between groups.

alphabetic	1	Jim Ryan was able to liquefy frozen oxygen; he kept it very cold.
figures	2	Flight 483 left Troy at 9:57 a.m., arriving in Reno at 12:06 p.m.
direct reaches	3	My brother served as an umpire on that bright June day, no doubt.
easy	4	Ana's sorority works with vigor for the goals of the civic corps.

| 1 | 2 | 3 | 4 | 5 | 6 | 7 | 8 | 9 | 10 | 11 | 12 | 13 |

New Functions

41b

help keywords
tables; create a table

Create Tables

Tables consist of columns and rows of data—either alphabetic, numeric, or both.

Column: Vertical list of information labeled alphabetically from left to right.

Row: Horizontal list of information labeled numerically from top to bottom.

Cell: An intersection of a column and a row. Each cell has its own address consisting of the column letter and the row number (cell A1).

Use Show/Hide to display end-of-cell marks in each cell and end-of-row marks at the end of each row. End-of-cell and end-of-row markers are useful when editing tables. Use Print Layout View to display the table move handle in the upper left of the table and the Sizing handle in the lower right of the table.

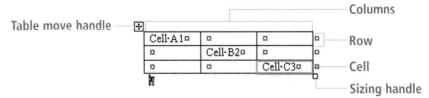

Applications

28c-d1
Memo

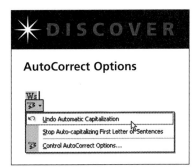

AutoCorrect Options

- Undo Automatic Capitalization
- Stop Auto-capitalizing First Letter of Sentences
- Control AutoCorrect Options...

1. Follow the steps for formatting a memo provided on the previous page.
2. Insert the current date using the Date and Time feature.
✳ 3. If the first letter of your reference initials is automatically capitalized, point to the initial until the AutoCorrect Options button appears. Click the button; then choose **Undo Automatic Capitalization**.
4. Proofread and correct all errors, following the steps under *Proofreading and Finalizing a Document*; then save the memo as **28c-d1**. Compare your document to the example on page 88.

↓2.1" **Set line spacing to DS; strike ENTER three times**

TO: All Transcom Employees

FROM: Cynthia Pham, RN

DATE: *Insert current date*

SUBJECT: Relieve Shoulder Tension at the Computer

Several employees have e-mailed our clinic inquiring about suggestions for relieving tension that seems to collect in the shoulders. Here are a few tips on how you can relieve pain and stiffness in the upper back and neck caused by working at a computer for a long period of time. ↓2

Shoulder rotations. Sit comfortably with your hands on your knees, and slowly rotate your shoulders forward, making large circles. Make five circles forward; then make five large circles backwards. Synchronize your breathing with your movements. Inhale when raising your shoulders, and exhale when lowering your shoulders. ↓2

Chest expander. Stand and clasp your hands behind your lower back, interlocking your fingers and resting your hands on your buttocks. Inhale and gently raise your arms high. Hold the stretch for three full breaths; then slowly lower your arms. ↓2

xx

 ## 28c-d2
Memo

Key this memo, check spelling, and save it as **28c-d2**.

Remeber to add your reference initals.

↓2.1"

TO: All Laurel Aircraft Employees

FROM: Melvin Galvez, Manager

DATE: *Insert current date*

SUBJECT: New Production Center

Laurel Aircraft is pleased to announce the completion of our new production center, located in B-107. Our center is able to produce high-resolution digital imaging for both color and black-and-white documents. You can bring us your PC or Mac files on disk, CD-ROM, or Zip disk, or you can e-mail them directly to our center.

Our staff is here to serve you and help you with all your in-house graphic needs from conception through completion. Stop by and visit our new center.

Drill 1
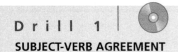

SUBJECT-VERB AGREEMENT

1. Review the rules and examples on the previous page.
2. Open **subjectverb1** from the data files. Save it as **subjectverb-drill1**.
3. Follow the specific directions provided in the data file.
4. Save again and print.

Drill 2

SUBJECT-VERB AGREEMENT

1. Open **subjectverb2** from the data files. Save it as **subjectverb-drill2**.
2. Follow the specific directions provided in the data file.
3. Save and print.

Drill 3

SUBJECT/VERB AND CAPITALIZATION

1. Key the ten sentences at the right, choosing the correct verb and applying correct capitalization.
2. Save as **subjectverb-drill3** and print.

1. both of the curies (was/were) nobel prize winners.
2. each of the directors in the sales department (has/have) given us approval.
3. mr. and mrs. thomas funderburk, jr. (was/were) married on november 23, 1936.
4. my sister and her college roommates (plan/plans) to tour london and paris this summer.
5. our new information manager (suggest/suggests) the following salutation when using an attention line: ladies and gentlemen.
6. the body language expert (place/places) his hand on his cheek as he says, "touch your hand to your chin."
7. the japanese child (enjoy/enjoys) the american food her hosts (serve/serves) her.
8. all of the candidates (was/were) invited to the debate at boston college.
9. the final exam (cover/covers) chapters 1-5.
10. turn south onto interstate 20; then take exit 56 to bossier city.

Drill 4

EDITING SKILLS

Key the paragraph. Correct all errors in grammar and capitalization. Save as **editing-drill4**.

This past week I visited the facilities of the magnolia conference center in isle of palms, south carolina, as you requested. bob bremmerton, group manager, was my host for the visit.

magnolia offers many advantages for our leadership training conference. The prices are reasonable; the facilities is excellent; the location is suitable. In addition to the beachfront location, tennis and golf packages are part of the group price.

Objective Assessment
Answer the questions below to see if you have mastered the content of Module 3.

1. In *Microsoft Word*, a paragraph is defined as any line that ends with a(n) _____ .

2. Which menu provides you with the option to display toolbars on your screen? _____

3. An ellipsis following a command on a pull-down menu indicates that a(n) _____ will display.

4. A(n) _____ command on a menu indicates that it is not available for use.

5. The _____ command is used to bring a previously stored document to the screen.

6. The _____ command on the Standard toolbar displays all nonprinting characters.

7. The _____ option on the File menu allows you to center a document vertically on the page.

8. Use the _____ command to see how the document will look before it is printed.

9. _____ _____ are messages sent to persons within the organization. They contain a heading, a body, and one or more notations.

10. The current date can be entered automatically using the _____ feature.

Performance Assessment

words

Document 1
Rough Draft Memo

1. Key the memo at the right. Make corrections as marked.

2. Save as **checkpoint3-d1**, proofread, and print.

```
TO:    J. Ezra Bayh                                              4
FROM:  Greta Sangtree                                            8
DATE:  August 14, 200-                                          13
SUBJECT: Letter-Mailing Standards                               20

Recently the post office delivered late a letter that          35
caused us some embarassment.  To avoid recurrence, please      47
ensure that all administrative assistants and mail person-     58
nel follow postal service guidelines.                          67

Perhaps a refresher seminar on correspondence guidelines is    79
in in order.  Thanks or you help.                               86
```

DS
, because of the delay
chk sp
U.S.
for your

Document 2
Edit memo

1. Open **checkpoint3-d1**. Save as **checkpoint3-d2**.

2. Select the four-line heading and delete it.

3. Bold U.S. Postal Service guidelines.

4. Change the spacing of paragraphs 1 and 2 to double. Delete the hard return between paragraphs 1 and 2. Indent each paragraph using TAB.

5. Key your name at the top of the document (not the top of the page). Strike ENTER twice below your name.

6. Format your name in 14-point bold. Key the filename below your name. Align it at the left.

7. Delete the hard returns above your name. Center the page vertically.

8. Save the document again and print.

COMMUNICATION SKILLS 2

Subject/Verb Agreement

Use a singular verb

1. With a **singular subject**. (The singular forms of *to be* include: am, is, was. Common errors with *to be* are: you was, we was, they was.)

> She monitors employee morale.
> You are a very energetic worker.
> A split keyboard is in great demand.

2. With most **indefinite pronouns**: *another, anybody, anything, everything, each, either, neither, one, everyone, anyone, nobody.*

> Each of the candidates has raised a considerable amount of money.
> Everyone is eager to read the author's newest novel.
> Neither of the boys is able to attend.

3. With singular subjects joined by *or/nor, either/or, neither/nor.*

> Neither your grammar nor punctuation is correct.
> Either Jody or Jan has your favorite CD.
> John or Connie has volunteered to chaperone the field trip.

4. With a **collective noun** (*family, choir, herd, faculty, jury, committee*) that acts as one unit.

> The jury has reached a decision.
> The council is in an emergency session.
> But:
> The faculty have their assignments. (Each has his/her own assignments.)

5. With words or phrases that express **periods of time, weights, measurements,** or **amounts of money**.

> Fifteen dollars is what he earned.
> Two-thirds of the money has been submitted to the treasurer.
> One hundred pounds is too much.

Use a plural verb

6. With a **plural subject**.

> The students sell computer supplies for their annual fundraiser.
> They are among the top-ranked teams in the nation.

7. With **compound (two or more) subjects** joined by *and.*

> Headaches and backaches are common worker complaints.
> Hard work and determination were two qualities listed by the references.

8. With *some, all, most, none, several, few, both, many,* and *any* when they refer to more than one of the items.

> All of my friends have seen the movie.
> Some of the teams have won two or more games.

module 4

Business Letter Formats

OBJECTIVES

* Format block and modified block business letters.
* Create envelopes and labels.
* Insert the date automatically.
* Set and modify tabs.
* Improve keying speed and accuracy.

LESSON 29 | Block Letter Format

Skillbuilding

29a
Warmup

Key each line twice SS; DS between 2-line groups.

Use *CheckPro 2002* if available for this lesson.

alphabetic 1 Which oval-jet black onyx ring blazed on the queen's prim finger?
figures 2 Cy will be 19 on May 4; Jo, 27 on May 6 or 8; Mike, 30 on June 5.
adjacent 3 We acquire few rewards for walking short treks to Union Terminal.
easy 4 To augment and enrich the visual signal, I turn the right handle.

| 1 | 2 | 3 | 4 | 5 | 6 | 7 | 8 | 9 | 10 | 11 | 12 | 13 |

29b
Timed Writing

Take two 3' timings.

all letters

gwam 3'

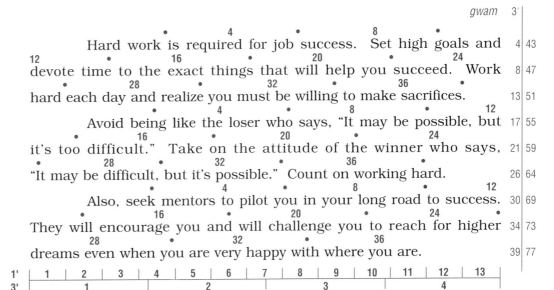

Hard work is required for job success. Set high goals and	4 43
devote time to the exact things that will help you succeed. Work	8 47
hard each day and realize you must be willing to make sacrifices.	13 51
Avoid being like the loser who says, "It may be possible, but	17 55
it's too difficult." Take on the attitude of the winner who says,	21 59
"It may be difficult, but it's possible." Count on working hard.	26 64
Also, seek mentors to pilot you in your long road to success.	30 69
They will encourage you and will challenge you to reach for higher	34 73
dreams even when you are very happy with where you are.	39 77

1' | 1 | 2 | 3 | 4 | 5 | 6 | 7 | 8 | 9 | 10 | 11 | 12 | 13 |
3' | 1 | 2 | 3 | 4 |

MODULE 5 Checkpoint

Objective Assessment

Answer the questions below to see if you have mastered the content of Module 5.

Part A:

1. Margins for unbound reports are _____ side margins, _____ top margin (first page), _____ top margin (second page), and _____ bottom margin.

2. To set margins, choose _____ from the _____ menu.

3. Use ____ -point font for main headings. Use _____-point for side headings.

4. The _____ format displays the first line of text at the left margin and indents all other lines to the first tab.

5. To prevent a single line of a paragraph from printing at the bottom or top of a page, apply _____.

6. To number the pages of a multipage report, choose _____ from the _____ menu. Numbers are positioned at the _____.

7. To prevent the middle initial in the name Thomas J. Swenson from being separated from the first name, insert a _____ after the first name.

8. Use the _____ feature to expand or condense the space between characters.

Part B: Study each format below. Circle the correct format.

9. Which of the following illustrates a hanging indent format?

   A Bruce, Lawrence A. *The Report Guide: Selected Form and Style*. Boise: State of Idaho Press, 2000.

   B Bruce, Lawrence A. *The Report Guide: Selected Form and Style*. Boise: State of Idaho Press, 2000.

10. Which of the following illustrates use of the right indent feature?

   A E-mail is a popular and effective means of communication that is being used by both companies and individuals.

   B E-mail is a popular and effective means of communication that is being used by both companies and individuals.

Performance Assessment

Document 1
Edit Report

1. Open **checkpoint5** from the data files. Make the edits below and save as **checkpoint5-d1**.

   a. Position the main heading and format it correctly; insert an em dash to replace the two hyphens.

   b. Format the side headings correctly.

   c. Format the report as a DS, unbound report.

   d. Format correctly the two long quotations that are displayed in red font. Change the red text to black.

   e. Format the references in hanging indent format. Begin references on a separate page. Position the first line correctly.

   f. Create a header for page numbers. Suppress the number on the first page.

Document 2
Prepare Title Page

1. Prepare a creative title page for **checkpoint5-d1**. You may use page borders, horizontal lines, or a design of your choice. Save as **checkpoint5-d2**.

   Prepared for

   Mr. Derrick Novorot, President

   Altman Corporation

   388 North Washington Street

   Starkville, MS 39759

   Prepared by

   Your Name, Communication Consultant

   Your Street Address

   Your City, State ZIP Code

Document Design
29c

Business Letters

Business letters are used to communicate with persons outside of the business. Business letters carry two messages: one is the tone and content; a second is the appearance of the document. Appearance is important because it creates the critical first impression. Stationery, use of standard letter parts, and placement should convey that the writer is intelligent, informed, and detail minded.

Stationery

Letters should be printed on high-quality (about 24-pound) letterhead stationery. Standard size for letterhead is $8^{1}/_{2}$" x 11". Envelopes should match the letterhead in quality and color.

Letter parts

Businesspeople expect to see standard letter parts arranged in the proper sequence. The standard parts are listed below. Other letter parts may be included as needed.

Letterhead: Preprinted stationery that includes the company name, logo, address, and other optional information such as a telephone number and fax number.

Dateline: Date the letter is prepared.

Letter address: Complete address of the person who will receive the letter. Generally, the address includes the receiver's name, company name, street address, city, state (followed by one space only), and ZIP code. Include a personal title (*Mr.*, *Ms.*, *Dr.*) with the person's name. Key the address four lines below the dateline, and capitalize the first letter of each word.

Salutation: Key the salutation, or greeting, a double space (DS) below the letter address. If the letter is addressed to an individual, include a courtesy title with the person's last name. If the letter is addressed to a company, use *Ladies and Gentlemen*.

Body: Begin the body, or message, a DS below the salutation. Single-space (SS) paragraphs and DS between paragraphs.

Complimentary closing: Begin the complimentary closing a DS below the body. Capitalize only the first letter of the closing.

Writer's name and title: Key the writer's name and job title four lines below the complimentary closing to allow space for the writer's signature. Key the name and title on either one or two lines, whichever gives better balance to the signature block. Separate the writer's name and title with a comma if they are on one line.

Reference initials: Key the initials of the typist in lowercase letters a DS below the typed name and title. If the writer's initials are also included, key them first in ALL CAPS followed by a colon (BB:xx).

Block Format

In block format, all letter parts are keyed at the left margin. For most letters, use open punctuation, which requires no punctuation after the salutation or the closing. For efficiency, use the default settings and features of your software when formatting letters.

Side margins: Default (1.25") or 1"

Dateline: About 2" (strike ENTER six times), center the page vertically, or at least 0.5" below the letterhead. If the letter is short, center the page vertically.

Spacing: SS paragraphs; DS between them. Follow the directions for spacing between other letter parts provided above.

Block Letter

Envelope

Copyright Laws

To avoid copyright infringement, the Internet user must be 301
knowledgeable about copyright law. Two important laws include The Copyright 316
Law of 1976 and the Digital Millennium Copyright Act, which was enacted in 331
1998 to update the copyright law for the digital age. Zielinski (1999, 40) 346
explains that under the Copyright Law of 1976: 356

Copyright is automatic when an original work is first 'fixed' in a 370
tangible medium of expression. That means material is protected by 383
copyright at the point when it is first printed, captured on film, drawn, 398
or saved to hard drive or disk. . . . The farsighted statute covers fixed 412
works 'now known or later developed'. 419

Insert the file copyright here.

REFERENCES 422

Lee, John E. "Technology Aids in Stopping Copyright Offenders." *Hopper* 437
Business Journal, (Fall 2000): http://www.hpj.edu/technologyaids.htm 451
(26 December 2000). 455

Zielinski, Dave. "Are You a Copyright Criminal?" *Presentations*, Vol. 13, No. 471
6, (June, 1999), 36-46. 476

40c-d2
Unbound Report

1. Open **present** from the data files. Save it as **40c-d2**.
2. Convert this leftbound report to an unbound report.
3. Format main and side headings correctly. Position the main heading on the correct line.
4. Be alert to a widow line on page 1.
5. Prepare the header as shown below; suppress it on the first page.

Effective·Presentations   →   →   Page·2·of·2

40c-d3
Title Page for
Leftbound Report

1. Prepare a title page for the leftbound report prepared in **40c-d1**.
2. The report is prepared for **Webb & Morse Company Employees** by **Your Name, Information Technology Manager**.
3. Expand character spacing in the title, add a page border, and change the font color.
4. Save the document as **40c-d3**.

E- Market, Group

10 East Rivercenter Boulevard
Covington, KY 41016-8765

Dateline Current date ↓4

Letter address Mr. Ishmal Dabdoub
Professional Office Consultants
1782 Laurel Canyon Road
Sunnyvale, CA 93785-9087 DS

Salutation Dear Mr. Dabdoub DS

Body Have you heard your friends and colleagues talk about obtaining real-time stock quotes? real-time account balances and positions? Nasdaq Level II quotes? extended-hours trading? If so, then they are among the three million serious investors that have opened an account with E-Market. DS

We believe that the best decisions are informed decisions made in a timely manner. E-Market has an online help desk that provides information for all levels of investors, from beginners to the experienced serious trader. You can learn basic tactics for investing in the stock market, how to avoid common mistakes, and pick up some advanced strategies. DS

Stay on top of the market and your investments! Visit our web site at http://www.emarket.com to learn more about our banking and brokerage services. E-Market Group is the premier site for online investing. DS

Sincerely ↓4   **Complementary Closing**

Margaritta Gibson

Writer's name Ms. Margaritta Gibson
Title Marketing Manager DS

Reference initials xx

40c-d1
Leftbound
Report

1. Key this leftbound report with DS.
2. Number the pages in a header at the top right; suppress the header on the first page.
3. Add a footer with using the title of the report.
4. Insert the file **copyright** from the data files where indicated in the report.
5. Key the references on a separate references page at the end of the report.
6. Save the report as **40c-d1**.

words

COPYRIGHT LAW IN THE INTERNET AGE
7

Copyright owners continue to face copyright challenges as technology advances more rapidly than ever before. History shows us that copyright infringements occur at the introduction of each new invention or emerging technology. Examples include the phonograph and tape recorder and mimeograph and copy machines. Today, the Internet age provides Internet users the ease of copying and distributing electronic files via the Internet.
19
34
49
63
76
92
94

Copyright owners of content published on the Web, photographers who view their photographs on Web pages, and recording artists whose music is downloaded from the Internet are only a few examples of copyright issues resulting from the Internet age. Compounding the issue is that many Internet users may not be aware they are violating copyright law (Zielinski, 1999, 38). The following list shows actions taken daily that are considered copyright infringements:
107
121
134
148
163
179
187

- Copying content from a Web page and pasting it into documents.
200

- Reproducing multiple copies of a journal article that was printed from an online journal.
214
219

- Distributing presentation handouts that contain cartoon characters or other graphics copied from a Web page.
233
241

- Presenting originally designed electronic presentations that contain graphics, sound and video clips, and/or photographs copied from a Web page.
255
269
271

- Duplicating and distributing copies of music downloaded from the Web.
284
286

Applications

29d-d1
Block Letter

At 2.1"   Ln 7   Col 1

1. Key the model letter on page 93 in block format with open punctuation. Assume you are using letterhead stationery.
2. Strike ENTER to position the dateline about 2.1" on the status bar. The position will vary depending upon the font size.
3. Insert the current date using the Date and Time feature.
4. Include your reference initials. If the first letter of your initials is automatically capitalized, point to the initial until the AutoCorrect Option button appears, click the button, and then choose **Undo Automatic Capitalization**.
5. Follow the proofreading procedures outlined in Lesson 28. Use Print Preview to check the placement.
6. Use **Show/Hide** to compare paragraph markers with the model at the left. Print the letter when you are satisfied. Create the folder **Module 4 Keys** and save the letter as **29d-d1** in this folder. Save all drills and documents for Lessons 29–34 in the **Module 4 Keys** folder.

29d-d2
Block Letter

1. Key the letter below in block format with open punctuation. Use **Date and Time** to insert the current date. Add your reference initials in lowercase letters.
2. Save the letter as **29d-d2**. Proofread and print the letter. Keep the document displayed for the next exercise.

↓2.1"
Current date ↓4

Ms. Alice Ottoman
Premiere Properties, Inc.
52 Ocean Drive
Newport Beach, CA 92747-6293 ↓2

Dear Ms. Ottoman ↓2

Internet Solutions has developed a new technique for you to market your properties on the World Wide Web. We can now create 360-degree panoramic pictures for your Web site. You can give your clients a virtual spin of the living room, kitchen, and every room in the house. ↓2

Call today for a demonstration of this remarkable technology. Give your clients a better visual understanding of the property layout—something your competition doesn't have. ↓2

Sincerely ↓4

Lee Rodgers
Marketing Manager ↓2

xx

29d-d3
Block Letter and Center Page

1. Document **29d-d2** should be displayed on your screen. Save it as **29d-d3**.
2. Replace the letter address with the one below in proper format.
   Ms. Andrea Virzi, J P Personnel Services, 2351 West Ravina Drive, Atlanta, GA 30346-9105
3. Supply the correct salutation. Turn on **Show/Hide (¶)**. Delete the six hard returns above the dateline. Align the page at vertical center (**File, Page Setup**). Proofread and save. Use Print Preview to view placement. Note that a short letter looks more attractive centered on the page rather than positioned at 2.1".

LESSON 40 | Assessment

Skillbuilding

40a
Warmup
Key each line twice SS;
DS between groups.

one-hand 1 In regard to desert oil wastes, Jill referred only minimum cases.

sentences 2 Carra agrees you'll get a reward only as you join nonunion races.

3 Few beavers, as far as I'm aware, feast on cedar trees in Kokomo.

4 Johnny, after a few stewed eggs, ate a plump, pink onion at noon.

5 A plump, aged monk served a few million beggars a milky beverage.

| 1 | 2 | 3 | 4 | 5 | 6 | 7 | 8 | 9 | 10 | 11 | 12 | 13 |

40b
Timed Writings
Key one 3' timing; then
key one 5' timing.

 all letters

gwam 3' | 5'

How is a hobby different from a business? A very common way	4	2 32
to describe the difference between the hobby and the business is	8	5 35
that the hobby is done for fun, and the business is done as work	13	8 38
which enables people to earn their living. Does that mean that	17	10 40
people do not have fun at work or that people do not work with their	22	13 43
hobbies? Many people would not agree with that description.	26	15 45
Some people begin work on a hobby just for fun, but then they	30	18 48
realize it has the potential to be a business. They soon find out	34	21 51
that others enjoy the hobby as well and would expect to pay for	39	23 53
the products or services the hobby requires. Many quite successful	43	26 56
businesses begin as hobbies. Some of them are small, and some grow	48	29 59
to be large operations.	49	30 60

3' | 1 | 2 | 3 | 4 |
5' | 1 | 2 | 3 |

Applications

40c
Assessment: Leftbound and Unbound Reports and Title Page

 Continue

 Check

With CheckPro 2002: *CheckPro* will keep track of the time it takes you to complete the entire production test and compute your speed and accuracy rate on each document and summarize the results.   When you complete a document, proofread it, check the spelling, and preview for placement. When you are completely satisfied with the document, click the **Continue** button to move to the next document. You will not be able to return and edit a document once you continue to the next document.   Click the **Check** button when you are ready to error-check the test. Review and/or print the document analysis results.

Without CheckPro 2002: On the signal to begin, key the documents in sequence. When time has been called, proofread all documents again; identify errors, and determine *g-pwam*.

$$g\text{-}pwam = \frac{\text{total words keyed}}{25'}$$

LESSON 30 | Block Letters with Envelopes

Skillbuilding

30a
Warmup
Key each line twice SS; DS between 2-line groups.

alphabetic 1 Buddy Jackson is saving the door prize money for wax and lacquer.
figures 2 I have fed 47 hens, 25 geese, 10 ducks, 39 lambs, and 68 kittens.
one hand 3 You imply Jon Case exaggerated my opinion on a decrease in rates.
easy 4 I shall make hand signals to the widow with the auditory problem.
| 1 | 2 | 3 | 4 | 5 | 6 | 7 | 8 | 9 | 10 | 11 | 12 | 13 |

30b
Rhythm Builder
Key lines 5–8 twice.
Take two 30" timings on lines 9 and 10.

Balanced-hand words, phrases, and sentences.

5 am an by do go he if is it me or ox or so for and big the six spa
6 but cod dot dug eye end wit vie yam make also city work gage them

7 is it| is it| is it he| is it he| for it| for it| paid for it| it is she
8 of it| pay due| pay for| paid me| paid them| also make| such as| may end

9 Sue and Bob may go to the zoo, and he or she may pay for the gas.
10 Jim was sad; Ted saw him as we sat on my bed; we saw him get gas.
| 1 | 2 | 3 | 4 | 5 | 6 | 7 | 8 | 9 | 10 | 11 | 12 | 13 |

Communication

30c

Letter Addresses and Salutations

The salutation, or greeting, consists of the person's personal title (*Mr.*, *Ms.*, or *Mrs.*) or professional title (*Dr.*, *Professor*, *Senator*, *Honorable*), and the person's last name. Do not use a first name unless you have a personal relationship. The salutation should agree in number with the addressee. If the letter is addressed to more than one person, the salutation is plural.

	Receiver	Salutation
To individuals	Dr. Alexander Gray	Dear Dr. Gray
	Dr. and Mrs. Thompson	Dear Dr. and Mrs. Thompson
To organizations	TMP Electronics, Inc.	Ladies and Gentlemen
Name unknown	Advertising Manager	Dear Advertising Manager

Drill 1 | PRACTICE LETTER PARTS

1. Review the model document on page 93 for correct placement of letter parts.
2. Key the letter parts for each activity, spacing correctly between parts. In the first exercise, strike ENTER six times to begin the dateline at 2.1"; use the Date and Time feature.
3. Press ENTER five times between drills. Do not save the drills.
4. Take a 2' timing on each drill. Repeat if you finish before time is up.

A Current date

Ms. Joyce Bohn, Treasurer
Citizens for the Environment
1888 Hutchins Ave.
Seattle, WA 98111-2353

Dear Ms. Bohn

B Please confirm our lunch date.

Sincerely yours

James D. Bohlin
District Attorney

xx

REFERENCES

Gilreath, Erica. "Dressing Casually with Power." 504
http://www.dresscasual.com (23 March 2001). 513

Monaghan, Susan. "Business Dress Codes May Be Shifting." *Business* 527
Executive, April 2000, 34–35. 533

Sutphin, Rachel. "Your Business Wardrobe Decisions Are Important 546
Decisions." *Business Management Journal*, January 2000, 10–12. 559

Tartt, Kelsey. "Companies Support Business Casual Dress." 571
Management Success, June 1995, 23–25. 578

39d-d3
Unbound Report

1. Reformat report **39d-d2** as an unbound report.
2. Change the numbered list to a bulleted list.
3. Change the heading font to Arial. (Use Format Painter.)
4. Edit the footer to include a bottom border.
5. Preview the document for correct pagination; then save it as **39d-d3**.

COURTESY OF © PHOTODISC, INC.

N E W S | on e-mail privacy

Is e-mail private? The answer is definitely not. In some companies, the e-mail administrator is able to read any and all e-mail messages. Some companies actually monitor employee e-mail wanting to ensure that employees are not spending time on personal activities or leaking confidential company information. Also remember that most companies back up their systems on a regular basis so that information is not lost (including e-mail).

Occasionally, e-mail software malfunctions causing your e-mail to be delivered to the wrong person or you to receive e-mail intended for someone else. In addition, there are many hackers who, if they try hard enough, can bypass security measures and read your e-mail. So remember, e-mail is not private. Don't send anything by e-mail that you would not want to find on the company bulletin board.

New Function
30d

Envelopes

The envelope feature can insert the delivery address automatically if a letter is displayed; postage can even be added if special software is installed. The default is a size 10 envelope (4⅛" by 9½"); other sizes are available by clicking the Options button on the Envelope tab. An alternative style for envelope addresses is uppercase (ALL CAPS) with no punctuation.

Ms. Alice Ottoman
Premiere Properties, Inc.
52 Ocean Drive
Newport Beach, CA 92747-6293

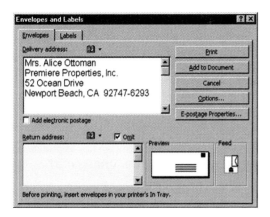

To generate an envelope:

1. With the letter you have created displayed, click **Tools** on the menu, and then **Letters and Mailings.** Click **Envelopes and Labels,** and if necessary, click the **Envelopes** tab. The mailing address is automatically displayed in the Delivery address box. (To create an envelope without a letter, follow the same steps, but key the address in the Delivery address box.)

2. If you are using business envelopes with a preprinted return address (assume you are), click the Return address Omit box. To include a return address, do not check the Omit box, click in the Return address box, and enter the return address.

   Note: To format a letter address on the envelope in all caps, click **Add to Document** to attach the envelope to the letter, and then edit the address.

Drill 2 | CREATE ENVELOPE

1. Create an envelope for the addressee in Drill 1.

2. Attach the envelope to a blank document.

3. Save the document as **30d-drill2.**

Change Case

Change Case enables you to change the capitalization of text that has already been keyed.

Sentence case capitalizes the first letter of the first word of a sentence.

Lowercase changes all capital letters to lowercase letters.

Uppercase changes all letters to uppercase.

Title case capitalizes the first letter of each word.

Toggle case changes all uppercase letters to lowercase and vice versa.

To change case, select the text to be changed, choose **Change Case** from the Format menu, and then choose the appropriate option.

TRENDS FOR BUSINESS DRESS

Casual dress in the workplace has become widely accepted. According to a national study conducted by Schoenholtz & Associates in 1995, a majority of the companies surveyed allowed employees to dress casually one day a week, usually Fridays (Tartt, 1995, 23). The trend continued to climb as shown by the 1997 survey by Schoenholtz & Associates. Fifty-eight percent of office workers surveyed were allowed to dress casually for work every day, and 92 percent of the offices allowed employees to dress casually occasionally (Sutphin, 2000, 10).

Decline in Trend

The trend to dress casually that started in the early 1990s may be shifting, states Susan Monaghan (2000, 34):

> Although a large number of companies are allowing casual attire every day or only on Fridays, a current survey revealed a decline of 10 percent in 1999 when compared to the same survey conducted in 1998. Some experts predict the new trend for business dress codes will be a dress up day every week.

What accounts for this decline in companies permitting casual dress? Several reasons may include:

1. Confusion of what business casual is with employees slipping into dressing too casually (work jeans, faded tee-shirts, old sneakers, and improperly fitting clothing).

2. Casual dress does not portray the adopted corporate image of the company.

3. Employees are realizing that promotion decisions are affected by a professional appearance.

Guidelines for Business Dress

Companies are employing image consultants to teach employees what is appropriate business casual and to plan the best business attire to project the corporate image. Erica Gilreath (2000), the author of *Casual Dress,* a guidebook on business casual, provides excellent advice on how to dress casually and still command the power needed for business success. She presents the following advice to professionals:

- Do not wear any clothing that is designed for recreational or sports activities, e.g., cargo pants or pants with elastic waist.

- Invest the time in pressing khakis and shirts or pay the price for professional dry cleaning. Wrinkled clothing does not enhance one's credibility.

- Do not wear sneakers.

- Be sure clothing fits properly. Avoid baggy clothes or clothes that are too tight.

In summary, energetic employees working to climb the corporate ladder will need to plan their dress carefully. If business casual is appropriate, it's best to consult the experts on business casual to ensure a professional image.

Drill 3 | ADD ENVELOPE

1. Open **29d-d2**. Create and attach an envelope to the letter.

2. Select the entire address and convert it to uppercase. Delete the punctuation.

3. Save the document as **30d-drill3** and print it. Your instructor may have you print envelopes on plain paper.

Applications

30e-d1
Edit Letter

1. Open letter **29d-d1**, save it as **30e-d1**, and then make the changes shown below.

2. Center the letter vertically. Use **Show/Hide** to remove any extra paragraph markers (¶).

3. Change the date to the current date, preview the letter, and print one copy.

~~Mr. Ishmal Dabdoub~~ Dr. Arthur Goralsky
~~Professional Office Consultants~~ Global Enterprises, Inc.
~~1782 Laurel Canyon Road~~ 2000 Corporate Way
~~Sunnyvale, Ca 93785~~ Lake Oswego, OR 97035

Dear ~~Mr. Dabdoub~~ Dr. Goralsky

Have you heard your friends and colleagues talk about obtaining real-time stock quotes? real-time account balances and positions? Nasdaq Level II quotes? extended-hours trading? If so, then they are among the ~~three~~ four million serious investors that have opened ~~an~~ accounts with ~~E-Market~~ E-Trade.

We believe that the best decisions are informed decisions made in a timely manner. ~~E-Market~~ E-Trade has an online help desk that provides information for all levels of investors, from beginners to the experienced serious trader. You can learn basic ~~tacties~~ strategies for investing in the stock market, avoiding common mistakes, and picking up some advanced strategies.

Stay on top of the market and your investments! Visit our Web site at http://www. ~~emarket~~ etrade.com to learn more about our banking and brokerage services ~~E-Market Group~~ E-Trade is the premier site for online investing.

Sincerely

~~Ms. Margaritta Gibson~~ Keisha Knight
Marketing Manager

xx

Document Design

39c

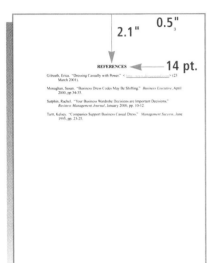

References Page

References cited in the report are listed at the end of the report in alphabetical order by authors' last names. The reference list may be titled REFERENCES or BIBLIOGRAPHY. Become familiar with the three types of references listed below:

1. A book reference includes the name of the author (last name first), work (italicized), city of publication, publisher, and copyright date.

2. A magazine reference shows the name of the author (last name first), article (in quotation marks), magazine title (italicized), date of publication, and page references.

3. A reference retrieved electronically includes the author (inverted), article (in quotation marks), publication (italicized), publication information, Internet address, and date the document was retrieved or accessed (in parentheses).

Begin the list of references on a new page by inserting a manual page break at the end of the report. Use the same margins as the first page of a report, and number the page at the top right of the page. The main heading (REFERENCES or BIBLIOGRAPHY) should be approximately 2" from the top of the page. References should be SS in hanging indent format; DS between references.

Applications

39d-d1
References Page

1. Open **38e-d1**. Save it as **39d-d1**.

2. Position the insertion point at the end of the report. Press CTRL + ENTER to begin a new page. Key **REFERENCES** approximately 2" from the top of the page.

3. Key the references in hanging indent style. (*Hint:* Try the shortcut, CTRL + T.)

Lehman, C. M., and Dufrene, D. D. *Business Communication.* 13th ed. Cincinnati: South-Western/Thomson Learning, 2002.

Publication Manual of the American Psychological Association. 4th ed. Washington, D.C.: American Psychological Association, 1994.

39d-d2
Leftbound Report

1. Key the following leftbound report DS. SS the direct quote, and indent it 0.5".

2. Create a header to number the pages at the top right; suppress it on the first page.

3. Create a footer that includes **Donovan National Bank Policy Manual** in the left position.

4. Key the references on a references page at the end of the report.

5. Switch to Print Layout view to verify the page numbers and ensure there are no widows or orphans.

6. Save the report as **39d-d2**.

30e-d2
Block Letter

1. Key the following letter in block style. Use the Date feature to insert the current date. Proofread and check the spelling.
2. Center the page vertically. Preview the letter and check the placement before printing. Save the letter as **30e-d2** and print one copy.

Current date | Mr. Trace L. Brecken | 4487 Ingram Street | Corpus Christi, TX 78409-8907 | Dear Mr. Brecken

We have received the package you sent us in which you returned goods from a recent order you gave us. Your refund check, plus return postage, will be mailed to you in a few days.

We are sorry, of course, that you did not find this merchandise personally satisfactory. It is our goal to please all of our customers, and we are always disappointed if we fail.

Please give us an opportunity to try again. We stand behind our merchandise, and that is our guarantee of good service.

Cordially yours | Mrs. Margret Bredewig | Customer Service Department | xx

30e-d3
Block Letter

1. Follow the directions for **30e-d2** and key the following letter in block style.
2. Save the letter as **30e-d3** and print one copy.

Current date | Mrs. Rose Shikamuru | 55 Lawrence Street |Topeka, KS 66607-6657 | Dear Mrs. Shikamuru

Thank you for your recent letter asking about employment opportunities with our company. We are happy to inform you that Mr. Edward Ybarra, our recruiting representative, will be on your campus on April 23, 24, 25, and 26 to interview students who are interested in our company.

We suggest that you talk soon with your student placement office, as all appointments with Mr. Ybarra will be made through that office. Please bring with you the application questionnaire the office provides.

Within a few days, we will send you a company brochure and more information about our offices; plant; salary, bonus, and retirement plans; and the beautiful community in which we are located. We believe a close study of this information will convince you, as it has many others, that our company builds futures as well as small motors.

If there is any other way we can help you, please write to me again.

Yours very truly | Miss Myrle K. Bragg | Human Services Director | xx

help keywords
Create a header or footer

Footer with Number of Pages Field

The **Footer** function places information at the bottom of each page in a document. Footers print 0.5" from the bottom edge of the paper. If necessary, select the footer to apply 12-point type. Footers can only be viewed from Print Layout view.

In legal documents such as wills and corporate minutes, it is necessary to print on each page the total number of pages in a document, e.g., Page 1 of 10. This feature can be used in either the header or the footer.

To create a footer to track the number of pages in a document:

1. Choose **View** from the menu, and then choose **Header and Footer**. The Header and Footer toolbar and a grid area display.

2. Click **Switch Between Header and Footer** to move to the footer area. (*Note:* The footer also has three positions: left, center, and right.)

Insert auto text   Switch between header and footer button

3. Press TAB to move to the right position of the footer.

4. Click the **Insert AutoText** down arrow; then choose **Page X of Y**.

5. Click **Close**. View the footer in Print Layout view.

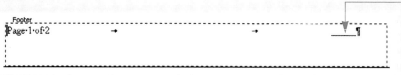

LESSON 31 | Tabs

Skillbuilding

31a
Warmup
Key each line twice SS; DS between 2-line groups.

alphabet	1	I quickly explained to two managers the grave hazards of the job.
figures	2	All channels—16, 25, 30, and 74—reported the score was 19 to 8.
shift	3	Maxi and Kay Pascal expect to be in breezy South Mexico in April.
easy	4	Did the man fight a duel, or did he go to a chapel to sign a vow?

| 1 | 2 | 3 | 4 | 5 | 6 | 7 | 8 | 9 | 10 | 11 | 12 | 13 |

31b
Review Letter Parts
Arrange letter parts correctly. Ignore top margin requirements.

Press ENTER five times between drills. Do not save.

1 May 15, 200- | Mr. Brad Babbett | 811 Wier Avenue, W. |Phoenix, AZ 83018-9087 | Dear Mr. Babbett

2 Current date | Ms. Lois J. Bruce | 913 Torch Hill Road | Columbus, GA 30904-4133 | Dear Ms. Bruce

3 Sincerely yours | George S. Murger | Assistant Manager | xx

4 Very cordially yours | Marvin J. Cecchetti, Jr. | Media Editor

New Functions

31c

Tabs

Tabs are used to indent paragraphs and align text vertically. Pressing the TAB key aligns text at the **tab stop**. *Word* has five types of tabs, which are listed below. The left, right, and center tabs are similar to paragraph alignment types.

⌞	**Left tab**	Aligns text at the left.
⌟	**Right tab**	Aligns text at the right.
⊥	**Center tab**	Aligns text evenly on either side of the tab stop.
⊥.	**Decimal tab**	Aligns numbers at the decimal point.
│	**Bar tab**	Aligns text to the right of a vertical bar.

Tabs can be set and cleared on the Horizontal Ruler. The numbers on the ruler indicate the distance in inches from the left margin. The small gray lines below each half-inch position are the default tab stops. The Tab Alignment button at the left edge of the ruler indicates the type of tab. To change the tab type, click the Tab Alignment button.

Tab alignment   **Left tab**   **Right tab**   **Decimal tab**

To set a tab:	Click the Tab Alignment button, and choose the desired tab type. Click the Horizontal Ruler where you want to set the tab.
To delete a tab:	Click the tab marker, and drag it straight down off the ruler.
To move a tab:	Click the tab marker, and drag the tab to the new location.

Tabs can also be set in the Tab dialog box (**Format** menu, **Tabs**). The Tab dialog box provides more options and allows you to set precise settings.

LESSON 39 | Two-Page Report with References

Skillbuilding

39a
Warmup
Key each line twice SS.
DS between groups.

alphabetic 1 Melva Bragg required exactly a dozen jackets for the winter trip.

figures 2 The 1903 copy of my book had 5 parts, 48 chapters, and 672 pages.

direct reach 3 Olga, the French goalie, defended well against the frazzled team.

easy 4 Rodney and a neighbor may go to the dock with us to work for Ken.

| 1 | 2 | 3 | 4 | 5 | 6 | 7 | 8 | 9 | 10 | 11 | 12 | 13 |

New Functions

39b

Help keywords
Hanging indent;
paragraph; about text
alignment and spacing

Hanging Indent

Hanging indent places the first line of a paragraph at the left margin and indents all other lines to the first tab. It is commonly used to format bibliography entries, glossaries, and lists. Hanging indent can be applied before text is keyed or after.

To create a hanging indent:

1. Display the Horizontal Ruler (click **View**; then **Ruler**).

2. From the Horizontal Ruler, drag the hanging indent marker to the position where the indent is to begin. ⟵ Hanging Indent

3. Key the paragraph. The second and subsequent lines are indented beginning at the marker. (*Shortcut:* CTRL + T, then key the paragraph; or select the paragraphs to be formatted as hanging indents, and press CTRL + T.)

Drill 1 | HANGING INDENT

1. Drag the Hanging Indent marker 0.5" to the right; then key the references that follow.

2. Turn Hanging Indent off by dragging the Hanging Indent marker back to the left margin.

3. Save the document as **39b-drill1**.

Fowler, H. Ramsey and Aaron, Jane E. *The Little, Brown Handbook*. 6th ed. Boston: HarperCollins College Publishers, 1995.

Osaji, Allison. "Know the Credibility of Electronic Citations." *Graduate Education Journal*, April 2000, 45–51.

VandenBos, Gary R. "Software Helps Writers Conform to APA Style." *APA Monitor Online*, (1999) http://www.apa.org/monitor/jan99/soft.html (10 November 2000).

Walters, Daniel S. dswalters2@umt.edu. "Final Report Available on Intranet." E-mail to Stephen P. Cobb, spcobb@umt.edu (14 September 2000).

D r i l l 1 | SET AND MOVE TABS

1. Display the Horizontal Ruler if necessary (**View** menu, **Ruler**).
2. Set these tabs: Left 1.5", right 3.5", and decimal 4.5".

3. Key the first three lines of the drill at these tab stops.
4. Move the left tab to 1", the right tab to 3", and the decimal tab to 5". Key the last three lines. Save it as **31c-drill1**.

Left tab 1.5"	Right tab 3.5"	Decimal tab 4.5"
Schneider	5,000	100.503
Langfield	17,200	98.9
Almich	9,500	.0198

Left tab 1"	Right tab 3"	Decimal tab 5"
McCoy	12,000	12.1
Buswinka	198,250	.98
Oritz	500	1.345

Leader tabs

A **leader tab** displays a series of dots that lead the eye to the next column. Leaders can be combined with a left, center, right, or decimal tab. Leaders are often used in documents such as table of contents, agendas, and financial statements. Leader tabs can only be set from the Tab dialog box.

To set a leader tab:

1. Click **Tabs** on the Format menu to display the Tab dialog box.
2. Enter the position of the tab in the Tab Stop Position box.
3. Choose the **Alignment** type.
4. Choose the **Leader** style, for example 2; click **Set**; then click **OK**.

D r i l l 2 | LEADER TABS

1. In the Tabs dialog box, set a right leader tab at 6" using Leader style 2.
2. Key the first name at the left margin and press TAB. Note that the leaders extend to the right margin.

3. Key the title. Notice that it aligns at the right tab stop.
4. Complete the drill and save it as **31c-drill2**.

John Sneider	President
JoAnn Rouche	Vice President, Education
Janice Weiss	Vice President, Membership
Lotus Fijutisi	Chief Financial Officer
Loretta Russell	Recording Secretary

- All ideas of others must be cited so that credit is given appropriately.

- The reader will need to be able to locate the material using the information included in the reference citation.

- Format rules apply to ideas stated as direct quotations and ideas that are paraphrased.

- A thorough list of references adds integrity to the report and to the report writer.

Good writers learn quickly how to evaluate the many printed and electronic references that may have been located to support the theme of the report being written. Those references judged acceptable are then cited in the report. Writers of the *Publication Manual of the American Psychological Association* (1994, 174-175) share these simple procedures for preparing a reference list that correlates with the references cited in the report body:

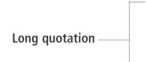
Long quotation

> Note that a reference list cites works that specifically support a particular article. In contrast, a bibliography cites works for background or for further reading. . . . References cited in text must appear in the references list; conversely, each entry in the reference list must be cited in text.

Using a Style Manual

Three popular style manuals are the *MLA Handbook, The Chicago Manual of Style,* and the *Publication Manual of the American Psychological Association.* After selecting a style, carefully study the acceptable formats for citing books, magazines, newspapers, brochures, online journals, e-mail messages, and other sources. Visit Web sites such as http://www.wisc.edu/Writing/Handbook/DocChicago.html, http://www.mla.org, and http://www.apa.org/journals/webref.html for assistance in understanding these styles.

With the availability and volume of excellent electronic resources, writers are including a number of electronic citations along with printed journals, books, and newspapers. Electronic citations may include online journal articles or abstracts, articles on CD-ROM, e-mail messages, discussion list messages, etc. To format references for documents retrieved electronically, Lehman and Dufrene (2002, B-9) offer the following guidelines:

Long quotation

> The various referencing styles are fairly standardized as to the elements included when citing documents retrieved electronically. . . . Include the following items: author (if given), date of publication, title of article and/or name of publication, electronic medium (such as online or CD-ROM), volume, series, page, path (Uniform Resource Locator or Internet address), and date you retrieved or accessed the resource.

38e-d2
Leftbound Report

Convert the unbound report **38e-d1** to a leftbound report. Save the report as **38e-d2**.

38e-d3
Title Page

Prepare a creative title page for report **38e-d2**. Save the document as **38e-d3**.

Applications

31d-d1
Leader and Right Tabs

1. Set a left leader tab using Leader style 2 at 5.25". Set a right tab at 5.75".
2. Key the name at the left margin; press TAB to insert the leaders; press TAB again and key the numbers.
3. Change the line spacing of the document to 1.5. Save the document as **31d-d1**.

Right tab 5.75"

Leader tab 5.25"

Nathaniel Hartwell—Small Forward	220
Cedric McCoy—Power Forward	250
Robert Marschink—Center	190
Joseph Manning—Point Guard	90
Barry English—Shooting Guard	130

31d-d2
Memo with Tab

1. Key the following memo in correct format (see Lesson 29).
2. After keying the second paragraph, strike ENTER twice. Set a tab at 2.5", and key the last several lines. Save the document as **31d-d2**.

TO: All Sunwood Employees

FROM: Julie Patel, Human Relations

DATE: Current date

SUBJECT: Eric Kershaw Hospitalized

We were notified by Eric Kershaw's family that he was admitted into the hospital this past weekend. They expect that he will be hospitalized for another ten days. Visitations and phone calls are limited, but cards and notes are welcome.

A plant is being sent to Eric from the Sunwood staff. Stop by our office before Wednesday if you wish to sign the card. If you would like to send your own "Get Well Wishes" to Eric, send them to:

Left tab 2.5" ——— Eric Kershaw
County General Hospital
Room 401
Atlanta, GA 38209-4751

31d-d3
Challenge
Form with
Underline Tabs

1. Another option for leaders is a solid line (Leader style 4). Format this document, setting a right underline tab at 6". Set DS; key the first two lines of the document.
2. On the third line of the document, set a right underline tab at 3" and a left tab at 3.5". (The right underline tab at 6" is still set.) Complete the document. Save it as **31d-d3**.

Right underline tab 6"

Employee Name _____

Title _____

Reports to _____   Date _____

Review Period from _____   to _____

Right tab 3"   Left tab 3.5"

Internal citations

Internal citations are an easy and practical method of documentation. The last name of the author(s), the publication date, and the page number(s) of the cited material are shown in parentheses within the body of the report (Crawford, 2002, 134). This information cues a reader to the name Crawford in the reference list included at the end of the report. When the author's name is used in the text to introduce the quotation, only the year of publication and the page numbers appear in parentheses: "Crawford (2002, 134) said that . . . ."

Short, direct quotations of three lines or fewer are enclosed within quotation marks. Long quotations of four lines or more are indented 0.5" from the left margin and SS. A DS or one blank line comes before and after the long quotation. The first line is indented an additional 0.5" if the quotation is the beginning of a paragraph.

If a portion of the text that is referenced is omitted, use an ellipsis (. . .) to show the omission. An ellipsis is three periods, each preceded and followed by a space. If a period occurs at the end of a sentence, include the period or punctuation.

deserves more attention that it gets. "Successful businesses have long known the importance of good verbal communication." (Catlette, 2000, 29).

Short Quotation

Probably no successful enterprise exists that does not rely for its success upon the ability of its members to communicate:

> Make no mistake; both written and verbal communication are the stuff upon which success is built . . . . Both forms deserve careful study by any business that wants to grow. Successful businesspeople must read, write, speak, and listen with skill. (Schaefer, 1999, 28)

Long Quotation

Applications

38e-d1
Two-page Report with Direct Quotations

1. Key the unbound report that follows.
2. Press ENTER to leave an approximate 2" top margin. SS the two-line main heading as shown. DS the report.
3. Create a header with the page number displaying at the right; suppress the header on the first page.
4. Check for side headings alone at the bottom of the page.
5. Save the report as **38e-d1**.

COMPLETE AND ACCURATE DOCUMENTATION ESSENTIAL FOR EFFECTIVE REPORTS

Preparing a thorough and convincing report requires excellent research, organization, and composition skills as well as extensive knowledge of documenting referenced materials. The purpose of this report is to present the importance of documenting a report with credible references and the techniques for creating accurate citations.

Documenting with References

For a report to be credible and accepted by its readers, a thorough review of related literature is essential. This background information is an important part of the report and provides believability of the writer and of the report. When sharing this literature in the body of the report, the report writer understands the following basic principles of report documentation:

LESSON 32 | Modified Block Letter Format

Skillbuilding

32a
Warmup
Keep fingers curved, hands quiet as you key each line twice SS; DS between 2-line groups.

1st finger
1 My 456 heavy brown jugs have nothing in them; fill them by May 7.
2 The 57 bins are numbered 1 to 57; Bins 5, 6, 45, and 57 are full.

2d finger
3 Ed decided to crate 38 pieces of cedar decking from the old dock.
4 Mike, who was 38 in December, likes a piece of ice in cold cider.

3d finger
5 Polly made 29 points on the quiz; Wex 10 points. Did they pass?
6 Sall saw Ezra pass 200 pizza pans to Sean, who fixed 20 of them.

| 1 | 2 | 3 | 4 | 5 | 6 | 7 | 8 | 9 | 10 | 11 | 12 | 13 |

32b
Timed Writing
Take two 3' timings.

 all letters

gwam 3'

So now you are operating a keyboard and don't you find it	4	38
amazing that your fingers, working with very little visual help,	8	43
move easily and quickly from one key to the next, helping you to	13	47
change words into ideas and sentences. You just decide what you	17	51
want to say and the format in which you want to say it, and your	21	56
keyboard will carry out your order exactly as you enter it. One	26	60
operator said lately that she sometimes wonders just who is most	30	64
responsible for the completed product—the person or the machine.	34	69

3' | 1 | 2 | 3 | 4 | 5 |

Document Design

32c

Modified-Block Format

In the modified block letter style the dateline and the closing lines begin at the center point of the page. Paragraphs may be blocked or indented to the first tab stop; however, it is more efficient not to indent paragraphs. Set a tab at the center of the page to key the date and the closing lines. To determine the position of the tab, subtract the side margins from the center of the paper.

4.25"	Center of the paper
−1.25"	Margins
3"	Tab setting

Letter Parts

In Lesson 29 you learned the standard letter parts. Listed below are optional parts.

Enclosure notation: If an item is included with a letter, key an enclosure notation a DS below the reference initials. Press TAB to align the enclosures. Variations include:

          Tab
Enclosures: Check #831
             Order form

Enclosures: 2

Copy notation: A copy notation (c) indicates that a copy of the document has been sent to the person listed. Key the copy notation a DS below the reference initials. Press TAB to align the names.

To indent text from the right margin:

1. Display the Horizontal Ruler (click **View**; then **Ruler**).

2. On the Horizontal Ruler, drag the Right Indent marker to the position where the right indent is to begin.

Right indent

3. Key the paragraph. The text will wrap to the next line when the right indent marker is reached.

Drill 1 | INDENT

1. Key the copy that follows. DS paragraph 1; strike TAB to indent the paragraph.
2. To format paragraph 2, at the left margin, click **Increase Indent**. Change to SS. Strike TAB, and then key paragraph 2.
3. For paragraph 3, click **Decrease Indent**; change to DS.
4. Save as **38c-drill1**. Leave the document open for Drill 2.

However, the thrust to use e-mail almost exclusively is causing a tremendous challenge for both e-mail recipients and companies.
DS

TAB   With the convenience of electronic mail resulting in its widespread use, many users are forsaking other forms of Indent → communication—face-to-face, telephone (including voice mail), and printed documents. Now companies are challenged to create clear e-mail policies and to implement employee training on effective use of e-mail (Ashford, 2000, 2).
DS

Communication experts have identified problems that may occur as a result of misusing e-mail. Two important problems include information overload (too many messages) and inappropriate form of communication.

Drill 2 | INDENT FROM BOTH MARGINS

1. Save **38c-drill1** as **38c-drill2**.
2. Click in paragraph 2.
3. Drag the right indent marker to 5.5" (or to the left 0.5").
4. Save the document again.

Document Design

38d
Documentation

Report Documentation

Reports must include the sources of all information used in the report. Documentation gives credit for published material, whether electronic or printed, that is quoted or closely paraphrased by the writer. The writer may document sources by using footnotes, endnotes, or internal citations. In this module, you will use internal citations.

At the end of the report, the writer provides the reader with a complete alphabetical listing of all references. With this complete information provided in the references, the interested reader may locate the original source. You will learn to format a reference list in Lesson 39.

NATIONAL
ASSOCIATION OF
INFORMATION
PROCESSING
PROFESSIONALS

Left tab 3"
January 11, 200- ↓
4

Mr. Richard Harrison
Jobs-OnLine, Inc.
7490 Oregon Avenue
Arvada, CO 80002-8765 **DS**

Dear Mr. Harrison
DS

Please consider this personal invitation to join the National Association of Information
Processing Professionals (NAIPP). Membership is offered to the top 25 percent of the
graduating class. NAIPP is a nonprofit organization comprised of technical
professionals who are striving to stay current in their field. Member benefits include:
DS

Career Development Opportunities—Resume preparation services, job search
program, 120-day internship in many cities, and access to our online job bulletin board.
DS

Educational Benefits—Industry Standard Skill Testing and Credentialing, discounts on
continuing education courses at "Curriculum Approved" colleges and universities, and
online recertification programs. **DS**

Professional Benefits—Discounts on technical publications and computer hardware,
competitive rates for medical and hospitalization insurance, retirement and financial
planning programs, and free international travel services. **DS**

Sign on to our Web site at http://www.naipp.org to learn more about our organization.
Enclosed is a parking pass for the Multimedia Symposium on February 27. **DS**

Sincerely ↓
4

Lorraine Beasly, President
NAIPP Board of Directors **DS**

LB:xx
DS
Enclosure

LESSON 38 | Two-Page Report with Long Quotations

Skillbuilding

38a
Warmup
Key each line twice SS.
DS between groups.

alphabetic 1 Two exit signs jut quietly above the beams of a razed skyscraper.

figures 2 Send 345 of the 789 sets now; send the others on August 1 and 26.

direct reach 3 I obtain many junk pieces dumped by Marvyn at my service centers.

easy 4 Enrique may fish for cod by the dock; he also may risk a penalty.

| 1 | 2 | 3 | 4 | 5 | 6 | 7 | 8 | 9 | 10 | 11 | 12 | 13 |

gwam 1' | 3'

38b
Timed Writings
Key a 1' timing on each paragraph, and a 3' timing on all paragraphs.

 all letters

	1'	3'
Does a relationship exist between confidence and success? If	12	4 42
you think it does, you will find that many people agree with you.	26	9 46
However, it is very hard to judge just how strong the bond is.	38	13 50
When people are confident they can do a job, they are very	12	17 54
likely to continue working on that task until they complete it	24	21 58
correctly. If they are not confident, they give up much quicker.	38	25 63
People who are confident they can do something tend to enjoy	12	29 67
doing it more than those who lack confidence. They realize that	25	34 71
they do better work when they are happy with what they do.	37	37 75

1' | 1 | 2 | 3 | 4 | 5 | 6 | 7 | 8 | 9 | 10 | 11 | 12 | 13 |
3' | | 1 | | 2 | | 3 | | 4 |

New Functions

38c
Indent

Indent

When a writer paraphrases or quotes material longer than three lines from another source, the writer must set off the long quote from the rest of the report. Quoted material is set off by indenting it 0.5" from the left margin.

The Indent feature moves all lines of a paragraph to the next tab. In contrast, TAB moves only the first line of a paragraph to the next tab. Indent is a paragraph command. The Indent feature enables you to indent text from either the left or right margin or from both margins.

To indent text from the left margin:

1. Click the **Increase Indent** button on the toolbar. (*Shortcut:* CTRL + M)

2. Key the paragraph and press ENTER. The left indent will continue until you click the **Decrease Indent** button. (*Shortcut:* CTRL + SHIFT + M)

Indent can also be applied to text that has already been keyed by selecting the text and then clicking **Increase Indent**.

Help keywords
Increase the left indent of an entire paragraph

 Increase Indent

Decrease Indent

Applications

32d-d1
Modified Block Letter

1. Open a new document, and set a left tab at 3". Insert the current date at 2.1" at the tab.
2. Key the letter on the previous page in modified-block style. Check spelling and correct errors.
3. Save the letter as **32d-d1**, preview the document, and print it when you are satisfied.

32d-d2
Modified Block Letter

1. Add your reference initials and a copy notation to your instructor.
2. Proofread carefully, save the letter as **32d-d2**, and print.

Current date ↓4

Ms. Ana Gonzalez
One-Stop Printing Co.
501 Madison Road
Cincinnati, OH 45227-6398

Dear Ms. Gonzalez

Do you know that more and more people are opting to go on a shopping spree on the Internet rather than the mall? Businesses, ranging from small mom and pop stores to global multinational corporations, are setting up shop on the Web if they haven't already. They are selling goods, services, and themselves!

Consumers expect businesses to have a Web site. Those that don't will give their business to their competitor.

E-Business, Inc. has helped hundreds of businesses nationwide establish their business on the Internet. May we help you integrate your online and offline sales strategies? Call us today at 800-555-1000 and arrange for one of our consultants to analyze your e-commerce strategies to increase your volume. ↓2

Sincerely yours ↓4

Ellen Soey
Marketing Manager ↓2

32d-d3
Letter with Envelope

1. Open **32d-d2** and add an envelope to the letter. Change the address to all caps with no punctuation.
2. Save the document as **32d-d3**.

32d-d4
Data Files

The CD-ROM in the back of your textbook contains extra files you will use in this course. This text refers to these files as **data files**. They are organized by module. Your instructor may already have installed these files for classroom use.

1. Ask your instructor how to access the files, or install the files on the hard drive following the instructions on the CD-ROM. When the files are installed, locate the data path or folder where these files are stored. (The default path is: *c:\College Keyboarding L1-60 Data.*)
2. Double-click the **Module 3** folder to open it. Open the file **Decker**. Correct the spacing between letter parts; assume spacing below Enclosure is correct. Set a right underline tab at 3" and 5.9" on the line immediately above *Date* and *Signature*; strike TAB to insert the underlines. Position the letter vertically on the page so that it looks attractive. Use Print Preview. Save the document as **32d-d4** in the **Module 4 Keys** folder and print.

- Format references using the hanging indent feature.
- Use typographic or special symbols to enhance the report. Examples include ¶ for paragraph, ™ for trademark, ® for registered, ≠ for not equal to, and ✂ to indicate cut along this line.

Writers also take advantage of the online thesaurus for choosing the most appropriate word and the spelling and grammar features to ensure spelling and grammar correctness. Additionally, electronic desk references and style manuals are just a click away.

Finally, all the report needs is the title page. Effective writers know that it pays dividends to create a custom title page that truly reflects the quality of the report that it covers. Use page borders and shading as well as graphics to create an attractive title page.

Four simple steps followed in a systematic order will assist you in your goal to learn to win at writing. Knowing the approach is the first step; the second step is to practice, practice, and practice.

37d-d2
Title Page

1. Prepare a title page for the leftbound report prepared in **37d-d1**. Set the left margin at 1.5".
2. Prepare the title page for **XYZ Employees by Jennifer Schoenholtz, Office Manager**.
3. Expand character spacing, add a page border, and change the font color.
4. Save the title page as **37d-d2**.

COURTESY OF © PHOTODISC, INC.

N E W S | on cell phones

Are cell phones dangerous to your health? Studies are being conducted to determine whether or not cell phones can cause serious health problems such as brain tumors and high blood pressure. So far, there is no conclusive evidence to support this theory. However, it is true that cell phones have caused an increased number of automobile crashes. The Cellular Telecommunications Industry has issued some cell phone safety tips. Use a hands-free device when possible. Try to place calls while you are not moving. Do not engage in stressful conversations that could divert your attention from the road. Never try to take notes or look up phone numbers while driving.

LESSON 33 | Letter Review

Skillbuilding

33a
Warmup
Key each line twice SS; DS between 2-line groups.

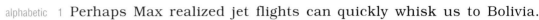

alphabetic	1	Perhaps Max realized jet flights can quickly whisk us to Bolivia.
fig/sym	2	Send 24 Solex Cubes, Catalog #95-0, price $6.78, before April 31.
1st finger	3	The boy of just 6 or 7 years of age ran through the mango groves.
easy	4	The auditor did sign the form and name me to chair a small panel.

| 1 | 2 | 3 | 4 | 5 | 6 | 7 | 8 | 9 | 10 | 11 | 12 | 13 |

33b
Review Letter Parts
Arrange the letter parts correctly. Ignore top margin requirements. Press ENTER five times between activities.

1 Sincerely yours | Manuel Garcia | Council President | MG:xx | c Ron N. Besbit

2 Yours truly | Ms. Loren Lakes | Secretary General | xx | Enclosure | c Libby Uhl

3 Ms. Mara Pena | 8764 Gold Plaza | Lansing, MI 48933-8312 | Dear Ms. Pena

Applications

33c-d1
Modified-Block Letter

1. Format the letter in modified block style. Insert the current date at 2.1".
2. Supply the correct salutation, a complimentary closing, and your reference initials. Add an enclosure line and a copy notation to **Laura Aimes, Sales Representative**.
3. Proofread carefully. Preview for good placement. Save as **33c-d1**. Print.
4. Attach an envelope to the letter, and save it again as **33c-d2**.

33c-d2
Envelope

Ms. Mukta Bhakta
9845 Buckingham Road
Annapolis, MD 21403-0314

Thank you for your recent inquiry on our electronic bulletin service. The ABC BBS is an interactive online service developed by All Business Communication to assist the online community in receiving documents via the Internet.

All Business Communication also provides a *Customer Support Service* and a *Technical Support Team* to assist bulletin board users. The Systems Administrators will perform various procedures needed to help you take full advantage of this new software.

For additional information call:

> Customer and Technical Support
> Telephone: 900-555-1212
> 9:00 a.m.-5:00 p.m., Monday-Friday, Eastern Time

Please look over the enclosed ABC BBS brochure. I will call you within the next two weeks to discuss any additional questions you may have.

Alex Zampich, Marketing Manager

Applications

37d-d1
Two-Page Report

1. Key the leftbound report that follows.

✳ 2. From the data disk, insert the file **writing** below the second paragraph. (*Note:* Be sure to position the insertion point where you want the text to appear before inserting the file.)

3. Format the first side heading *Researching* correctly. Use **Format Painter** to format the other side headings.

4. Format the bulleted list SS with a DS between items.

5. Revise the side headings to make them parallel (grammatically consistent).

6. Create a header for the page numbers; do not print the header on page 1. (*Optional:* Include a border under the header.)

7. Apply **Keep with next** to protect side headings from being left alone at the bottom of a page.

8. Switch to Print Layout view to verify page numbers.

9. Save the report as **37d-d1**. Check the spelling, and print the document.

LEARN TO WIN AT WRITING

Being able to communicate effectively continues to be one of the most demanded work skills. Today's high demand for clear, concise, and logical communication makes it impossible for an employee to excuse himself or herself from writing by saying, "I'm just not a writer," or "I can't write."

Realizing you need to improve your writing skills is the first step to enhancing them. Then you must apply a systemized approach to writing as detailed in this report.

Insert the data file writing here.

The effective writer understands the importance of using technology to create an attractive document that adheres to correct style rules. Review the list below to determine your use of technology in the report writing process.

- Number preliminary pages of the report with small Roman numerals at the bottom center of the page.
- Number the report with Arabic numbers in the upper-right corner.
- Create attractive headers or footers that contain helpful information for the reader.
- Suppress headers, footers, and page numbering on the title page and on the first page of the report.
- Invoke the widow/orphan protection feature to ensure that no lines display alone at the bottom or top of a page.
- Use the block protection command to keep side headings from appearing alone at the bottom of the page.

continued

33c-d3
Rough-Draft Letter
Block Style

1. Key the following letter in block style. Apply what you have learned about correct letter placement and letter parts.

2. Save the document as **33c-d3**, and print one copy.

Mr. John Crane
5760 Sky Way
Seattle, WA *05671-0321*

Would you like to invest in a company that will provide you with *a* *sp* 180%

return on your investment? Consider investing in a ~~company~~ *firm* that specializes in

importing and exporting with China. China's domestic product (GDP) is

expected to be over a trillion dollars. *gross*

(bold & italic) Ameri-Chinois has made a significant number of business arrangements

with key organizations in China to source goods and to participate in global two-

way trade. Trade between China and ~~other countries~~ *the rest of the world* is expected to grow over

sp 20% this year. China's exports are expected to rise to $244 billion in the year

2001. Imports will grow to $207 billion. *are expected to*

Contact Lawrence Chen at Century Investments to learn how you can be

an investor in the growing company of Ameri-Chinois. The current price is

$0.52; the targeted price is $9.00. Call today! *per share*

800-555-1034 Sincerely

Lawrence Chen

33c-d4
Edit Block Letter

1. Open **33c-d3**; and save it as **33c-d4**. Select the letter address, and then delete it.

2. Address the letter to: **Mr. Tom K. Onehawk, 139 Via Cordoniz, Evansville, IL 44710-3277.** Supply an appropriate salutation.

3. Add **Please study the enclosed portfolio and then** at the beginning of paragraph 3. Be sure to change the *c* in contact to lowercase.

4. Add an enclosure notation.

33c-d5
Label

✶ 1. Open the letter to Mr. Onehawk (**33c-d4**). Prepare a label to send the portfolio in a larger envelope. Create an Avery 5160 address label. *Note:* Once you click the Options button on the Labels tab, select **Avery Standard** in the Label products. Then select **Avery 5160** from the Product Number list box.

2. Open document **33c-d1,** and create and print an address label for this letter as well. Choose an **Avery 5168** label.

Document Design

37c
Two-Page Reports

Report Format Guidelines

Reports are widely used in various environments. Study the information that follows:

Side margins: Set according to type of binding, e.g., leftbound or topbound.

Top margin: 2" for first page of report, preliminary pages, and Reference page; 1" on other pages.

Page numbers: Include page numbers for the second and succeeding pages of a report. Position at the right top margin.

Single lines: Avoid single lines at the top or bottom of a report (called *widow/orphan lines*). Do not separate a side heading from the paragraph that follows between pages.

To format a report:

1. At the top of the document, change the line spacing to double. Strike ENTER three times to position the insertion point to leave an approximate 2" top margin.

2. Check that the font size is 12 point.

3. Insert a header for page numbers. Suppress the header on the first page.

4. Key the main heading in ALL CAPS. Strike ENTER twice, then select the heading and apply 14 point and bold. Center-align the heading.

5. Move the insertion point to below the heading, and begin to key the report.

6. Position the references on a new page. If necessary, insert a hard page break. Format the title REFERENCES in 14 point, bold, at approximately 2".

7. Protect side headings that may get separated from the related paragraph with the Keep with next feature.

8. View the report using Print Layout view.

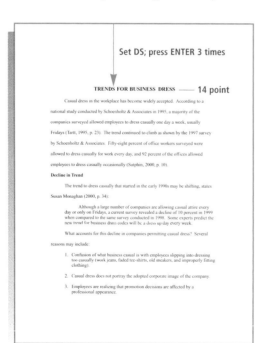

LESSON 34 | Assessment

Skillbuilding

34a
Warmup
Key each line twice SS; DS between 2-line groups.

alphabetic 1 Johnny Willcox printed five dozen banquet tickets for my meeting.

fig/sym 2 Our check #389 for $21,460—dated 1/15/01—was sent to O'Neil & Co.

1st finger 3 It is true Greg acted bravely during the severe storm that night.

easy 4 In the land of enchantment, the fox and the lamb lie by the bush.

| 1 | 2 | 3 | 4 | 5 | 6 | 7 | 8 | 9 | 10 | 11 | 12 | 13 |

gwam 3'

34b
Timed Writings
Take two 3' timings.

  all letters

Many young people are quite surprised to learn that either | 4 | 48
lunch or dinner is included as part of a job interview. Most of | 8 | 52
them think of this part of the interview as a friendly gesture from | 13 | 56
the organization. | 15 | 58

The meal is not provided just to be nice to the person. The | 18 | 62
organization expects to use that function to observe the social | 22 | 66
skills of the person and to determine if he or she might be effective | 27 | 71
doing business in that type of setting. | 30 | 73

What does this mean to you if you are preparing for a job | 33 | 77
interview? The time spent reading about and learning to use good | 38 | 81
social skills pays off not only during the interview but also after | 42 | 86
you accept the job. | 44 | 87

1' | 1 | 2 | 3 | 4 | 5 | 6 | 7 | 8 | 9 | 10 | 11 | 12 | 13 |
3' | 1 | 2 | 3 | 4 |

Applications

34c
Assessment
Timed production

 Continue button

 Check button

General Instructions: Format the letters in the style indicated; add additional letter parts if necessary. Use the Date and Time feature for the current date. Add a proper salutation and your reference initials for all letters. Position each letter at 2.1". Check spelling, preview for proper placement, and carefully proofread each letter before proceeding to the next document.

With CheckPro 2002: *CheckPro* will keep track of the time it takes you to complete the entire production test, compute your speed and accuracy rate on each document, and summarize the results. When you complete a document, proofread it, check the spelling, and preview for placement. When you are completely satisfied with the document, click the Continue button to move to the next document. You will not be able to return and edit a document once you continue to the next document.   Click the **Check** button when you are ready to error-check the test. Review and/or print the document analysis results.

Without CheckPro 2002: On the signal to begin, key the documents in sequence. When saving documents, name them in the usual manner (for example, **34c-d1**). When time has been called, proofread all documents again, identify errors, and determine *g-pwam*.

$$g\text{-}pwam = \frac{\text{total words keyed}}{25'}$$

D r i l l 3   LINE AND PAGE BREAKS

1. Open **Report2** from the data files. Save it as **37b-drill3**.
2. Create a header for page numbers. Suppress the header on the first page.
3. Select the heading *In Conclusion* and the paragraph that follows. Apply **Keep with next**.
4. Position the main heading at about 2".
5. Format all headings correctly.
6. Change to Print Layout view to verify the page numbers and the top margin.
7. Save and print. Compare your document to the model on page 125.

help keywords

Insert a symbol;
Insert a special character

Symbols and Special Characters

Symbols and special characters can be printed using the Symbol command even though they do not appear on the keyboard. Symbols that you use frequently can be assigned to a shortcut key. (See Help, Insert Symbol or Character.) Examples of symbols and special characters include:

Em dash —   En dash –   Copyright ©   Registered ®   Trademark™

To insert symbols or special characters:

1. Position the insertion point where the symbol or special character is to be inserted.
2. Click **Insert** on the menu, and then click **Symbol**.
3. Click the **Symbols** tab to insert a symbol or click the **Special characters** tab to insert a special character. You may also select from the Recently used symbols box.

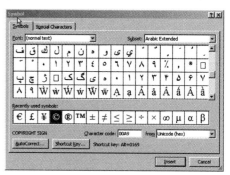

4. Select the symbol or special character to be inserted. When selecting symbols, you may also want to select a different font to display various symbols, e.g., Wingdings, Wingdings2, and Wingdings3.
5. Click **Insert** and **Close**. (*Hint:* To increase the size of the symbol, select and enlarge font size.)

D r i l l 4   SYMBOLS

1. Key the following lines as a numbered list.
2. Insert the symbols and special characters shown.
3. Save it as **37b-drill4**.

Special Characters

1. Parker House—Best Dining (em dash)
2. Pages 13–25 (en dash)
3. July 20 (nonbreaking space)
4. 92°F (degree and nonbreaking space)
5. Revise ¶3.

Symbols

6. ☺ Have a nice day.
7. ⇨ Room 253.
8. ✎ Sign here.
9. ✓ Yes, send today.
10. ❑ Yes ❑ No

34c-d1
Block-Format Letter
Supply the salutation.

Current date | AMASTA Company, Inc. | 902 Greenridge Drive | Reno, NV 13
69505-5552 19

We sell your videocassettes and have since you introduced them. Several 33
of our customers now tell us they are unable to follow the directions on the 49
coupon. They explain that there is no company logo on the box to return to 64
you as you requested. 68

What steps should we take? A copy of the coupon is enclosed, as is a 82
Super D Container. Please read the coupon, examine the box, and then let 97
me know your plans for extricating us from this problem. 109

Sincerely yours| John J. Long | Sales Manager | Enclosures: 2 122

34c-d2
Modified-Block Letter
Supply the salutation.

words

Current date | Mr. John J. Long, Sales Manager | The Record Store | 9822 11
Trevor Avenue | Anaheim, CA 92805-5885 22

With your letter came our turn to be perplexed, and we apologize. When 36
we had our refund coupons printed, we had just completed a total redesign 51
program for our product boxes. We had detachable logos put on the 65
outside of the boxes, which could be peeled off and placed on a coupon. 79

We had not anticipated that our distributors would use back inventories 94
with our promotion. The cassettes you sold were not packaged in our new 108
boxes; therefore, there were no logos on them. 118

I'm sorry you or your customers were inconvenienced. In the future, 131
simply ask your customers to send us their sales slips, and we will honor 146
them with refunds until your supply of older containers is depleted. 160

Sincerely yours | Bruna Wertz | Sales and Promotions Dept. | xx 173

34c-d3
Memo with Leader Tabs
Set a left leader tab at 5" and a right tab at 6".

words

TO: Arethea Scheib-Race | **FROM:** Bruna Wertz | **DATE:** Current | 12
SUBJECT: New Employees 17

Please add the following new employees and their extension numbers to 31
your phone list. 34

Jordan, Shalini 1359 39

Mundy, Paul 1203 42

Mahindra, Allison 6346 47

A new phone directory will not be printed for at least two months. 61

34c-d4
Modified-Block Letter

1. Open **Brackmun** from the data files. Save it as **34c-d4**.
2. Send the letter to: **Vidadex Corporation, 3945 Alexandria Boulevard, Detroit, MI 48230-9732.** Replace the salutation.
3. Change the letter from block to modified-block format.

D r i l l   2 | HEADER

1. Open **36d-d3**. Save it as **37b-drill2**.

2. Create the header shown below for the two-page report, and suppress the header on the first page.

3. Key the report title at the left position.

4. Tab to the right position. Key **Page** and space once; then insert the page number.

✳ 5. Use the Border button on the Formatting toolbar to create a bottom border under the header.

6. View the header.

7. Make the revisions shown below to the report.

8. Close the document and save your changes.

> Header
> Basic Tips for Designing Attractive Brochures   Page 2

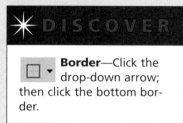

Border—Click the drop-down arrow; then click the bottom border.

Summary (Use Format Painter to format)

Remember to plan your page layout with the three basic elements of effective page design. Always include sufficient white space to give an uncluttered appearance. Learn to add bold when emphasis is needed, and do consider your audience when choosing typestyles. Finally, use typestyles to add variety to your layout, but remember, no more than two typestyles in a document.

[handwritten edits: keeping, in mind, add italic when required, and, page, limit, to]

Line and Page Breaks

help keywords
Format paragraph and line and page breaks.

Pagination or breaking pages at the appropriate location can easily be controlled using two features: Widow/Orphan control and Keep with next.

Widow/Orphan control prevents a single line of a paragraph from printing at the bottom or top of a page. A check mark displays in this option box indicating that Widow/Orphan control is "on" (the default).

Keep with next prevents a page break from occurring between two paragraphs. Use this feature to keep a side heading from being left alone at the bottom of a page. To use Keep with next:

1. Select the side heading and the paragraph that follows.

2. Click **Format**; then **Paragraph**.

3. From the Line and Page Breaks tab, select **Keep with next**. Click **OK**. The side heading moves to the next page.

MOUS TIP

You can also insert a page break by pressing CTRL + Enter or choosing Page Break from the Insert menu.

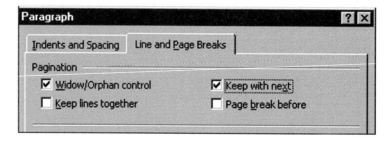

Objective Assessment

Answer the questions below to see if you have mastered the content of Module 4.

1. When a business letter is addressed to a company, the correct salutation is _____ .

2. From the dateline, strike ENTER _____ times before keying the letter address.

3. Use 1.25" or _____ side margins for a business letter.

4. Letters are positioned vertically on the page by using the _____ command.

5. When keying a modified block letter, set a tab at the center point of the page, which is _____".

6. When an item is included with a letter, a(n) _____ notation is keyed a DS below the reference initials.

7. Envelopes and labels are accessed from the _____ menu.

8. The _____ button at the left edge of the Ruler indicates the type of tab.

9. If the Ruler is not displayed on your screen, click the _____ menu and select Ruler.

10. The _____ notation is used to indicate that a copy of the letter is being sent to another person.

Performance Assessment

Document 1
Block Letter with Envelope

1. Key the letter in block format. The letter is from Darin Parson, Marketing Manager. Add the necessary letter parts.

2. Attach an envelope to the letter.

3. Save as **checkpoint4-d1**. Proofread and print when you are satisfied.

Ms. Lucy Marino | 2155 Mack Avenue | Los Angeles, CA | 90115-0989

The keynote speaker for our annual sales conference this year will be Dr. Helen McBride, from the University of Southern California. She will be giving her opening speech at 2:00 p.m. on Tuesday, May 25, 200–.

Dr. McBride, a well-known psychologist who has spent a lot of time researching and writing on employee productivity, will address "Stress Management." I am sure you will find her speech to be both informative and entertaining.

A copy of Dr. McBride's resume is enclosed for use in preparing news releases and announcements for the sales conference.

Document 2
Edit Letter

1. Open **checkpoint4-d1**.

2. Select the date and closing lines; set a tab appropriate for a modified block letter. Format the document in modified block.

3. Delete the letter address. Send this letter to **Mr. Joseph Rodrigues, 55 La Brea Avenue, Santa Monica, CA 90155-9876**. Perform all necessary changes to make this a mailable business letter.

4. Save as **checkpoint4-d2**. Print.

LESSON 37 | Two-Page Reports

 Skillbuilding

37a
Warmup
Practice each line;
repeat the drill.

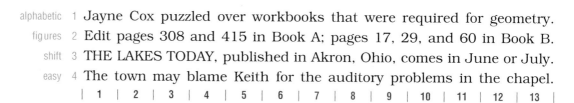

alphabetic 1 Jayne Cox puzzled over workbooks that were required for geometry.
figures 2 Edit pages 308 and 415 in Book A; pages 17, 29, and 60 in Book B.
shift 3 THE LAKES TODAY, published in Akron, Ohio, comes in June or July.
easy 4 The town may blame Keith for the auditory problems in the chapel.
| 1 | 2 | 3 | 4 | 5 | 6 | 7 | 8 | 9 | 10 | 11 | 12 | 13 |

New Functions

37b

Help keywords
Create a header or footer

Header and Footer

The **Header** feature enables you to place information at the top of each page in a document. The default header allows for three lines, but this space may be increased or decreased. Headers print 0.5" from the top edge of the paper. Headers can only be viewed in Print Layout view.

To create a header for page numbers:

1. Click **View** on the menu bar, and then click **Header and Footer**. The Header and Footer toolbar and a grid area in which you will key the header display.

2. The header has three positions: left margin, center, right margin. Press the TAB key twice to move the insertion point to the right margin position.

3. Click the **Insert Page Number (#)** button to insert the page number.

4. Click the **Page Setup** button on the Header and Footer toolbar. Choose **Different First Page**; then click **OK** to suppress the header on first page.

5. Choose **Close** on the Header and Footer toolbar. View the header in Print Layout view (View menu).

Drill 1 | HEADER

1. Open **header** from the data files. Save it as **37b-drill1**.

2. Create the header to number the pages in the top right position for the two-page report.

3. Choose **Different First Page** to suppress the header on the first page.

4. View the document by clicking **Print Layout** on the View menu.

5. Close the document and save your changes.

COMMUNICATION SKILLS 1

Capitalization Guides

Capitalize:

1. **First word of a sentence and of a direct quotation.**

   We were tolerating instead of managing diversity.

   The speaker said, "We must value diversity, not merely recognize it."

2. **Proper nouns**—specific persons, places, or things.

   Common nouns: continent, river, car, street

   Proper nouns: Asia, Mississippi, Buick, State St.

   Exception: Capitalize a title of high distinction even when it does not refer to a specific person (e.g., President of the United States).

3. **Derivatives** of proper nouns and capitalize **geographical** names.

   Derivatives: American history, German food, English accent, Ohio Valley

   Proper nouns: Tampa, Florida, Mount Rushmore

4. **A personal or professional title** when it precedes the name; capitalize a title of high distinction without a name.

   Title: Lieutenant Kahn, Mayor Walsh, Doctor Welby

   High distinction: the President of the United States,

5. **Days of the week, months of the year, holidays, periods of history, and historic events.**

   Monday, June 8, Labor Day, Renaissance

6. **Specific parts of the country** but not compass points that show direction.

   Midwest   the South   northwest of town   the Middle East

7. **Family relationships** when used with a person's name.

   Aunt Carol   my mother   Uncle Mark

8. **A noun preceding a figure** except for common nouns such as line, page, and sentence.

   Unit 1   Section 2   page 2   verse 7   line 2

9. **First and main words of side headings, titles of books, and works of art.**
   Do not capitalize words of four or fewer letters that are conjunctions, prepositions, or articles.

   Computers in the News   *Raiders of the Lost Ark*

10. **Names of organizations and specific departments** within the writer's organization.

    Girl Scouts   our Sales Department

11. **The salutation of a letter and the first word of the complimentary closing.**

    Dear Mr. Bush   Ladies and Gentlemen: Sincerely yours,

    Very cordially yours,

Set DS; Press ENTER 3 times

About 2.1"

PLANNING A SUCCESSFUL PRESENTATION

Presenters realize the need to prepare for a successful presentation. Two areas of extensive preparation are the development of a thorough audience analysis and a well-defined presentation purpose.

Audience Analysis

The presenter must conduct a thorough audience analysis before developing

1.5" the presentation. The profile of the audience includes the following demographics. 1.25"

- Age and gender
- Education
- Ethnic group
- Marital status
- Geographic location
- Group membership

Interviews with program planners and organization leaders will provide insight into the needs, desires, and expectations of the audience. This information makes the difference in preparing a presentation that is well received by the audience.

Purpose of the Presentation

After analyzing the audience profile, the presenter has a clear focus on the needs of the audience and then writes a well-defined purpose of the presentation. With a clear focus, the presenter confidently conducts research and organizes a presentation that is on target. The presenter remembers to state the purpose in the introduction of the presentation to assist the audience in understanding the well-defined direction of the presentation.

Drill 1

CAPITALIZATION

Review the rules and examples on the previous page. Then key the sentences, correcting all capitalization errors. Number each item and DS between items. Save as **capitalize-drill 1.**

1. according to one study, the largest ethnic minority group online is hispanics.
2. the american author mark twain said, "always do right; this will gratify some people and astonish the rest."
3. the grand canyon was formed by the colorado river cutting into the high-plateau region of northwestern arizona.
4. the president of russia is elected by popular vote.
5. the hubble space telescope is a cooperative project of the european space agency and the national aeronautics and space administration.
6. the train left north station at 6:45 this morning.
7. the trademark cyberprivacy prevention act would make it illegal for individuals to purchase domains solely for resale and profit.
8. consumers spent $7 billion online between november 1 and december 31, 2000, compared to $3.1 billion for the same period in 1999.
9. new students should attend an orientation session on wednesday, august 15, at 8 a.m. in room 252 of the perry building.
10. the summer book list includes *where the red fern grows* and *the mystery of the missing baseball.*

Drill 2

CAPITALIZATION

1. Open the file **capitalize2** from the data files and save it as **capitalize-drill2**.
2. Follow the specific directions provided in the data file. Remember to use the correct proofreaders' marks:

   ≡ Capitalize   sincerely
   lc Lowercase   My Đear Sir
3. Resave and print. Submit the rough draft and final copy to your instructor.

Drill 3

CAPITALIZATION OF LETTER PARTS

Key the letter parts using correct capitalization. Number each item and DS between each. Save as **capitalize-drill3**.

1. dear mr. petroilli
2. ladies and gentlemen
3. dear senator kuknais
4. very sincerely yours
5. dear reverend Schmidt
6. very truly yours
7. cordially yours
8. dear mr fong and miss landow
9. respectfully yours
10. sincerely
11. dear mr. and mrs. Green
12. dear service manager

Drill 4

CAPITALIZATION

1. Open the file **capitalize4** from the data files. Save it as **capitalize-drill4**.
2. This file includes a field for selecting the correct answer. You will simply select the correct answer. Follow the specific directions provided in the data file.
3. Resave and print.

Document Design

36c

Leftbound report

The binding on a report usually takes about 0.5" inch of space. Therefore, when a report is bound on the left, set the left margin to 1.5" for all pages.

The same right, top, and bottom margins are used for both unbound and leftbound reports.

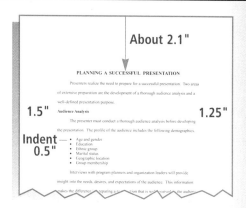

Applications

36d-d1
Leftbound Report

1. Key the leftbound report on page 121. Save the report as **36d-d1**.
2. To create the bulleted list, key the items; then select the items and apply bullets.
3. With the items selected, click the **Increase Indent** button to align the bullets with the paragraph indent.

36d-d2
Title Page

1. Create a title page for the leftbound report prepared in Document 1. Set the left margin at 1.5".
2. Prepare the title page for **John E. Swartsfager, Marketing Director**, by you as the **Information Technology Manager**.
3. Expand character spacing by 1.5 pt. in the report title.
✳ 4. Add a dark red page border, and change the text font color to dark red.
5. Save the document as **36d-d2**.

36d-d3
Leftbound Report

1. Open **35e-d2** and format the document as a leftbound report.
2. Add the last paragraph shown below, and save the document as **36d-d3**.

Summary (Use Format Painter to format.)

Remember to plan your page layout with the three basic elements of effective page design. Always include sufficient white space to give an uncluttered appearance. Learn to add bold when emphasis is needed, and do consider your audience when choosing typestyles. Finally, use typestyles to add variety to your layout, but remember, no more than two typestyles in a document.

module 5

Simple Reports

OBJECTIVES

✳ Format two-page reports with references and title pages.
✳ Indent long quotations and bibliography entries appropriately.
✳ Create headers and footers.
✳ Apply bullets and numbers.

LESSON 35 | Unbound Report with Title Page

▣ Skillbuilding

35a
Warmup
Key each line twice SS.
DS between groups.

alphabetic	1	Dave Cagney alphabetized items for next week's quarterly journal.
figures	2	Close Rooms 4, 18, and 20 from 3 until 9 on July 7; open Room 56.
up reaches	3	Toy & Wurt's note for $635 (see our page 78) was paid October 29.
easy	4	The auditor is due by eight, and he may lend a hand to the panel.

| 1 | 2 | 3 | 4 | 5 | 6 | 7 | 8 | 9 | 10 | 11 | 12 | 13 |

gwam 1' | 3'

35b
Timed Writings
Take two 3' timings.

 all letters

Have simple things such as saying please, may I help you, and thank you gone out of style? We begin to wonder when we observe front-line workers interact with customers today. Often their bad attitudes shout that the customer is a bother and unimportant. But we know there would be no business without the customer. So what can be done to prove to customers that they really are the king?

First, require that all your staff train in good customer service. Here they must come to realize that their jobs exist for the customer. Also, be sure workers feel that they can talk to their bosses about any problem. You do not want workers to talk about lack of breaks or schedules in front of customers. Clients must always feel that they are kings and should never be ignored.

	1'	3'
	12	4
	25	8
	39	13
	52	17
	66	22
	79	26
	12	30
	25	35
	38	39
	51	43
	64	48
	77	52

1' | 1 | 2 | 3 | 4 | 5 | 6 | 7 | 8 | 9 | 10 | 11 | 12 | 13 |
3' | 1 | 2 | 3 | 4 |

Bullets   Numbering

Numbered and bulleted lists are commonly used to emphasize information in reports, newspapers, magazine articles, and overhead presentations. Use numbered items if the list requires a sequence of steps or points. Use bullets or symbols if the list contains an unordered listing. *Word* automatically inserts the next number in a sequence if you manually key a number.

Single-space bulleted or numbered items if each item consists of one line. If more than one line is required for any item, single-space the list and double-space between each item. Study the illustrations shown below.

- Word processing
- Spreadsheet
- Database
- Presentation
- Desktop publishing

1. Preheat oven to 350°.
2. Cream butter and sugar; add eggs.
3. Add flour.

To create bullets or numbers:

1. Key the list without bullets or numbers. Select the list and click the **Bullets** or **Numbering** button on the Formatting toolbar. If a double space is required between items, press SHIFT + ENTER at the end of each line.
2. To add or remove bullets or numbers, click the **Bullets** or **Numbering** button.
3. To convert bullets to numbers or vice versa, select the items to change and click either the **Bullets** or **Numbering** button.

D r i l l   2 | BULLETS

1. Key the text below; do not key the bullets.
2. Apply bullets to the list by selecting the text to be bulleted and clicking the **Bullets** button.
3. Convert the bullets to numbers. Select the bulleted items and click the **Numbering** button.
4. Add **Roll Call** as the second item.
5. Delete the number before *Next Meeting*.
6. Save the document as **36b-drill2** and print it.

- Call to Order
- Reading and Approval of the Minutes
- Announcements
- Treasurer's Report
- Membership Committee Report
- Unfinished Business
- New Business
- Adjournment
- Next Meeting: November 3, 200-

D r i l l   3 | BULLETS

1. Open **bullets** from the data files.
2. Select the bulleted items, and convert them to numbers.
3. Add a blank line between each numbered item without adding an additional number by pressing SHIFT + ENTER at the end of each item.
4. Save as **36b-drill3**.

New Functions
35c

Format Painter

 Use **Format Painter** to copy paragraph and character formats to other text in a document. The Format Painter button is located on the Standard toolbar.

To copy paragraph formats:

1. Click the **Show/Hide** button to display the paragraph marker (¶). Select the entire paragraph, including the paragraph marker.

2. Click the **Format Painter** button once to apply the format to a single paragraph. Double-click the **Format Painter** button to apply the format to more than one paragraph.

3. Click in the paragraph(s) to be reformatted.

4. If the Format Painter button is still active, click it again to turn it off.

To copy character formats:

1. Place the insertion point in the text with the formatting to be copied.

2. Click **Format Painter**. (Double-click **Format Painter** if the formatting will be applied in more than one location.)

3. Select the text to be reformatted.

4. If Format Painter is still active, click the button again to turn it off.

Drill 1 | APPLY FORMATS

1. Open **functions** from the data files. In this drill, you will use Format Painter to apply the format of the first term and definition to the remaining items in the document.

2. Click **Show/Hide** to display tabs and paragraph markers. Select the word **Bullets.**

3. Double-click the **Format Painter** button. Click each of the remaining functions in the first column to apply the format; then click the **Format Painter** button off.

4. Select the paragraph that defines the first function and the paragraph marker following it. Use Format Painter to format the remaining definitions.

5. Create the folder **Module 5 Keys**, and save the document as **35c-drill1** in this folder.

FUNCTIONS¶		
¶ Bullets	→	Inserts·various·style·bullets·or·symbols·to·emphasize· a·list.¶

Drill 2 | APPLY FORMATS

1. Open **design** from the data files.

2. Bold the first side heading, *White Space*; change the font to Arial.

3. Use Format Painter to format the other side headings (*Attributes* and *Typestyles*).

4. Save the document as **35c-drill2** in the **Module 5 Keys** folder.

LESSON 36 | Leftbound Report

Skillbuilding

36a
Warmup
Practice each line;
repeat the drill.

alphabetic 1 The explorer questioned Jack's amazing story about the lava flow.

fig/sym 2 I cashed Cartek & Bunter's $2,679 check (Check #3480) on June 15.

1st/2d finger 3 Hugh tried to go with Katrina, but he did not have time to do so.

easy 4 The eighty firms may pay for a formal audit of their field works.

| 1 | 2 | 3 | 4 | 5 | 6 | 7 | 8 | 9 | 10 | 11 | 12 | 13 |

New Functions

36b

Help keywords:
Change page margins

Margins

Margins are the distance between the edge of the paper and the print. The default settings are 1.25" side margins and 1" top and bottom margins. Default margins stay in effect until you change them.

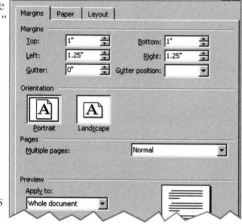

To change the margins:

1. Click **File**; then **Page Setup**.

2. From the Margins tab, click the up or down arrows to increase or decrease the default settings.

3. Apply margins to the Whole document unless directed otherwise. Click **OK**.

D r i l l 1 | MARGINS

1. Set 1" side margins. Key the paragraph below. Save as **36b-drill1**; then preview the document.

2. Position the insertion point at the beginning of sentence 4. Press ENTER twice.

3. With the insertion point in paragraph 2, change the top and side margins to 2". Preview the document.

4. At the end of sentence 4, press ENTER twice. Key and complete this sentence with the better response, (a) or (b).

The margin command affects the appearance of the (a) entire document (b) paragraph containing the insertion point.

5. Save the document again.

6. Change the left, right, and top margins to 1.5". Apply margin settings to the whole document.

7. Save the document as **36b-drill1b**.

Attractive document layout begins with margins set an equal distance from the left and right edges of the paper. When margins are equal, the document appears balanced. One exception to the equal-margin rule is in the formatting of reports bound at the left. To ensure the appearance of equal left and right margins in a leftbound report, you must add extra space to the left margin to allow for the binding.

Document Design

35d
Report Format Guides

Unbound Report Format

Reports prepared without binders are called **unbound reports**. Unbound reports may be attached with a staple or paper clip in the upper-left corner.

Margins, Spacing, and Page Numbers

Top margins: Approximately 2" for the first page; strike ENTER to position the insertion point; 1" for second and succeeding pages.

Side margins: Default margins 1.25" or 1".

Bottom margins: Approximately 1"; last page bottom margin may be deeper.

Font size and spacing: Use 12-point size for readability. Generally, educational reports are double spaced (DS) and business reports are single spaced (SS). Indent paragraphs 0.5" when the body of the report is DS. Begin the paragraphs at the left margin when the report is SS, and DS between paragraphs.

Enumerated items: Align bulleted or numbered items with the beginning of a paragraph. SS each item and DS between items.

Page numbers: The first page of a report is not numbered. The second and succeeding pages are numbered in the upper-right corner in the header position.

Headings

Headings have a hierarchy. Spacing and font size indicate the level of heading. The main heading informs readers of the report title. Side headings within the report break a lengthy report into smaller, easier-to-understand parts.

Main heading: Center and key the title in ALL CAPS. Use 14 point and bold.

Side headings: Key at left margin in bold. Capitalize the first letters of main words; DS above and below side headings if the report is SS.

Main heading

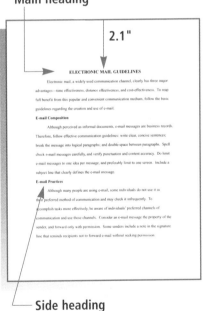

Side heading

Title Page

The cover or title page should have a concise title that identifies the report to the reader. A title page includes the title of the report, the name and title of the individual or the organization for which the report was prepared, the name and title of the writer, and the date the report was completed.

Center-align each line and center the page vertically. Allow near equal space between parts of the page (strike ENTER about eight times).

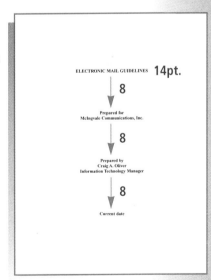

35e-d4
Title Page with Borders
Challenge

1. Open **35e-d3**, and save it as **35e-d4**.
2. Add a page border following the directions below.
✳ 3. Expand the space between characters in the report title using the Character Spacing feature. Expanding the space between characters will cause the heading to be more prominent (stand out more).

Page Borders

1. The title page, **35e-d4**, should be open.
2. Choose **Format**; then **Borders and Shading**.
3. Click the **Page Borders** tab; then choose a setting, e.g., **Box**. Choose the desired line style, line color, and line width. Click **OK**.
4. Close the document and save your changes.

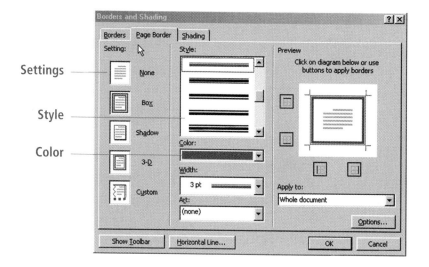

NEWS | on e-mail etiquette

Keep your messages short and to the point. Limit the amount of punctuation, especially exclamation points at the ends of sentences. Use a single font; don't try to be fancy. Use only commonly understood abbreviations. Avoid the use of emoticons (symbols used to convey the writer's emotions such as a smiley face). Do not send any e-mail message that you would not want anyone else to read. Do not use your company computer for personal e-mail.

COURTESY OF © PHOTODISC, INC.

about 2.1" top margin

ELECTRONIC MAIL GUIDELINES ← 14pt

Electronic mail, a widely used communication channel, clearly has three major

advantages—time effectiveness, distance effectiveness, and cost-effectiveness. To reap

full benefit from this popular and convenient communication medium, follow the basic

guidelines regarding the creation and use of e-mail.

DS

Side heading · **E-mail Composition**

DS

Although perceived as informal documents, e-mail messages are business records.

Therefore, follow effective communication guidelines: write clear, concise sentences;

Default or 1" · break the message into logical paragraphs; and double-space between paragraphs. Spell · Default or 1"

check e-mail messages carefully, and verify punctuation and content accuracy. Do limit

e-mail messages to one idea per message, and preferably limit to one screen. Include a

subject line that clearly defines the e-mail message.

DS

Side heading · **E-mail Practices**

DS

Although many people are using e-mail, some individuals do not use it as

their preferred method of communication and may check it infrequently. To

accomplish tasks more effectively, be aware of individuals' preferred channels of

communication and use those channels. Consider an e-mail message the property of the

sender, and forward only with permission. Some senders include a note in the signature

line that reminds recipients not to forward e-mail without seeking permission.

Applications

35e-d1
Unbound Report

1. Key the model report on the previous page. Change the line spacing to double. Strike ENTER three times to leave a top margin of about 2". Use default side margins.

2. Key the main heading in ALL CAPS. Strike ENTER once. Select the heading; then change the font size to 14-point bold and center-align the heading. (*Tip:* Striking ENTER before formatting the main heading prevents the format of the heading from being applied to the body of the report.)

3. After keying and formatting the report, save it as **35e-d1**.

35e-d2
Unbound Report

1. Open **report** from the data files.

2. Select the entire document, and set the line spacing to double.

3. Position the main heading at about 2" by striking ENTER three times.

4. Change the font of paragraph 1 to Garamond.

5. Apply the format of paragraph 1 to the remaining paragraphs using Format Painter. Do not format the side headings.

6. Bold the first side heading, *Working with Blocks*; change the font to Univers.

7. Apply the side heading format to the second side heading and the main heading.

8. Center the main heading and change to 14 point.

9. Save the document as **35e-d2**.

35e-d3
Title Page

1. Prepare a title page for the unbound report completed in 35e-d1. See the illustration on page 117.

2. Use bold and 14 point for all lines.

✳ 3. Center-align each line using the Click and Type feature.

4. Center the page vertically. Save the document as **35e-d3**.

✳ DISCOVER

Click and Type—Switch to Print Layout View. Point to the center of the page to display centered text icon; double-click and key.

ELECTRONIC MAIL GUIDELINES

↓8

Prepared for
McIngvale Communications, Inc.

↓8

Prepared by
Craig A. Oliver
Information Technology Manager

↓8

Current date

Standard Coding Number	Certification Skill Sets	Content Pages	Drill and Page	Application Number and Page
W2002-1	**Insert and modify text**			
W2002-1-1	**Insert, modify, and move text and symbols**	85 (text) 124 (symbols) 126 (file)	Drill 7, p.85 Drill 4, p.124	27b-d1, 27b-d2, p.86 37d-d1, p.126
	Cut, Copy, Paste	168 170	Drill 1, p.169 Drill 2, p.170 Drill 4, p.170	46c-d1, step 1d, 1e, p.171 47d-d1, step 1, p.174 47d-d3, step 4, p.174
	Paste special	181	Drill 4, p.181	50c-d1, step 3, p.186 51c-d1, p.190 53d-d2, step 4, p.203
	Find and replace text	172	Drill 1, p.173	47d-d1, p.174 47d-d3, step 5, p.174
	AutoCorrect to insert frequently used text	87 210 (Discover)	Drill 1, p.87	56e-d1, step 5, p.210 (Project directions, paragraph 1, p.226)
W2002-1-2	**Apply and modify character format**	81 84 96 113	Drill 2, p.82 Drill 3, p.83 Drill 3, step 2, p.97 Drill 1-2, p.113 Drill 1, step 4, p.204	27b-d2, p.86 Doc. 2, p.90 35e-d2, d3 35e-d4, p.116 46c-d1, step 1f, p.171
W2002-1-3	**Correct spelling and grammar usage**	87	Drill 1, p.87 Drill 2, step 3, p.88	28c-d1-d2, p.89 30d-d2, p.98
	Thesaurus	173	Drill 2, p.173	47d-d1, p.174 47d-d3, p.174
W2002-1-4	**Apply font and text effects**	81; 120; 170	Drill 2, p.82 Drill 3, p.83 Drill 5, p.171	27b-d1, p.86 27b-d2, p.86 28c-d1, p.89 28c-d2, p.89 36d-d2, step 4, p.120 37d-d2, step 3, p.127
	Apply character effects	117; 170	Drill 5, p.171 Drill 3, p.185	35e-d2, p.116 37d-d2, step 3, p.127 46c-d1, p.171
	Apply highlights	180	Drill 3, p.180	49d-d1, p.182 50c-d1, p.187
W2002-1-5	**Enter and format date and time and modify formats**	88	Drill 2, p.88	28c-d1-d2, p.89 29d-d1, p.94
W2002-1-6	**Apply character styles**	81 183	Drill 2, p.82 Drill 3, p.83 Drill 1, p.184	27b-d1, p.86 28c-d1-d2, p.89 33c-d1, p.105
W2002-2	**Create and modify paragraphs**	82	Drill 3, p.83 Drill 4, p.84 Drill 1-2, p.113 Drill 4, p.185	27b-d1, p.86 27b-d2, p.86 29d-d3, p.94 Document 7, p.229
	Apply borders and shading to paragraphs	123 179	Drill 2, p.123 Drill 2, p.180	39d-d3, step 4, p.136 50c-d1, step 4, p.186
	Indent paragraphs	128 129 132	Drill 1, p.129 Drill 2, p.129 Drill 1-3, p.132	38e-d1, p.130 39d-d1, p.134 40c-d1, p.139

MOUS CERTIFICATION CORRELATION REF1

MOUS Certification Correlation REF2

Standard Coding Number	Certification Skill Sets	Content Pages	Drill and Page	Application Number and Page
W2002-2-2	**Set and modify tabs**	99 148	Drill 1, p.100 Drill 2, p.100 Drill 1, p.148	31d-d1-d3, p.101 32d-d1-d2, p.104 34c-d3, p.108
W2002-2-3	**Apply bullet, outline, and numbering format to paragraphs**			
	Apply bullets and numbering	119	Drill 3, p.119 Drill 4, p.120	36d-d1, 36d-d3, p.121 37d-d1, p.126 39d-d3, p.136 40c-d1, p.138
	Create outlines	178	Drill 1, p.179	51c-d2, p.190
W2002-2-4	**Apply paragraph styles**	183; 186	Drill 1-2, p.184 Drill 4, p.186	50c-d1, 50c-d2, p.186 51c-d1, p.190
W2002-3	**Formatting documents**			
W2002-3-1	**Create and modify a document header and footer**	122 133 186	Drill 1, p.122 Drill 2, p.123 Drill 4, p.133 Drill 5, p.186	38e-d1, p.130 39d-d2, 39d-d3, p.134 40c-d1, p.138 40c-d2, step 5, p.139 46c-d1, step 1, p.171 Document 1, p.192 Document 7, p.229
W2002-3-2	**Apply and modify column settings**	204 206	Drill 1, p.204 Drill 2, p.206	54b-d2, 54b-d3, p.206 54b-d5, p.206
	Create newsletter columns	204-205	Drill 1, p.204 Drill 2, p.205	54-55b-d3, p.206 56e-d1, p.210
	Revise column layout	204-205	Drill 1, p.204 Drill 2, p.205	54b-d3, 54b-d4, 54b-d5, p.206 56e-d1, step 8, p.210
W2002-3-3	**Modify document layout and Page Setup options**			
	Insert page breaks	123; 209	Drill 3, p.124 Drill 4, step 4, p.133 Drill 1, p.209	37d-d1, p.126 40c-d1, step 5, p.138 Document 1, 1e, p.140 56c-d1, p.209
	Insert page numbers	122	Drill 1, p.122 Drill 2, p.123 Drill 3, p.124	37d-d1, p.126 38e-d1, p.130 39d-d2, p.134 40c-d1, step 2, p.138 Document 1, p.140
	Modify page margins; page orientation	118; 151	Drill 1, p.118 Drill 2, p.119	36d-d1, p.120 36d-d3, p.120 37d-d1, step 1, p.126 42c-d4, p.151 44c-d4, step 4, p.159
W2002-3-4	**Create and modify tables**	143-144; 146	Drill 1, p.144 Drill 2, p.145 Drill 3, p.146	41d-d1, p.147 41d-d2, p.147 45d-d4, p.162
	Apply AutoFormat to tables	149	Drill 3, p.150	42c-d3, p.151 44c-d3, 44c-d4, p.158

Standard Coding Number	Certification Skill Sets	Content Pages	Drill and Page	Application Number and Page
	Modify table borders and shading	149 157	Drill 2, p.149 Drill 2, p.157 Drill 3, p.157	42c-d2, p. 150 42c-d4, p.151 44c-d2, p.158 44c-d4, p.159 45d-d1, p.161 Document 2, p.227
	Revise tables (insert/delete rows; modify cell formats)	152 153 156	Drill 1-3, p.152 Drill 4, p.154 Drill 1, p.156	43c-d1-d2, p.154 43c-d3-d4, p.155 44c-d1-d4, p.185
W2002-3-5	**Preview and print documents, envelopes, and labels**			
	Use Print Preview	76	Drill 5, p.77 Drill 6, p.84	27b-d1, p.86 29d-d1, p.94 30d-d1, 30d-d2, p.97 39d-d3, step 5, p.136
	Print documents, envelopes, and labels.	77 96 106	Drill 5, p.77 Drill 2, p.96 Drill 3, p.97	30d-d1, p.97 32d-d3, p.104 33c-d1, p.105 33c-d5, p.106
W2002-4	**Manage documents**			
W2002-4-1	**Manage files and folders for documents**	xiii-xvi 75 104 216	Drill 4, p.76 Drill 1, step 5, p.113 Drill 1-2, p.145 Drill 1, p.217	29d-d1, step 6, p.94 32d-d4, p.104 Overview, p.226
W2002-4-2	**Create documents from a template**	175	Drill 1, p.175 Drill 2, p.176 Drill 3, p.176	48b-d1, 48b-d2, 48b-d3, p.177 51c-d3, p.191 Document 1, p.192
W2002-4-3	**Save documents using different names and file formats**	xvi; 75 86	Drill 4, p.76 Drill 6, p.78	26b-d1, 26b-d2, p.79 27b, step 8, p.86
W2002-5	**Working with graphics**			
W2002-5-1	**Insert images and graphics**	193-194	Drill 1, p.194 Drill 3, p.197	52c-d1, 52c-d2, p.198 54b-d2, 54b-d4, p.206 56e-d1, steps 2, 7, 10, p.210 60c, step 3, p.223
W2002-5-2	**Create and modify diagrams and charts**	199; 200; 201	Drill 1-5, pp.200-202 Drill 2, p.210	53d-d1, 53d-d2, p.203 Document 1, step 5, p.225
W2002-6	**Workgroup Collaboration**			
W2002-6-1	**Compare and merge documents**	219	Drill 1, p.219	59c-d1, step 3, p.221 59c-d2, step 3, p.221 60c-d3, step 2, p.224
W2002-6-2	**Insert, view, and edit comments**	220	Drill 2-5, p.220	59c-d2, steps 6 and 7, p.221 Document 7, p.229
W2002-6-3	**Convert documents into Web pages** (Preview documents and save them as Web pages)	216	Drill 1, p.217	58c-d1-d3, 218 60c-d2, step 5, p.224 Document 2, p.225

For a complete listing of applications, see the Instructor's Resource CD and Instructor's Manual.

MOUS CERTIFICATION CORRELATION

Function Summary

Function	Menu Command	Page	Keyboard Shortcut	Toolbar Button
Alignment: Left, Center, Right, Justify	Format, Paragraph, Indents and Spacing	82		
AutoCorrect	Tools, AutoCorrect Options	87, 210		
Bold	Format, Font, Font tab	81	CTRL + B	**B**
Borders—Page	Format, Borders and Shading	123, 179		
Bullets	Format, Bullets and Numbering	119		
Charts	Drawing Toolbar	201		
Clip Art and Images	Insert, Picture, Clip Art	194		
Close	File, Close	78	CTRL + W	
Columns	Format, Columns	204		
Comments	Insert, Comments	220		
Compare and Merge	Tools, Compare and Merge Documents	219		
Copy	Edit, Copy	168, 170	SHIFT + F2	
Cut	Edit, Cut	168	CTRL + X	
Date and Time	Insert, Date and Time	88		
Diagrams	Drawing Toolbar	200		
Envelopes and Labels	Tools, Letters and Mailings, Envelopes and Labels	96, 106		
Exit	File, Exit	78		
Find	Edit, Find	172	CTRL + F	
Fonts	Format, Fonts	81		Times New Roman
Format Painter		113		
Go to	Edit, Go To	182	CTRL + G	
Hanging Indent	Format, Paragraph, Indents and Spacing tab	132	CTRL + T	
Headers and Footers	View, Headers and Footers	122, 133		
Highlight		180		
Indent	Format, Paragraph, Indents and Spacing tab	128		Increase Indent / Decrease Indent
Insert file	Insert, File, Locate file	126		
Italic	Format, Fonts, Font tab	81	CTRL + I	

Function	Menu Command	Page	Keyboard Shortcut	Toolbar Button
Landscape	File, Page Setup, Margins tab, Landscape	151		
Line Spacing	Format, Paragraph, Indents and Spacing tab	83		
Margins	File, Page Setup, Margin tab	118		
New	File, New	78	CTRL + N	
Numbering	Format, Bullets and Numbering	119		
Open	Format, Open	78	CTRL + O	
Page Numbers	Insert, Page Numbers	122		
Paste	Edit, Paste	168	CTRL + V	
Paste Special	Edit, Paste Special	180		
Print	File, Print	77	CTRL + P	
Print Preview	File, Print Preview	76	CTRL + F2	
Redo	Edit, Redo	84	CTRL + Y	
Replace	Format, Replace	172		
Save as/Save	File, Save as	75	F12/CTRL + S	
Section breaks	Insert, Break	209		
Shading	Format, Borders and Shading, Shading	179		
Show/Hide		82		
Spelling and Grammar	Tools, Spelling and Grammar	87	F7	
Styles—Apply	Click down arrow on Style button and make selection	183		
Symbols	Insert, Symbols	124		
Tables—Create	Insert, Table	143		
Tabs: Set	Horizontal Ruler: set Tab Alignment, click Ruler; Format, Tabs	99		
Template	File, New, General Template	175		
Text effects	Format, Fonts, Text Effects	170		
Thesaurus	Tools, Language, Thesaurus	173	SHIFT + F7	
Undo	Edit, Undo Typing	84	CTRL + Z	
WordArt	Drawing Toolbar	197		

FUNCTION SUMMARY